Praise for Books by Douglas A. Gray

THE COMPLETE CANADIAN SMALL BUSINESS GUIDE (with Diana Gray)

"This guide is truly a gold mine . . . an admirable job . . . taps into the author's expertise."

Profit Magazine

"I can say with absolute certainty that this guide is *the best*. . . . It is well organized, written in an informative way and at the right level of detail. . . . The samples, check-lists, glossary and sources of information can be best be described as exemplary. Just a great piece of work . . . recommended to everyone I deal with."

Steve Guerin
Former Project Manager
Office of Research and Innovation
Ryerson Polytechnical University, Toronto

"Thorough and wide-ranging . . . bursts with practical tips and explanations"

Vancouver Sun

"Excellent . . . geared especially to Canadians, unlike most small business guides"

Financial Times

"If you're thinking of launching your own business, or if you want to pick up invalu-able tips on running the one you already own, this Canadian book on small business is a terrific resource tool."

"This Week in Business," Montreal

"Contains a wealth of information to help you maximize your chances of success. . . . If you can't be bothered reading an excellent book like this, you probably shouldn't bother going into business for yourself."

Mike Grenby
National Syndicated Financial Columnist

"The strength of the book is its attention to the practical needs of small business . . . provides a broad overview of 18 major topic areas . . . full of numerous 'street-smart' tips on how to successfully open and operate a business . . . contains a plethora of 'how-to' features and useful resource information."

Ottawa Citizen

"Written in an easy-to-read, matter-of-fact manner which helps take much of the mystique out of starting and developing a business . . . provides a signpost guide through the key areas of small business development . . . a wealth of practical infor-mation . . . this book is a must for every Economic Development Officer's library"

Christopher Brant
Past Director, Economic Development Program
University of Waterloo

"Detailed, very informative, scrupulously objective as well as being written in a style that is refreshingly clear of jargon . . . this one is a 'must' buy"

B.C. Business

HOME INC.: THE CANADIAN HOME-BASED BUSINESS GUIDE (with Diana Gray)

"Outstanding . . . peppered with practical no-nonsense tips . . . invaluable information throughout."

Calgary Herald

"Should be required reading for all potential home-basers . . . authoritative, current and comprehensive."

Edmonton Journal

"An absolute necessity for your bookshelf . . . crammed with useful information."

Victoria Times-Colonist

MAKING MONEY IN REAL ESTATE: THE CANADIAN RESIDENTIAL INVESTMENT GUIDE

MORTGAGES MADE EASY: THE CANADIAN GUIDE TO HOME FINANCING

HOME BUYING MADE EASY: THE CANADIAN GUIDE TO PURCHASING A NEWLY-BUILT OR PRE-OWNED HOME

"Gray delivers the goods. It is all-Canadian, and not a retread book full of tips that are worthless north of the U.S. border. It's chock-full of practical streetsmart strategies and advice, pitfalls to avoid, samples, what-to-look-out-for-checklists and information. . . . The information that Gray passes along is invaluable, thorough and eminently usable . . . the book has an easy style to it that is almost conversational."

Business in Vancouver

"Gray's latest endeavour is a good educational tool . . . no legalese here, just some good ol' street-level English that explains — mostly for the benefit of novices — all the real and perceived complexities of mortgages."

Calgary Herald

"The prolific output of real estate and financial books establishes Gray as a Canadian voice . . . provides consumer insights into securing the best deal and avoiding the pitfalls . . . Gray's legal background has given him valuable insights."

Edmonton Journal

"Author knows what he is talking about . . . full of street-smarts and practical advice."

Halifax Chronicle-Herald

RAISING MONEY: THE CANADIAN GUIDE TO SUCCESSFUL BUSINESS FINANCING (with Brian Nattrass)

"The most informative and comprehensive guide on this subject matter."

The Toronto Star

RISK-FREE RETIREMENT: THE COMPLETE CANADIAN PLANNING GUIDE (with Graham Cunningham, Les Solomon, Tom Delaney, Dr. Des Dwyer)

"This book is a classic . . . will be invaluable for years to come . . . arguably the most comprehensive guide to retirement planning in Canada today."

Vancouver Sun

HOME INC.

SECOND EDITION

THE
CANADIAN HOME-BASED
BUSINESS GUIDE

HOME INC.

SECOND EDITION

THE
CANADIAN HOME-BASED BUSINESS GUIDE

By
DOUGLAS A. GRAY
&
DIANA L. GRAY

McGraw-Hill Ryerson
Toronto Montreal

HOME INC.

Revised edition published in 1994 by
McGraw-Hill Ryerson Limited
300 Water Street
Whitby, Ontario, Canada
L1N 9B6

    3 4 5 6 7 8 9 10   0 1 2 3 4 5 6 7 8 9

Canadian Cataloguing in Publication Data

Gray, Douglas A.
  Home Inc.: the Canadian home-based business guide

2nd ed.
ISBN 0-07-551558-X

1. Home-based businesses — Canada.   2. Home-based businesses — Canada — Management.   3. New business enterprises — Canada.   4. New business enterprises — Canada — Management.   I. Gray, Diana Lynn. II. Title

HD8037.C3G73 1994   658′.041   C94-930545-6

The material in this publication is provided for information purposes only. Laws, regulations and procedures are constantly changing, and the examples given are intended to be general guidelines only. This book is sold with the understanding that neither the authors, nor the publisher, are engaged in rendering professional advice. It is recommended that legal, accounting and other advice or assistance be obtained before acting on any information contained in this book. Personal services of a competent professional should be sought.

The authors, publisher and all others directly or indirectly involved with this publication do not assume any responsibility or liability, direct or indirect, to any party for any loss or damage by errors or omissions, regardless of the cause, as a consequence of using this publication, nor accept any contractual, tortious or other form of liability for the publication's contents or any consequences arising from its use.

Cover design by Dave Hader/Studio Conceptions
Editorial services provided by Word Guild, Toronto

Printed and bound in Canada

CONTENTS

PREFACE

Home Inc.: The Canadian Home-Based Business Guide is written for the growing number of Canadians who are choosing to run their businesses from their homes — whether on a full-time or a part-time basis. It is written to assist those who have dreamed of having a business at home, those who have made definite plans to start, and those who are already in business and want to operate more effectively and profitably.

More and more people are seeing the advantages and opportunities of this career option. It has been common for many years for home-based businesses to be operated by consultants, craftspersons, and tradesmen. What we are now seeing is a trend for others to opt for this form of self-employment. Working parents, retirees, students, and the handicapped are some examples. Many have the drive to be their own boss, independent of external controls and able to take a dream and run with it. Their need for challenge, personal fulfillment, and unlimited financial potential are other catalysts. There are also distinct tax and lifestyle advantages of operating from home.

But how do you turn your skills and interests into a money-making venture? How do you make sure your business is going to be profitable? How do you combine the dynamics of working at home with personal and family lifestyle?

Home Inc. has been designed to answer the above questions and many more. Self-employment and home business operation is not for everyone, though, and by the time you finish this book, you will be in a much better position to decide whether the timing is right to consider this option.

The book is divided into four sections, each with a different educational approach to enhance the learning experience.

Section One provides the important "how-to" steps that apply to any type of home-based business. It is full of "street-smart" tips and practical ideas that will help you to save money and avoid the pitfalls. Topics range from municipal zoning and income tax to marketing strategies and your home business environment.

Section Two covers how to select a home-based business and discusses the differences between service-related and product-related businesses. Brief overviews of some profitable types of home businesses are given as well as lists of other examples to stimulate creative ideas.

Section Three contains profiles based on personal interviews of selected home-based business entrepreneurs from across Canada. It includes both individuals who are still operating from home and individuals who have chosen to continue their business outside the home. They have shared their experiences and ideas, tips, advice, and insights. The profiles are intended to provide you with a positive, motivating influence and to be a source of encouragement to those with the requisite vision.

Section Four includes worksheets, checklists, and samples, and lists of recommended reading and sources of further information. This will save you research time and will help you to put into practice some of the many tips and suggestions.

The message of this book is that you *can* achieve financial independence and personal satisfaction in operating your home-based business — but don't expect instant success. It takes time to make a business work and to attain an attractive profit. This is part of the challenge of being your own boss. You will need to find out what combination of factors provides success for you, as each individual and each business is unique. The success of your business is directly related to your planning, persistence, skill, energy, discipline, commitment, flexibility, and resilience.

Do you think you can do it? Of course you can! Your decision to read *Home Inc.* has been the first step in the process.

Your candid feedback on how this book can better meet your needs is welcomed. This will help us in future editions. Please refer to the last page of this book for the address for reader input and for obtaining further information.

PREFACE TO THE SECOND EDITION

We have received a great deal of positive and constructive feedback since our first edition was published five years ago. This new edition is revised, updated and expanded, and incorporates suggestions, fresh insights and legislative changes (such as the GST), and additional sources of information.

We have also updated the business profiles to reflect how these businesses have matured. We hope you enjoy the book and find it practical and encouraging.

Douglas A. Gray
Diana Lynn Gray
Vancouver, B.C.
March 1994

ACKNOWLEDGEMENTS

We are indebted to the thousands of Canadian home-based business owners who have shared their ideas and experiences with us over the years through our seminars, consulting practice, and business relationships. We are particularly appreciative of the time and candid feedback provided by the home business owners profiled in this book.

We are also grateful for the extensive assistance given us by the Federal Business Development Bank and small business departments of all the provincial governments and the governments of the Yukon and Northwest Territories. Their contribution in identifying and contacting home-based entrepreneurs profiled in this book was most helpful.

Many thanks to Bob Jamison, C.A., and Steve Reed, C.A., of Manning Jamison, chartered accountants, for their review of the chapter on tax. We appreciated the assistance of Annette Lorek, M.L.S., of Infoplex Information Associates Inc. in compiling research data for reference sources in Section Two. To Adèle Hevey: We thank you for your assistance in the interviews in French and their translation.

Sincere appreciation is extended to the staff of McGraw Hill Ryerson for their continued support and encouragement.

SECTION ONE

THE BASICS OF STARTING AND OPERATING A HOME-BASED BUSINESS

CHAPTER
1

Exploring the Home-Based Business Idea

A. INTRODUCTION

Do you dream about being your own boss and having the freedom to take your business idea and turn it into a profitable reality? Many people do. In fact, studies show that over 70% of the adult population fantasizes at some point about taking the entrepreneurial step. However, many people never proceed any further than the dream, because of fear of failure, risk, or uncertainty. In the comfort of your own home or apartment, you can take your entrepreneurial desires and creative ideas and test them with minimal financial resources and risk.

Operating a home-based business is becoming increasingly popular in Canada. Recent studies indicate that two to two-and-a-half million Canadians work from home on a part-time or full-time basis. It is estimated that by the year 2000 up to 40% of the labour force in North America will be working out of the home. Some of these people will be employees, but most will be self-employed. Today, as many as 50% of small businesses in Canada are started out of the home, and over 50% of them are begun by women. The natural starting place for many of these businesses is the den, spare room, basement, or garage. Homemakers, parents of young children, the disabled, the unemployed, retirees, hobbyists, and people interested in a second income are but a few of those attracted to home enterprises.

Before you invest your time, skill, and resources, it is important to have a good conceptual understanding of what is involved in running a home business. Whether you are thinking of working full-time or part-time at home, you have to take the decision-making process one step at a time. You have to realistically look at the advantages and disadvantages of running a business in general, and from your home specifically. You should understand the personality traits of successful entrepreneurs, and undertake a candid and honest assessment of your personal skills, attributes, and talents. These subject areas and others will be discussed in this first chapter.

The rest of the chapters in Section One will discuss the necessary preliminary business startup issues as well as operational considerations. Subjects covered include planning your home business and legal, tax, accounting, insurance, financial, and marketing information. How to select professional advisors, deal with personnel, and apply effective time and stress management techniques, and why home businesses succeed or fail, are also explained.

Section Two of the book covers the process of deciding what home-based business is right for you and gives an overview of 20 sample businesses.

Section Three provides advice and comments from successful Canadian home-based entrepreneurs who share their thoughts on home business ownership and its advantages and disadvantages. (Some of these "role models" no longer operate from their homes, but their initial business success occurred at home.)

Section Four of this book includes checklists, samples, sources of further information, and recommended reading to assist in your preparation for business success.

B. HOME-BASED BUSINESS — IS IT FOR YOU?

The small business sector is a dynamic, innovative, and growing force that provides challenge, fulfillment, and financial security to more than one million small business owners in Canada. Studies show that over 75% of these small businesses have five employees or less. A small business, as defined by the Canadian Federation of Independent Business (CFIB), is an independently owned firm of up to 20 employees. The Federal Business Development Bank (FBDB), on the other hand, defines "small businesses" as those firms with gross annual sales of less than $2 million.

The types of businesses that can be operated from the home are diverse, ranging from consulting firms, bed and breakfast inns, craft workshops and photography studios, to landscaping, accounting, small manufacturing, and advertising agencies. Some of the trends which have encouraged the startup of home businesses are:

- **Economic changes**   With the restructuring and downsizing of many public- and private-sector operations, many middle managers and upper-management executives are being laid off or encouraged to take early retirement. This major economic change, along with the normal cyclic economic downturns or recessionary periods, has caused many people to be faced with the spectre of unemployment. As whole industries are affected and the prospect of lateral moves is diminished, the option of self-employment becomes more attractive as a protective buffer or career option.

- **Dislike of commuting**   Many people commute up to two to four hours a day to and from work. This causes stress, frustration, sleep deprivation, extra car expenses, and environmental pollution, as well as resulting in unproductive time. For these obvious reasons, the idea of eliminating the daily commute by having a home-based business is very appealing. Lifestyle enhancement and the desire to have balance in one's life are interrelated factors when considering a home-based business.

- **Low-risk incubator**   One of the positive benefits of working from home is the ability to test the idea with minimal risk on a part-time basis. Many people are financially risk-averse, especially if they have been laid off or might be. The beauty of a home business is the ability to see if the idea is financially viable, fun, challenging, and a good personal fit. Having a low startup expense and minimal extra overhead are other factors, coupled with many different tax-deduction advantages when operating from the home.

- **Cocooning**   Many people are preferring to centre their leisure time around the home. This lifestyle trend has been labelled "cocooning" and comes from the desire to eliminate a lot of outside stresses. This is reflected throughout the economy in an increase in the number and variety of goods and services available, such as home improvements, gardening equipment and supplies, delivery services, home electronics, home gymnasiums, and home entertainment.

- **Computerization**   This trend has had a profound impact on home-based businesses. Equipment such as facsimile (fax) machines, photocopiers, personal computers, modems, and specialized software is not only smaller and more compact (in many cases, portable), but affordably priced. Cellular phones, memory pagers, voice mail, and answering machines also make it possible to provide accessibility to the business world. A home office can have all the technical sophistication and professional image of a traditional business office outside the home.

- **Combining roles of career and raising a family** Many parents prefer to raise a family and operate a part-time or full-time business from home at the same time. There are many examples of both spouses operating businesses at home, either the same business or separate businesses.

- **Growth of the service industry** The service industry is growing faster than the retail, manufacturing, or agricultural industries. More than two-thirds of all national income (GNP) is created in the service industry, and estimates are that by 1996 nine out of 10 new jobs will be created in the service industry. Many home businesses are ideally suited for this industry. They generally require less startup capital, have lower ongoing operational expenses, and have minimal equipment cost.

- **Telecommuting** An increasing number of corporations are encouraging staff to work out of their homes and communicate with the office by computer and telephone. There are many benefits to the employer, including:

  - **Increased productivity** Studies show that when employees can work at their own pace during their "peak" hours, productivity increases from 20% to 60%.

  - **Reduced staff turnover** In some business sectors the turnover rate can be considerable — anywhere from 20% to 50%. Employees may leave the firm because of retirement, disability, child care responsibilities, or commuting time. The cost of losing a productive, reliable, and well-trained employee is high. Instead, by being flexible and allowing the employee to work at home, the benefit to the employer could be considerable.

  - **Saving on office rental** Office workspace is expensive when you consider the costs of a lease, furniture, and equipment, and other related expenses of running an office. Money can be saved by having some employees work at home.

People who are currently employed may find that they can operate effectively out of the home. They may therefore decide to quit their jobs and act as independent contractors or consultants for the same firm on a part-time or full-time basis. In addition, they could take on work for other clients. Many employers prefer to hire independent contractors, since they don't have to pay fringe benefits as they would for employees. Being employed at home might be the first step to becoming an entrepreneur.

But though there are benefits, there are also risks and frustrations. Many people have an idealized picture of the rewards and pleasures of running their own business. It is important to objectively look at both sides of the issue of small business ownership in order to make a realistic decision.

1. Advantages of Going into Business for Yourself

Some of the most common advantages are:

- You have the opportunity of making more money working for yourself than by being an employee. There is no ceiling on your potential income, as it is limited only by your energy, management skill, and good judgement. Hence, the financial rewards can be very great. (Studies show, however, that making money is not one of the main motivating factors of small business ownership.)
- You have the opportunity to satisfy your creative drive. This allows for personal growth, self-fulfillment, and freedom of expression. Small businesses are more creative, productive, and responsive to changing conditions in the marketplace than are large corporations.
- You can't be laid off. In that sense, you have job security as long as your business is successful.
- You have definite tax advantages over people who are not self-employed.
- You set your own priorities as the decision-maker. You have control over your own destiny, as you are the only person responsible for the success of your company.
- Your workday will not be routine, as you are constantly faced with a variety of new and different challenges.
- You have the opportunity to see your ideas through to completion.
- You have flexible work hours that can accommodate your personal and lifestyle needs.
- You can determine your own style and type of work environment.
- You will receive prestige, status, and recognition if your business is successful.

Home-based business ownership offers some additional advantages:

- Startup and operating costs are much lower, and therefore the business is easier to get established and less risky.
- Commuting time and related expenses are reduced or eliminated.

- There are more opportunities for your business to grow because of fewer financial constraints. Therefore, you can expect to turn a profit sooner and increase your chances of success.
- Such a business provides an atmosphere where commitment to a family and a career can be combined for the benefit of both.
- Spouse and family members can be employed by the business.

2. Disadvantages of Going into Business for Yourself

The most important negative aspects are:

- Your income may be irregular, fluctuating with the economy, competition, and other variables.
- Your involvement with the business will generally be very time-consuming, especially during the early startup years. This will tend to reduce the time available for friends, family, and recreation.
- You will be under pressure to succeed from family, friends, investors, and creditors. Others will rely on you to perform, because you have invested so much time, energy, and money.
- In many cases, you must commit considerable financial resources toward the operation of your business. This could vary, of course, according to partner or investor involvement or bank financing.
- You are faced with the risk of losing all your money in the venture due to circumstances within or outside your control. Health, family, marital, partnership, and competition problems may not always be avoidable or predictable.
- In order to maintain proper control over the business, you must be conversant and deal effectively with various management roles at the same time, such as selling, negotiating contracts, hiring and training staff, writing proposals, and monitoring accounts receivable and cash flow.
- There is a lack of fringe benefits such as health, dental insurance, paid vacations, and unemployment insurance.
- Considerable paperwork may be required by various levels of government which is a non-revenue-generating expenditure of time and money.

Operating your business from home has some additional disadvantages:

- There may be isolation from the companionship of and interaction with colleagues or fellow workers.
- There is a risk of working too hard because of a lack of separation between the work and home environments.

- Space may be cramped or inappropriate for an ideal working environment or for growth purposes. Your inventory storage and work area may spill over into your living space.
- Personal or family lifestyle patterns or priorities may be disrupted or have to be set aside.
- Distractions and disruptions due to the nearness of family or friends may interfere with concentration.
- Business and family privacy may be jeopardized.
- Tensions and frustrations may develop because of work blending into the family relationship.
- There can be a disturbing feeling that working at home may not be considered important by society. One's business may not be taken seriously by others due to the more relaxed business image that comes with working at home.
- It may be difficult to hire employees due to limited space or a lack of facilities.
- Business activity could create difficulties with neighbours.

Running a home-based business is not for everyone. What may be an advantage to one person may be a disadvantage to another. You will need to carefully assess your personal situation to decide whether the disadvantages are major or minor obstacles for you.

C. WOMEN IN BUSINESS

In Canada, women are going into business at a greater rate than men, almost three to one. Studies show that almost 65% of home-based businesses are run by women. They also show that twice as many women as men who are small business owners are still in business five years later. In various investigations conducted regionally and nationally of the reasons for the success of women in business generally, the same underlying factors are found. They include the following:

(a) Women do their research Before starting a business, a woman typically spends from six to 10 months researching the product or service, the best location for the business, and many other considerations. On average, less than four months is spent by their male counterparts.

(b) Women plan ahead While small business instructors extoll the benefits of having a written business plan, it is women who most often heed this advice. As a follow-through on the research they have done, the preparation of the written business plan becomes an easier task. By the time this stage is completed, they have a fully developed concept and can see clearly the stepping stones they need to follow to lead them to their ultimate goal. (A sample business plan is shown in Section Four, Sample 2.)

(c) Women take courses and seek advice   Women tend to readily accept the fact that they may not have all the necessary skills or business know-how. Consequently, they will enroll in courses that, for instance, teach them how to read financial statements or prepare a marketing plan. Also, women tend to act more cautiously in an area where they have little expertise, and seek the advice of others.

(d) Women have realistic expectations   In looking ahead to the profit potential, women tend to set conservative and realistic expectations, and tend to be less impulsive. They will write into their business plans an anticipated slow period for the concept to catch on, for example. They do not overextend themselves financially in hopes of making large sales tomorrow. This is a critical aspect of building a solid foundation from the outset, and gaining the trust and respect of your banker, suppliers, and staff. Women tend to take less money out of their businesses in the critical growth years. Studies show they take out less than half of the amount taken by male entrepreneurs.

(e) Women are committed to the business   Many women are not in business just for the money — theirs is often a "lifestyle" business. Thus, they tend to persevere during hardships. Such determination is usually accompanied by an openness to new ideas and approaches. A woman, in leaving no stone unturned in her attempts to succeed, usually does.

When research studies state that women tend to be more successful in small business than men, most often the word "successful" refers to surviving in business longer. Because of the commitment and the realistic expectations, a woman is more likely to "hang in there" during the slow growth of a business. While statistics are lacking in the area of overall profits made by men and women in business, it is perceived that men are far more successful than women. But this is because a man is likely to take greater risks, have greater access to finances, and therefore be able to generate larger amounts of money; these factors naturally translate into a higher "success" profile in the media and the business world.

D. TRAITS OF SUCCESSFUL ENTREPRENEURS

What kind of person becomes an entrepreneur? What characteristics must a successful entrepreneur have? Whether people are born with these traits or learn them is material for a good debate, but what we do know from numerous studies is that successful entrepreneurs tend to have several important personality characteristics in common. They are often strong individualists, optimistic and resourceful, and they usually have a high degree of problem-solving ability. There are many other traits that might describe an entrepreneur, some of which are listed below.

- **Strong goal orientation** Ability to set clear goals that are challenging but attainable; ability to continually reevaluate and adjust goals to make sure they are consistent with one's interests, talents, and values, as well as personal or business needs. Rather than being content at the attainment of goals, successful entrepreneurs enjoy the challenge that setting new goals brings.
- **Persistence** Steadfast pursuit of an aim; constant perseverance; continuing to strive for a goal despite obstacles; strong determination to reach goals regardless of personal sacrifice.
- **Ability to withstand business reversals without quitting** Though perhaps disappointed, not discouraged by failure; ability to use failures as learning experiences so that similar problems can be avoided in the future; attitude that setbacks are only temporary barriers to goals; strong capacity to build on successes.
- **Business and product/service knowledge** The entrepreneur must understand basic principles by which a business survives and prospers. That means comprehending the roles of management and the responsibilities of employees to maintain a viable business. Although the entrepreneur must be in control of overall goals, he or she can't perform each task without help. Awareness of the functions of marketing, accounting, tax, financing, planning, and management, and how to deal with them, is therefore required. Must have a good level of understanding of the product or service.
- **Willingness to accept calculated risks** Ability to identify risks and weigh their relative dangers; preference for taking calculated risks to achieve goals that are high but realistic. (Contrary to the stereotype that entrepreneurs are gamblers or high-risk-takers, the risks involved are often moderate due to the amount of planning behind them.)
- **Strong desire for independence** Genuine desire to be one's own boss, free from external direction and control; sincere willingness and proven ability to be self-disciplined in sometimes isolated working conditions; ability to organize activities to reach personal goals. Successful entrepreneurs are not usually joiners by nature. They often join only to network; that is, to make business contacts, further their ventures, or obtain useful information

to solve problems. Studies have shown that reliance on social interaction and friendship may inhibit entrepreneurial behaviour.

- **Ability to handle uncertainly well**   An entrepreneur must have an ability to live with the uncertainty of job security. He or she must face many crises, take risks, and allow for temporary failures without panic. Successful entrepreneurs accept uncertainty as an integral part of being in business.
- **Self-confidence and self-reliance**   Strong but realistic belief in self and ability to achieve personal or business goals. Successful entrepreneurs have an enduring faith in themselves that gives them the capacity to recover from serious defeat or disappointment.
- **Versatility and resourcefulness**   Capable of dealing effectively with many subjects or tasks at the same time; can assume different roles and switch back and forth as required. During the early stages of the business, the entrepreneur will assume numerous and diverse business responsibilities, including marketing, sales, credit and collection, finances, employee selection, accounting, planning, and negotiating.
- **The habit of seeking and using feedback**   The skill to seek and use feedback from employees, the management team, and professional advisors on personal performance and goals for the business; the skill to take any remedial action required.
- **Physical health, with high degree of stamina and energy**   Staying healthy is essential to the intense demands and ongoing pressures of one's own business, especially during its early years. The long hours and pressures of business demand emotional and mental well-being. Also, a high level of stamina and energy is important to meet the intense demands of running a business. One needs the ability to work hard for long hours, often with less sleep than one is accustomed to. One must be prepared to make personal sacrifices. Because the pressures may be great, the success of a business may be determined by whether or not one's spouse, family, and friends can pull together and provide emotional support and understanding.
- **The habit of looking for and creating opportunities**   Self-reliant nature; initiative; desire and willingness to initiate action without needing or taking direction from others; ability to solve problems, fill a vacuum, or lead others when the need exists; motivated by situations where personal impact on problems can be measured. Entrepreneurs perceive themselves as strong, capable, and in control, which allows them to be innovative and creative

in expressing their ideas; they are individuals who apply their ideas immediately so they can see results.

- **Self-determination**   Belief that one controls one's success or failure, and that it is not decided by luck, circumstance, or external events; belief in self-determined destinies and that one has the ability to achieve the goals one has set.
- **Objectivity and realism**   Ability to distinguish between oneself and the business, so that when a mistake occurs, one has the strength to admit it and take corrective action; desire to deal with business issues and decisions rationally and logically rather than emotionally and subjectively.
- **Openness to change**   Receptivity to change; ability to adjust perceptions, goals, or action on basis of an assessment of new information.
- **Ability to apply ideas in creative ways**   Strong desire to originate an idea or product, to develop something new, to be innovative, to make something happen, to imprint personality, dreams, and ideas on a concept in a unique and different way; powers of both observation and imagination to foresee possible market ideas.
- **Sense of purpose**   A feeling of mission must motivate the person to go into business; the activity must have meaning. The mission may be to make an attractive profit, to sell some necessary and unique product or service, or to develop ideas or skills without the constraints of others' expectations.
- **Human relations ability**   Ability to understand and interact well with people of varying personalities and values. This is important when dealing with employees, bankers, investors, partners, suppliers, or customers and is reflected in characteristics such as sociability, consideration, cheerfulness, cooperation, and tact.
- **Achievement orientation**   Desire to take on challenges and test abilities to the limit. Successful entrepreneurs are not ambivalent about success. They concentrate on ways to succeed, not on what will happen if they fail. Because they are objective, though, they build a "what if" scenario into the business plan, so that they anticipate problems and develop strategies to surmount obstacles in advance. Successful entrepreneurs adopt the attitude that if they do chance upon unexpected obstacles, they will find resourceful and effective ways to overcome them.

It is unrealistic to suggest that successful entrepreneurs possess all of the traits outlined. Many of the characteristics are interrelated and not all are necessary for business success, so do not be overly concerned if you feel you do not possess every one of these qualities. The key question is how significant the missing traits are to your type of business and your business goals.

You also have to fully identify and understand your personal strengths and weaknesses in the areas of management skills, product knowledge, and expertise. Once you have identified these areas, you are then in a much better position to compensate for them by hiring employees, bringing in partners, or taking further training.

E. SELF-ASSESSMENT

Most people start a business without ever completing an honest, thorough personal assessment. Without this self-appraisal, your personal success in business could be limited. This section is intended to assist you in focussing on your strong points, identifying your weaknesses, and dealing with areas that need improvement. This will enable you to clarify your personal and business goals. A listing of books on self-evaluation and development is provided in Appendix B, "Recommended Reading."

Your self-assessment will help you to identify areas of interest and possible business opportunities, and your skills, talents, and attributes. It will help you identify skills and attributes you may not have recognized in yourself. In the following categories expand as fully as you like on your answers. To get the most out of your self-assessment, you should be free from distractions and take as much time as necessary. Rank your answers to indicate the degree of importance or impact on your future business.

- **Autobiography** Summarize your own life history. Review and detail all aspects of your past, including credentials you have obtained, education, special projects, leisure time activities including sports and hobbies, and travel experiences. List the work you have done, including all full-time, part-time, and summer jobs. Beside each job list all the roles that you assumed or tasks that you performed (e.g., coordinating, supervising, writing). Start with the most current time period and work backward.
- **Skills** List all your skills. These are your developed or acquired abilities such as researching, administering, instructing, problem-solving, selling, etc. Once you have identified your skills, rank them by frequency of use. This will give you a good indication of how important these are in your activities. Which skills do you believe will assist you in attaining your business goals? You may wish to refer to the book *What Color Is Your Parachute?* by

Richard N. Bolles (see Appendix B) for a detailed list of skill areas to stimulate your awareness.

- **Personality attributes** List all your personality attributes. Attributes are inherent characteristics such as having an analytical, inquiring, or insightful mind, being compassionate or sociable, etc. The common characteristics of entrepreneurs discussed earlier in this chapter are good examples of personality attributes.

- **Accomplishments** List your most important job-related accomplishments. Examples may include negotiating a major contract for your employer, coordinating a major conference, or exceeding sales quotas. Then list your most significant non-job-related accomplishments (e.g., being elected as president of a club or organizing a fundraising event). Rank your accomplishments from the most important to the least important. Then identify and write down all the skills used, talents demonstrated, and attributes shown which were needed to attain each accomplishment.

- **Personal and recreational interests** Identify your personal interests (e.g., business, science, politics, health, environment, sports). List those activities (personal and business) that provide you with the greatest amount of personal enjoyment and satisfaction. List the recreational activities that you enjoy.

- **Community** List community or social activities that you have participated in (e.g., church, hospital, clubs, volunteer organizations).

- **Hobbies** List all your current and past hobbies (e.g., reading, painting, photography, gardening, cooking).

- **Things you like and dislike** Think of the activities or circumstances that you like or dislike the most (work or personal). List the events that cause you the greatest amount of pleasure, satisfaction, and happiness, and the events that cause you the greatest amount of anxiety, frustration, or unhappiness.

- **Strengths and weaknesses** List your personal strengths and weaknesses. Rank them in order of intensity. Can you eliminate, reduce, or compensate for your weaknesses? Ask someone who knows you well (e.g., a relative, a friend, your spouse) to list what they perceive to be your strengths and weaknesses, and to rank them. Do others see you as you see yourself?

- **The present** Think about your present situation under various headings: social, career, family, marital, physical, emotional, financial. list the strong and weak points in each category. What impact will self-employment have on each of these categories? Ask your spouse the same questions. Is his or her assessment similar to yours?

- **The future**   List the personal goals that you wish to attain in one, three, five, and 10 years. Will your business ambitions assist you in attaining these, and if so in what manner?

By carefully focussing on your previous experiences and recognizing hidden talents and abilities, you will be better able to identify your personal and business needs. Any business or career you select should address and satisfy those needs. Know your strengths and capitalize on them. Identify your weaknesses and reflect upon how you can minimize their effect on your business activities. Be confident of your abilities, because in business when you are selling a service or product, you are selling yourself. If others believe in you and trust you, they will want to do business with you.

This self-assessment process will probably be an enlightening experience. A close match between your attributes and personality style, and the type of business you choose, will make a difference in the fulfillment you receive from the business and the degree of success you attain. It will certainly help in the various other stages of business planning and evaluation.

CHAPTER

2

Planning Your
Home-Based Business

A. DEVELOPING YOUR BUSINESS PLAN

In the previous chapter we looked at the motivating factors for starting a business and the advantages and disadvantages. We also focussed on your skills and attributes to see if you have some of the inherent traits of entrepreneurs. If you were honest and thorough in your self-assessment, you have probably already made your decision: to proceed to set up a business in your home, to delay your plans until the timing is more suitable to you, or to shelve the idea altogether. We will assume that you have decided to proceed, and the remaining chapters in Section One will cover various aspects that you will have to consider before actually starting your business. This chapter will focus on starting your business plan, startup considerations, your business image, and where to go for further assistance on any aspects of your business plan or business growth.

1. What Is a Business Plan?

A business plan is a written summary of what you hope to accomplish by being in business and how you intend to organize your resources to meet your goals. It is the road map for operating your business and measuring progress along the way. Planning is an essential first step of any business venture. It is a means of testing out your business concept on paper before you invest any money and time. By making your business decisions on paper beforehand, you will have the tools necessary to get further input and advice from business associates, family members, accountants, lawyers, and bankers. Especially if you require financing, preparing a thorough business plan will increase your chances of being approved for a loan.

Some aspects of your business plan will require considerable research. You will need to find out if there is a need for your product or service. You should check out your competition to see where they are located, what they offer, and their pricing structure. In doing so, you may decide to modify your original concept to address a need that is presently not being met. Or, by changing your product slightly, you may be able to offer something unique in the product design, application, or packaging.

The business plan has two main components: the business concept (including the marketing plan) and the financial plan. A business plan format is shown in Sample 2. This outline will guide you through the various steps and indicate the type of information required.

2. The Business Concept

The business concept will include a description of the industry and a description of your business venture. How large is the industry? Is yours a new product or service? Will you be offering something different or unique to entice customers away from your competitors? Or will you be filling an unmet need where a demand already exists? Provide a statement of your business goals and objectives. Be specific with regard to what you hope to achieve by being in business. Include both your short- and long-term objectives. By clearly identifying what stage your business will be at after six months, one year, two years, and five years, you will have a guide for your course of action. Even though your goals and objectives may change along the way, the fact that you have your game plan on paper will help you decide whether you should stay on target or modify your plans in accordance with new circumstances.

Once your basic concept, business goals, and objectives are formulated on paper, it will be easier to complete your marketing plan. To identify your market (the people who will buy your product or service), you will need to put yourself in their shoes. Are you appealing to one gender more than the other, or to a certain income bracket more than another? Do you find these people in the workplace, at home, at school, or in shopping malls? Are they mostly within a certain age range, educational level, or residential area? A visit to a branch office of Statistics Canada will provide you with current geographic and demographic statistics of the Canadian population. The answers to these necessary questions will help you decide on how to price your product or service, and how to market and sell it most effectively. It will give you ideas on catchy words or phrases to use in your advertising to get the message to your target audience. If your product will appeal to different audiences, you may have to modify your approach for each. Your marketing plan, therefore, is made up of your pricing structure, identification of your market, and your strategies for marketing and selling your product or service.

On the basis of your marketing plan, you will need to prepare a sales forecast and production plan. At this point your projections may appear to be artificial, because you have no experience or actual data on which to base your projections. However, you must persevere. Try to set three levels of projections: conservative, realistic, and optimistic. This will give you goal posts to aim for.

The rest of the business concept section of your business plan will include a step-by-step action plan to take you from your business plan, through the research and further planning stages, up to the actual start of your business. Checklist 1 will help you with your action plan.

Also, look into the verious business plan software programs available through the Federal Business Development Bank and computer stores.

3. The Financial Plan

The financial plan will comprise a number of documents to bring together an overall financial picture of the business. It will include your financial forecasts, any financing and capitalization required, any present financing, business references, and appendices. Samples 3 and 4 provide formats for working out a personal cost-of-living budget and your projected financial needs for the first three months. Of course, these statements, along with your personal net worth statement, will indicate whether additional financing is required. Appendixes should include a personal net worth statement (see Sample 1), a list of supplies, equipment, and inventory to be purchased and their total value, proposed price lists, etc. A cash flow statement may also be required (see Sample 5). "Cash flow" means the way the cash flows in and out of a business. For instance, if your mortgage and loan payments are due on the first of the month, you will want to plan to collect on any sales made and receivables outstanding prior to the end of the previous month in order to have sufficient cash on hand to make your monthly payments. Other payables may be scheduled for the middle of the month so that the beginning-of-the-month financial burden is not amplified unnecessarily. Your accountant will be able to assist you in planning your cash flow activity.

If you find that you will need to go to the bank for financing, you should be certain to review and formalize your entire business plan in preparation for presenting it to the banker. Prior to taking it to the banker, however, you should have your lawyer and/or accountant review your plan and financial projections. They will be able to identify any weak areas that may need further work before making your presentation.

At the outset you may be unfamiliar with some of the terms and statements referred to in the samples. The topics discussed in the subsequent chapters are intended to provide you with more background information to enable you to better understand the business terms and to make informed decisions when planning your business on paper. This book alone cannot help you to make all your decisions. Statistics Canada population profiles, your local library, government small business offices, and telephone directories are but a few of the resources that will further assist you. A listing of sources of further information is provided in Appendix A.

Even after the business has been launched, the need for planning continues. Events may occur outside your control that may cause you to periodically revise your plan.

It is good business practice to review your plan on a regular basis, either monthly or quarterly. Check your sales to see whether you have met — or possibly exceeded — your projections. In consideration of your actual experience, revise your projections, goals, and course of action. If you have not accomplished what you had hoped to by that benchmark, try to identify the reasons. It may mean that you need to take a course on time management to help keep you on track. Make some decisions that will help you to progress further along your business plan by the next benchmark. If you stop planning, there is a large risk that your business will stop growing or, worse, it may stagnate and die prematurely.

B. STARTING YOUR HOME-BASED BUSINESS

Many people think about starting their own home business, but don't know how to begin. For some, starting their business on a part-time basis is an easy way of taking the first step. The following are four directions you can take in getting started.

1. **The buffer route** Find some means of attaining a financial reserve or buffer to sustain you while you start your business. You

should have sufficient resources to finance your business and personal expenses for a minimum of six to 12 months. The money could come from personal resources, family, friends, or a lender.

2. **The spinoff route** You could take a client or clients from your previous job (assuming there are no legal or ethical impediments). Alternatively, you could turn your employer into your first client by negotiating a contract as an independent contractor (consultant, broker, etc.).

3. **The moonlighting route** Develop your business as a sideline to your full-time job. Once your business starts to successfully generate sufficient income to meet your personal financial needs, quit your full-time job.

4. **The part-time job route** Find a part-time job to provide you the base income required to build up your home business. Ideally this would be in a field related to your business, so that you have the chance to develop ideas and contacts or client potential, but you should be on the lookout for a possible conflict of interest. Once the point is reached that your business net income is equal to your base part-time income, you could quit the part-time job.

It is important to start on a small scale. This enables you to test your concept without incurring large expenses. It also provides you with the flexibility to try out new ideas, test the market, determine what works and what doesn't, and develop confidence, experience, expertise, and "street smarts." Finally, it even allows you to change your mind completely about the business idea or business in general, all without much financial loss.

C. ESTABLISHING A BUSINESS IMAGE

A professional image and businesslike approach are important for any type of business. Ask yourself: How do I make my decision on the businesses I patronize? How do I develop my impressions? How does my perception of the image of that business influence my continued patronage?

To appear professional and businesslike is especially important for a home-based business. Many operators of home-based businesses fail at establishing and maintaining a positive, professional business image, or merely perceive it as a hobby or a means of making extra money. This could be due to the fact that the entrepreneur is not aware of the importance of or how to develop the right image. Possibly, the home business owner operates too casually, or on too tight a budget. The perception could develop that the owner is an amateur and cannot be capable of operating a viable business.

Think of your reaction to another question. Let's assume you see an ad for a business offering a product. The ad has a post office box as an address and a price for the product. You phone the number given, and a telephone answering machine responds and requests that you leave a message. What would be your initial impression of the business? One of stability, reliability, permanence? Would you send money to the address for the product? Would you phone back again? Probably not. This is a good example of an "image" problem that could have been avoided by a different approach.

This section will discuss some of the factors that make up the image your business conveys.

1. Name

The name of your business is particularly important. Keep it short and easy to spell, pronounce, and remember, and make sure it presents the image you want to convey.

Be sure to check in the telephone book to see whether anyone else is using the same name, and check with the partnership and corporate registry in your province to make sure no one else has registered the name.

2. Type of Legal Structure

The three types of legal structure (which will be discussed in Chapter 4) include proprietorship, partnership, and incorporated company. Incorporated companies are identified by the word "Incorporated," "Limited," or "Corporation" (or the abbreviated form) at the end of the company name. If you are dealing with other corporations, you may be at an image disadvantage if you are not incorporated. For some, it may create the impression that you don't have much business depth or longevity, or divulge unnecessarily that your firm is in an early stage of business evolution.

3. Address

Your address does create an image. It could be a positive one or negative one, depending on your type of business. If you work in a metropolitan area, a Canada Post office box address may create a "transient image" (e.g., P.O. Box 12345, Station "A", Anytown, Canada). This is not recommended, as there are better options. Obviously this would not be the case in a rural area, where postal box numbers are the norm.

If it is important for you to project a business image to corporate clients, renting a mailing address service could be an option to consider. There are various types. One option is a packaged office company. They rent offices but also provide a "business I.D." package for people who want to have a business image and address, even though you don't have an office there. Essentially, you would use the business address, and fax number of the place as well, if you wish, on your stationery and business cards. Your mail would be either forwarded or picked up by you, according to the arrangements that you have made. It is common to use a telephone answering service at the same location, to ensure that your business address is in the telephone book, and to consolidate your office needs. Look in the Yellow Pages of your telephone directly, under "Offices for Rent".

Another option is to rent a box from a mail box rental company. Many of these companies are franchises, with office locations throughout North America, in case you want to have a U.S. business presence. These businesses are located in business address locations. They frequently offer other services as well, such as faxing (you can use their fax number on your stationery), copying, printing, desktop publishing, and sending and receiving courier parcels on your behalf. If you have a mail box which you show as, for example, "#150 - 240 Front Street, Anytown, Canada", this will create the impression that it is a suite number. If you go to clients or customers, and not the other way around, this format could work well for you. Look for a location that is near you, ideally one with 24-hour/7-day access. You can find this type of business under "Mail Box Rentals" in the Yellow Pages of your telephone directory.

You may wish to consider the above options, in other words, to have an address other than your home address, for a variety of reasons. For example, for convenience (e.g., courier parcels if you are not home during the day); keeping your own address confidential, for image, privacy or security reasons; or for business marketing reasons. Another reason could be for the purpose of your business license.

4. Telephone

For most businesses, the telephone is the most important means of communication. Your selection of telephone equipment and how you answer the phone will have a profound effect on your image. (See Chapter 3.) Some general telephone tips are as follows:

- Have a separate telephone line for your business. In this way you can leave your personal line free for other family members to use without interfering with your business.
- Have a policy that your children do not answer or use your business phone.
- Locate your business phone away from household noises (stereos, televisions, appliances).
- Have a call alert feature, to give you the advantage of having a second line. In this way callers won't be frustrated by hearing a busy signal and having to call again.
- Answer your business phone in a professional manner, using either your business name or your own name.
- Use an answering machine or answering service when you are unable to answer the phone directly. While it costs more, an answering service is more personal and professional. You have to weigh the image impact against the increased cost. Also consider the fact that a lot of people don't like leaving messages on a telephone answering machine, and you could therefore lose potential clients because of it.
- If you have an answering machine, leave a clear, polite, and businesslike message.

5. Stationery, Logo, and Promotional Materials

Stationery is a very important image creator. The colour and quality of the letterhead and envelopes as well as the size and type of printing will create definite impressions. If it fits your business image, you may decide to use a unique and creative logo design or a colour of ink other than the standard black. The format and quality of the typing on your letters also creates an impression, so make sure you use a good-quality typewriter ribbon.

A logo makes your business distinctive and hopefully memorable. You may either design your own or have one designed for you. If you decide to create your own design, you may want to read *Design Your Own Logo* by Mark Haskett (Self-Counsel Press, 1984) to get some ideas. "Clip art" logos can be purchased from commercial stationers and printers.

The logo should create a graphic image of your business product or service. Use it to provide a coordinated image on all your printed material. Make sure that your promotional material is professional in its quality and appearance. Use good-quality paper and printing. You may want to test the effectiveness of the message on different types of brochures before having large quantities printed. Desktop publishing can be an effective and reasonable cost option as a means of designing the format, content, and graphics.

6. Dress

Dress to reflect your business image. If you are a tradesman, for example, you would dress in practical, casual, and clean working clothes. If you are meeting with your banker, lawyer, accountant, or consultant, you should dress in appropriate attire. You want to look well-groomed, successful, and self-confident.

7. Workspace

How much time, effort, and money you put into the appearance and contents of your workplace will of course depend on whether clients will be visiting your house, and the type of business you are running. At the very least, however, you will want your surroundings to be comfortable and conducive to the work you will be doing there. If you are going to have business visitors, you want to be aware of such factors as washroom facilities, privacy, quietness, comfortable surroundings, pleasing furniture, plants, attractive and tasteful pictures on the walls, and a neat and orderly office. If you have a telephone answering service, have them take your calls while you are meeting with clients, so you are not interrupted. Look at your business premises through your clients' eyes. What image is conveyed? Is that image consistent with the one you want to convey? Does your office have the feel of an office, albeit more relaxed and informal?

Of course, you may prefer not to have clients come to your home. Instead, you could rent a hotel suite or packaged office for a meeting, or meet at the client's office. You may offer pickup and delivery service and conduct the majority of your business by means of telephone and mail.

D. SOURCES OF COUNSELLING ASSISTANCE

You may feel that it would help your business success to have some business counselling before you start out. Assistance may also be needed when the business is moving from one stage of growth to the next. Some sources to contact are listed below. Look in the White, Yellow, or Blue Pages of your telephone directory for further information.

1. CASE (Counselling Assistance for Small Enterprises)

This is a program operated by the Federal Business Development Bank (FBDB) wherein retired business owners or executives provide counselling services to small business owners for a reasonable fee. The CASE counsellors have a wide range of expertise in specific areas. After an interview at your FBDB office to ascertain your needs, a meeting is set up with the appropriate counsellor. That person then works with you on a particular project or an ongoing basis as your need dictates.

2. Provincial Government

The small business department of each provincial government employs counsellors who are available without charge to provide counselling during the various stages of your enterprise. You may have a specific question to ask over the telephone, or you may need to set up an appointment. The small business counsellors have useful planning guides and how-to publications are available at no charge. In many cases there are branch offices throughout your province, and these offer free small business advice plus a toll-free information number.

3. Federal Government

Industry Canada has counsellors who will assist you free of charge. In addition, other government departments such as Statistics Canada, Foreign Affairs and International Trade Canada, and Public Works and Government Services can all assist you with free research information.

4. Universities/Community Colleges

Some universities, community colleges, and technology institutes have "enterprise development centres" which provide instructional seminars and training on small business management, as well as counselling assistance for a nominal fee. This one-on-one mentoring relationship can help new business owners establish a sound foundation for their operations.

5. Private Consultants

Private business consultants are available who offer many types of specialized assistance. In the Yellow Pages under "Business Consultants" you will find a listing of consultants along with their specialty, and you will frequently see ads in the business section of your newspaper and in trade journals. But perhaps the best source is referral from business associates or friends who can recommend a consultant they have used, or referral from your lawyer, accountant, or banker.

In summary, to start your home-based business on a secure foundation, you should thoroughly research, plan, and get advice before starting. The decision-making skills required in writing your business plan will prepare you for dealing with business decisions on a day-to-day basis.

CHAPTER

3

Arranging Your Work
Environment and Equipment

The work environment you set up for your home business will vary a great deal according to the type of business you are operating. If you have a craft business, your workspace will resemble that of a workshop, with a working table, shelving, and compartments for storage and easy access to tools and materials. Most product-type businesses will require a lot of storage space for inventory and raw materials, while service-related businesses may only require sufficient space for storage of any tools and equipment used. However, certain elements will always be necessary regardless of the type of business you select, as most businesses will require an "office" area for handling the paperwork and accounting functions. For this you will need a desk, proper chair, filing cabinet, telephone, computer and facsimile (fax) machine. Some helpful hints on selecting equipment are provided in the latter part of this chapter. Following is a discussion of design and image considerations to help you define your work environment.

A. SELECTING YOUR WORK AREA

The space you select for your home business will require your ingenuity and creativity in order to make the environment conducive to your productivity and comfort. If you are going to spend eight or more hours in that one location, careful judgement and planning is needed.

If you live in a one-bedroom apartment or condominium, your options are rather limited, but things are still manageable if space is not a major business requirement. In a house, your options are more extensive. You may want to use a spare room, the attic, the basement, or the garage, or make additions to your house. (Refer to *Home Offices and Workspaces*, published by Sunset Books.) For Revenue Canada's benefit (and your own sanity), you should have a clearly defined workspace. Here are some of the key factors to help you decide.

1. Image

The importance of creating a professional and businesslike image was covered in the previous chapter. You should consciously identify an image you wish to create for your business, and then portray that image in all your business dealings. If you are seeing clients in your home, you want your workspace to project an image that is in keeping with the type of business you are operating. Image is most often reflected through use of colour (walls, carpets), furniture (contemporary, colonial, antique) and decor (plants, pictures, ornaments). It is also reflected by the structured (formal) or unstructured and more relaxed atmosphere. For example, if you are operating a film production studio, your clients in the entertainment business would appreciate a creative decor. This, however, would not be suitable for a desktop publishing business that caters to corporate clients. If you are not seeing clients in your home, you may spend less time and money on creating an atmosphere and more on creating an efficient workspace. Even here, however, a neatly organized workshop with materials and supplies protected in separate compartments reflects a professional image and pride about the quality and care of products that is sure to affect your work attitude and habits.

2. Privacy

Maintaining privacy is an important element for productivity, freedom from distractions, and creating the correct image. Having a separate room or area with doors to close off the living area, and a separate business entrance, will provide you with maximum privacy. One approach would be converting a basement or garage for your business use. Of course, you may choose to sacrifice some privacy for reasons of expediency.

Once you have defined your workspace, you will have to educate other adults living in the house, children, and neighbours about your business boundaries. If these are unclear, others may feel that your office and its associated activity are an intrusion on their own privacy, freedom of movement, and spontaneity. Identify and resolve such issues in a tactful and constructive fashion.

If it is not possible to have a closed-off area, an appropriate compromise may be to schedule your business activities in such a way that they do not clash with family activities. For example, you may agree only to accept appointments in your home in the morning while your children and spouse are at school and work. You may plan to have lunch when your children are home for their lunch break to allow some quality family interaction time. If you have young children, you may have to build your work hours around their nap times. Discourage neighbours and relatives from stopping by for a coffee, and suggest that, if they strongly wish to do so, they phone first so you can suggest a time for the visit that would fit into your schedule.

You should also look for ways to conceal or put away your work when your office is not being used. For example, a screen or room divider could attractively and functionally conceal the area.

Older children may be able to understand and respect the meaning of your closed office door if you set a firm policy that you are not to be interrupted during certain hours unless there is an emergency. Young children, however, constitute the classic problem associated with the home business. Have a separate business telephone line into your office and keep the telephone answering machine out of reach of children.

3. Access

The access route to your home office is as important to your business image as the office itself. How will customers or clients enter your office — through a separate entrance, or will they have to walk through the kitchen, living room, or other family area? Or will they have to get through a security door system because you live in an apartment or condominium? If so, is this easily accessible?

4. Storage

Initially you will probably be storing your work-related materials in two-drawer filing cabinets and desk drawers. This would include copies of correspondence, office supplies, financial records, and reference materials. If you need more storage space, make sure that it does not use up your work space unnecessarily. For example, rather than buying a four-drawer filing cabinet, consider two two-drawer ones, so that you will be able to use the cabinet tops as a work surface.

As your needs increase, consider using areas outside the office. Examples would include hall closets, the garage, or the basement.

You can calculate the floor area utilized for these additional storage areas as part of your office-related square-footage calculations for tax purposes.

Be careful of factors such as heat, cold, and humidity if you are storing supplies such as computer diskettes, ribbons, or paper. These could be ruined by temperature or humidity extremes. Also, if you have any important client, legal, or financial documents, you should store them in a safety deposit box at a bank, or in a fireproof cabinet. This of course also applies to computer programs and diskettes.

5. Task-Oriented Design

To make your office effective and practical, you want to design the layout and contents to achieve your objective — to be creative and productive. Also, you may want to have different areas for different tasks. For example, if your workspace has windows that overlook your backyard and garden, this may be an ideal area for working on the creative aspects of your business. A well-lit corner of the room may be a suitable spot for your desk, filing cabinet, and computer. Having your equipment, supplies, and records all within reach of your desk will provide an efficient area for handling the paperwork aspects. Each work area should therefore be well organized, self-contained, and accessible. Multiple work areas that require you to stand up and move around will help you avoid back problems or muscle fatigue, and provide some exercise and diversity to the work function.

You will be able to work most efficiently if your workspace is customized to your specific requirements. It should be compatible with your needs for physical comfort, concentration, and productivity in order to minimize stress, physical ailments, and fatigue. Such factors as proper seating and desk height, back and arm rests, ideal viewing distance from a computer screen, the positioning and amount of lighting, and many other matters should be taken into account. When searching for office furniture and equipment, especially computer-related, consider the comfort design (sometimes referred to as "ergonomic") features.

6. Utility Hookups

The typical house electrical circuits may not be able to handle the increased electrical demands of the equipment that you might be using. Overloading the circuits can create circuit breaks and also a fire hazard. You can understand the problem when you think of the potential electrical demands of a computer, photocopier, fax machine, telephone answering machine, air conditioner, and space heater, plus any other items specific to your business needs.

Computer equipment has unique power needs. If you were operating your computer on the same circuit as your air conditioner, refrigerator, washing machine, or some other major household appliance, you could cause serious damage to your equipment or software. You also want to make sure your computer equipment is not near any magnetic field and is protected in the event of a power surge.

It is not worth the risk to attempt to do the electrical work yourself. Hire a qualified electrician to wire your home office to provide the power needs and protection you require. If you need extensive rewiring, you may want to have a separate meter installed so that you can determine and deduct the actual electrical usage costs. Otherwise, just estimate the percentage of your overall electrical bill that you believe relates to your office.

Other utility features you may require include multiline telephone (for fax line or computer modem connection), or special plumbing connections for a separate washroom or work area sink.

7. Washrooms

If you don't intend to have temporary or full-time help or business visitors at your home, you may not have to deal with the issue of installing a separate washroom. Local regulations may require you to provide washroom facilities, though, if your home office is used by employees or visited by the public. Even if you are not required to provide a washroom facility, you may want to have one installed for reasons of privacy and personal hygiene. In this way your personal washroom would not be needed to be shared by your staff or business clients.

Of course you can deduct the cost to construct an extra washroom, including all supplies required to stock it. If you have no alternative but to use your personal washroom, it is important to keep it clean and remove any items of personal hygiene you would not want to share.

8. Noise Control

Noise can be distracting and stressful if it is at more than a comfortable level. It has been found that a moderate-to-high level of background noise can cause various symptoms of stress such as a faster heartbeat, increased blood pressure, fatigue, and an inability to concentrate. On the other hand, a working environment devoid of sound can also be stressful: a completely silent and soundproof office could be so artificial that it creates a sense of isolation.

To protect your office from intrusive noise, you may want to soundproof it by using thick carpets with underpad, heavy drapes, acoustic ceiling tiles, weatherstripping on windows and doors, solid rather than hollow doors, and double- or triple-glazed windows. You may also want to consider outdoor sound barriers such as tall, thick shrubs or indoor sound barriers such as screens or room dividers.

9. Cost to Renovate

When looking at an area for possible office use, one consideration of course is the cost to renovate. For this purpose it is important to determine not only what immediate tasks will take place there, but also what future tasks. Once you do this, you can assess how much space will be required and the types of furnishings, equipment, and utility lines you need. When anticipating future needs, consider: the addition of employees or temporary help, which could mean an extra washroom, work area, chairs, and equipment; meetings with clients, which could mean extra chairs or a conference area; or additional computer or other equipment, which could mean extra phone lines or electrical circuits. You also have to consider the adequacy of storage space, heavy equipment that may require additional floor support, or materials that are extra-sensitive to temperature, dust, or other environmental factors. Consider any special requirements for your type of business. Chemical use, for example, will require very specific storage and venting facilities.

Draw up a realistic budget of current and projected financial costs associated with renovation.

10. Tax Considerations

The tax aspects of operating a home-based business are covered in Chapter 5, "Accounting and Tax." Technically, one of the requirements for home business tax deductions is that the space be used *exclusively* for business purposes. Therefore, there should be some way of defining where the office begins and the personal space ends. When trying to determine the office location, it makes it much easier if the office is separate in terms of definable boundaries.

However, in practical terms, you may have to use part of an area that is also being used for personal purposes. For example, you may be using 75% of the basement space for business storage, or 50% of a bedroom or other large room. In the latter example, to create a boundary for business/personal separation, you may want to divide the room by means of a bookcase or grouping of furniture. If you live in a one-bedroom apartment, you may have to be creative by having a screen to physically and psychologically separate your work area off.

The square-footage areas that you use for business purposes do not have to be adjacent. For example, you could have bookcases lining the hallways, files and inventory stored in the basement, attic, or garage, and supplies stored in a cupboard or closet. In this case you would estimate the total of all the square-footages.

11. Security

If the public will be coming to your home, how will you deal with the issue of security? Will you and your premises be safe when strangers enter? A separate entrance to the business workspace and only keeping daytime hours may provide you with some protection. If this is a major concern, you could arrange to offer pickup and delivery of your clients' work.

B. EQUIPPING YOUR HOME BUSINESS

As with the type of space most suitable to your type of business, your specific equipment needs will vary widely. When planning your workspace, prepare a list of the minimum equipment and supplies you will need. If you are currently working, look around you and make a record of all the items you see. Include supplies as well as furniture and equipment. The basic furniture you will probably require will be a desk, chairs, filing cabinets, tables, bookcases, storage racks, and lamps.

There is a wide variety of office equipment available on the market today to assist you in speeding your means of communication while keeping your costs down, and enhancing your image, productivity, and efficiency. Computers, printers, modems, fax machines, photocopiers, cellular telephones, answering machines, and other types of equipment can give your home business the same competitive force as larger businesses. Before you buy equipment, though, do your research thoroughly. You will want to assess your present needs, look at the costs involved on a per-time use, project your ongoing requirements, and estimate the actual benefit that you would attain. Then check out the suppliers — the office equipment business is highly competitive. Also consider the advantages and disadvantages of leasing or buying.

1. Tips on Selecting Equipment

The best advice that can be given is to make sure you know clearly what you need before shopping. Do your research, know what equipment and features are available, and draw up a feature comparison chart. If you start talking to salespeople before doing your homework, chances are you will spend a lot more time than necessary listening to aggressive sales pitches and becoming confused about the features you actually require.

(a) Assessing your needs

If you are replacing a piece of equipment, what is your present volume or use? What problems or frustrations do you have with the equipment? What is your cost per usage? If you are searching out the equipment for the first time, what are your anticipated needs? What applications of use or special features do you think will enhance your efficiency and productivity? List the features in order of importance. Do you anticipate your needs increasing drastically over the next few years in volume or types of applications? In addition to equipment needs, you may have supplier needs. For instance, you may prefer to deal with an established and reputable company, or directly with the manufacturer of the equipment. You may need a supplier that can provide initial and ongoing training support and equipment servicing. The amount of your equipment budget should also be listed with your needs.

(b) Comparing what's available

Once you are aware of your projected needs, identify at least three or four models of equipment that are designed to handle those needs. With the features and needs that you have prioritized listed down the left-hand side of a page, write the names of the three or four suppliers you have chosen and the respective model names across the top of the page in vertical column format. You may then use this chart to take notes when talking to suppliers about the various features. In this way you will remain focussed on *your* needs rather than being distracted by the salesperson's emphasis on items that may be of minimal or no benefit to you.

Perhaps you have made some initial enquiries and comparisons over the telephone. However, when buying a major piece of equipment, you must insist on a thorough demonstration to satisfy yourself that the equipment will do the job. Some suppliers will allow you a free trial period in which you may use the equipment at your home for a few days or a week. Suppliers of photocopiers, fax machines, and memory typewriters fall into this category.

Once your chart has been filled in with the necessary comparative data, highlight those factors which most closely meet your needs. For a photocopier, for example, where "auto feed" is an essential feature, highlight on your chart the model which demonstrated the auto feed feature to your greatest satisfaction. Perhaps you liked this feature equally well on another model; then highlight both. As well as highlighting the "best-liked" features, you should also circle in red those items which you were not impressed with, or which did not meet your needs. Be careful to make "apple to apple" comparisons. Perhaps one supplier's feature is included in the price, while another's is considered an add-on feature which may then raise the price of the equipment beyond your budget. Don't hesitate to check back with the salesperson if you are unsure on any items. By the time you have completed this exercise, it should be easier for you to decide which model would best suit your needs.

(c) Training, service, and supplies

Depending upon the type of equipment you are selecting, training and service support may have been listed with your essential needs. However, it is important to make specific reference to these factors before you make your final decision. Especially with more complicated equipment, you will want to know if training is provided as part of the purchase price, and if training and operations manuals are included. Many responsible suppliers will provide unlimited assistance to ensure that you are making effective use of their equipment. After all, this may lead to future purchases of other product lines, or word-of-mouth referrals to others.

Regarding servicing the equipment, you will need to know the length of the warranty on the equipment, and how much a service contract will cost you after the warranty period has expired. What is the hourly service rate if you opt not to enter into a service contract? What is the company's response time to service calls? Emergency calls?

Some equipment suppliers are also in the business of selling expendable supplies needed to operate their equipment, such as photocopier toner and developer, or fax paper. You should ask whether you are obliged to purchase your supplies from them, and at what cost. Some do insist on this, for quality and performance control.

(d) Negotiating the purchase contract

You are now ready to make your final decision. Perhaps your comparison chart has helped you to narrow down your selection to two models which are very close in features and price. It is helpful to keep in mind that the office equipment business is extremely competitive, with many aggressive salespeople willing to put up a good fight in order to earn their sales commissions. This being the case, a salesperson may be willing to reduce the price of the equipment in order to make the sale. Others, who may have little flexibility on the price, may offer a free starter kit of supplies, a free training course, free service on the equipment for a one-year period, etc. Using good negotiating skills you may be able to strike a favourable bargain and at the same time get the equipment of your choice.

A word of caution in relation to price: it is not a good business decision to purchase equipment that fits your budget but doesn't fit your needs. This will only lead to increased costs and frustrations. An alternative may be to lease, rather than purchase, the necessary equipment. The next section discusses some alternatives to buying equipment.

2. Alternatives to Buying Equipment

(a) Renting

Some vendors have rental arrangements for their equipment. While the cost tends to be higher, it generally includes delivery, installation, initial training and ongoing support, instruction manuals, and servicing of the equipment. Especially in a situation where the purchase price is unaffordable, or the technology is rapidly changing, the rental option protects you from being left with obsolete or outdated equipment within a relatively short period of time. In the rental contract you should look for flexibility of upgrading to a different model of equipment, duration of the rental agreement, and the cancellation policy.

(b) Leasing

The difficulty that many business owners have in finding sufficient financing has caused many to look at leasing as an alternative financing arrangement for acquiring furniture and equipment. Leasing requires no down payment and provides 100% financing, which allows the growing company to conserve its capital. Payments are usually spread over a three-year period, although a flexible payment schedule may be arranged if your business is seasonal. There is no equity buildup in the equipment because you do not own the asset; however, some leases have a buyout clause at the end of the term.

(c) Business centres

For those who cannot justify the purchase of a piece of office equipment due to minimal use, "business centres" or "packaged offices" can provide services. Typically, a business centre is equipped with a variety of state-of-the-art equipment, and offers use of the facilities on a user-fee basis. A business centre could become a one-stop shop for your business needs such as word processing, photocopying, printing, fax messages, telephone answering service, and boardroom. They are listed in the Yellow Pages under "Offices for Rent."

3. Telephones

For the business owner working from home, the telephone may be the main link to suppliers and customers. It is therefore important to discuss special features and telephone answering options available to ensure that a professional business image will be projected.

(a) Special features

Telephone companies are marketing a rapidly expanding portfolio of features that make use of Touch-Tone phones and special electronic equipment to enhance basic local service. The following is a brief guide to the features offered to residential and small business subscribers in three key areas:

Custom Calling

- Ident-A-Call — allows up to three different phone numbers, each with a distinctive ring, to be included on one phone line.
- Call Waiting — emits a beep when you are on the phone to tell you another caller is trying to reach you and, with a custom phone, allows you to put one call on hold, answer the second call, and switch back to the first caller.
- Three-Way Calling — resembles a conference call feature by allowing you to talk to people at two different locations at the same time.
- Call Forwarding — allows you to send your calls to another phone number or pager.
- Speed Calling — allows you to place a call with a one-digit code.

Call Management

- Call Return — lets you know when a busy line is free and lets you return the last call placed or received at the touch of a button.
- Call Display — shows you an incoming caller's number on an electronic display screen before you answer the phone.
- Name Display — an added option to call display, which identifies the name of a caller.
- Call Screen — allows you to block calls from up to 12 phone numbers from whom you do not wish to receive calls. Callers from those numbers hear a recorded message that you are not currently accepting calls.

TeleMessage

- Voice Mail — allows customers to send voice mail messages to other call answer customers without having to ring their phone.
- Call Answer — automatically answers calls if you are on the phone or unavailable.
- Family/Extension Call Answer — provides personal answering service for up to four people who use the same line.

Other helpful tips for saving time or money on telephone service are:

- Use touch-tone phones; rotary dial phones take four times as long to dial a number.
- Enquire about long-distance discount programs, and comparison shop the long-distance networks.
- Dialing direct can save you up to 60% of the long-distance costs of operator-assisted calls.
- Place long-distance calls during non-peak hours whenever possible to reduce rates.
- Choose a good time for returning calls, such as just before noon or near the end of the day. Conversations will be briefer at those times (lunch and quitting time).
- Use "800" numbers whenever possible. When you are calling an out-of-town business, it is a good idea to check an 800 directory or call the 800 operator for assistance (1-800-555-1212).
- Carefully check your telephone bills for errors. Report discrepancies promptly.

(b) Cellular phones

Originally perceived as a communications toy, cellular telephones have become a standard communications tool in industries such as real estate, construction, trucking, and selling. Cellular phones have become a competitive necessity where people are on the road constantly and need to keep in touch with clients and suppliers. Small business owners are able to conduct business from their cars, home workshops, and gardens. Some models offer call waiting, call forwarding, conference calls, voice mail, pager, a dictation function, and message-taking while you are away from the set.

(c) Telephone answering

In any business where the telephone is a prime source of new business, careful attention should be paid to the manner in which the phone is answered during business hours. Thousands of dollars of advertising can be wasted if your business telephone is left unattended or answered inappropriately. Especially for the one-person home business, you must recognize that you will not be available to answer calls at all times. Therefore, you need an efficient backup system that will ensure callers are greeted with courtesy and that an accurate message is taken.

When you are using an automatic answering machine, the recorded message should be appropriate to your type of business and kept as brief as possible. Callers may become frustrated having to wait through a long taped message merely to leave their name and telephone number. If you find your taped message is not working (you get beeps instead of messages), you might alter your message. And if that doesn't work, throw away the machine and hire a personalized answering service! When you compare the cost of a monthly answering service with the amount of potential lost sales during that same period, you will appreciate the benefits. Your business image and credibility will be enhanced, for your customers and suppliers will respect your businesslike communications. Because the answering service can be asked to relay an important message to a particular caller, you will have greater freedom to leave your home on errands. There will be periods when you need to complete a project, and the answering service can free you from interruptions.

(d) Voice mail
There are all kinds of statistics which point up the perils of simultaneous communications. When you make a phone call, the odds are in favour of the telephone company. A full 75% of all business calls are not completed on the first attempt. The effect is an incredible amount of wasted time and energy. In addition, half of all calls are for one-way transfers of information, and two-thirds of all phone calls are less important than the work they interrupt.

Here are some prime examples of the benefits of voice mail:

- **Reduces "telephone tag"** It lets people communicate the complete message without regard for confidentiality or complexity of the information. Messages are in the caller's own voice, with all the original intonations and inflections. For one-way transfer of information, this eliminates the need for callback. When a response is required, the call can be made more effectively when you have the necessary files in front of you. Or perhaps a fax response can best serve the purpose, relieving the need of having to call back.

- **Shorter calls save time and money on long-distance charges** When messages are left on voice mail, calls are invariably shorter, as the caller gets right to the point. Live communications encourage "chit chat" — wasting time and money. When you are out of town, you can call into the voice mail to receive your messages in the evening when the long-distance rates are lower.

- **24-hour availability means no more time zone/business hour dilemma** If you operate a business in B.C., customers in the East no longer have to wait until noon to call you. When you are out of town, you can retrieve your messages at your convenience.

• **Automatic paging of all voice mail messages quickens response to callers**   Your voice mail can be programmed to call you as soon as messages are left on the service. You can leave instructions as to where calls should be directed (cellular, pager, home, or associate's number) as they are received.

To obtain more information on voice mail, contact your local telephone company. Also, look in the Yellow Pages under "Voice Mail" to comparison shop on different features, benefits, and rates.

4. Fax Machines

The word "fax" is actually an abbreviated form of "facsimile." It refers to a method of transmitting printed information over the telephone lines. A person wishing to send a document (letter, report, diagram) will insert the document into a fax machine, dial the telephone number of the fax machine at the receiving end, and touch a start button. The fax machine will feed the document, one page at a time, through the machine and deposit the pages in a tray. A facsimile or photocopy of the material will be simultaneously received at the other end. Fax machines can be programmed for after-hours sending which allows you, for example, to take advantage of the reduced telephone rates after midnight.

Fax machines have been on the market for relatively few years, but are now becoming indispensable. Their cost has fallen to as low as $300 for a basic unit. Of course, the convenience of using this type of electronic mail is dependent upon a fax machine being available at your customer's or supplier's place of business. Some suppliers now insist on receiving orders by mail or fax (rather than by telephone) to avoid the risk of mistakes by the message-taker, and to eliminate the costs of an order-taker. Many small business owners in the import/export industry rely solely on fax communication to conduct their business overseas. When you compare the costs and time delays of communicating overseas by mail or courier, sending by fax is a very efficient method.

5. Personal Computers

What can a computer do for you? You must list the jobs you want the computer to do for you, review the benefits that you will gain, and look at the costs involved. To do business today, a computer is a fact of life.

(a) Computer uses

Computers can speed up basic administrative work and make available more information on which to base management decisions. The following are the more common business computer applications:

- **General information**   Storage and retrieval; customer profiles; profiles on existing and potential suppliers and their products; word-processing applications (price lists, personalized letters, mailing lists).
- **Accounting**   Sales invoices and purchase orders; accounts receivable and payable; general ledger.
- **Management**   Monitoring movement of inventory in order to maximize turnover; valuing inventory to assist in monitoring profitability; analyzing sales and profitability (which products or lines are the most profitable, which customers contribute most profit to the operation); preparing monthly financial statements.
- **Planning**   Preparing financial budgets; cash flow projections; forecasting sales; scheduling production runs.

Once you have completed the list of jobs you want the computer to do for you, detail the information that is required for each application. An invoice will require an invoice number, date, customer's order number, "ship to" address, item number and name, quantity, price, discounts, taxes, etc. You will need to quantify each application to know the size or capacity of computer system you will need. For instance, how many customer accounts do you have? How many sales invoices are generated monthly? How many suppliers and creditors do you have? How many items in inventory?

The next step is to review your list of computer applications and place them in order of priority: must have, should have, would like to have. This is because when selecting computer hardware or software, you will seldom find something that meets all of your needs. It is therefore important to remain focussed on the essential priority applications.

(b) Computer benefits

Your next step in identifying your needs is to list, for each computer application, the benefits that will be realized. Common benefits are listed below:

- respond faster to customer inquiries and orders
- improve cash flow and reduce interest expense
- speed collection of receivables
- keep projects within budget
- reduce costs of outside services
- reduce inventory and inventory carrying costs
- reduce lost sales as a result of fewer out-of-stock items
- reduce future labour costs

- improve timeliness and accuracy of financial statements
- improve company image through improved appearance of reports, proposals, correspondence.

(c) Hardware and software

Selecting the right computer system is very important, so be prepared to devote time to your deliberations. Because this is a very technical piece of equipment, you may wish to seek the advice of an independent computer consultant who can make recommendations on the appropriate hardware (the physical equipment) and software (the disks and programs) for your needs. The consultant may also assist with the initial training and startup programming. Also, attend computer trade shows and comparison shop. The market is highly competitive.

Today there are software packages available for a wide variety of functions as well as industry sectors. As a rule of thumb, it should be possible to find a package for your business that will meet 80% of your needs. Some businesses with unique needs opt to have a software program custom-written for them. However, the variety of programs readily available, the speed of implementation, and the lower costs make off-the-shelf packages the best bet.

Your software program selections will predict your hardware needs, not vice versa. You don't need a computer any bigger, faster, more sophisticated, or more expensive than is needed to do the job. It must, however, have the capacity to house the programming for each software program you intend to install. Also, allow for projected growth. Most businesses use a dot matrix printer for routine financial reports and customer records, charts, and graphs. If you expect to be producing high-quality reports and proposals, a laser printer is recommended.

(d) Pitfalls to avoid

- **Inadequate storage or growth capacity** Avoid purchasing a computer system with inadequate capacity, or one which cannot grow with your business. To add additional storage capacity or new software programs can literally double the original cost.
- **Starting with complex applications** Selecting a difficult or complex application as your first computer task will cause frustration and much wasted time. Learn by implementing basic functions. Avoid leading-edge or state-of-the-art technology. As an inexperienced user, stick to the tried and true.
- **Nonspecific objectives** Loosely stated or overly general benefits to be achieved will leave you not knowing if you have met your

goals. When you are listing your justification for buying a computer, your objectives should be measurable and easy to achieve.

- **Poor documentation**   Instruction manuals which are not "user-friendly" will cause considerable delays in learning the software. The instruction manual should be concise and easily understood, without overuse of computer jargon, and include section tabs, an extensive index, and a help section to assist the operator to quickly find the necessary information.

Much of the enjoyment and freedom of being your own boss will result from working in a customized and personalized home workplace. It does not necessarily need to be a costly remodelling of space. Rather, it should be based on your business and personal needs. Be pragmatic and conservative in your expenditures. And ensure you are comfortable and enjoy your working environment.

CHAPTER

4

Legal Matters

In researching and planning your business, as well as dealing with the day-to-day aspects once you get started, many decisions will have to be made. These will include legal and accounting matters, government regulations, and marketing decisions. The decision-making process will be much easier if you establish at the outset a circle of experts whom you can trust to give you information and advice that will be helpful to you. This chapter will cover how to select your advisors in general — and specifically how to select a lawyer — forms of legal structure of a business, and complying with government regulations, zoning laws, and licence requirements. Later, in Chapter 5, "Accounting and Tax," advice will be given on selecting an accountant.

A. SELECTING PROFESSIONAL ADVISORS

Professional advisors are essential to small business success, and a home-based business is no exception. Your team of professional advisors should include a lawyer and tax accountant, and ideally a consultant or mentor experienced in small business ownership. They can provide knowledge and expertise in areas which you have little experience. They will round out your own management skills so that your business is operating most efficiently.

It is important to recognize when it is necessary to call in an expert to assist you. Because of the costs associated with hiring a lawyer or accountant, some business owners are inclined to try the do-it-yourself approach. This can be a shortsighted decision and detrimental to your business. For instance, the person who processes his or her own income tax return rather than hiring a tax accountant may miss out on small business tax exemptions that could save much more than the cost of the accountant's time. Or a person who signs a lease or a contract without having it reviewed beforehand by a lawyer may regret it for many years to come.

You should be very selective in your screening process. The right selection will enhance your prospects for profit and growth; the wrong selection will be costly in terms of time, money, and stress.

There are many factors you should consider when selecting advisors. Some are more related to paid professional advisors than "free" advisors, but all are important. For example, the person's professional qualifications, experience in your specific area, and the fee for services are factors you will want to consider. It is helpful to prepare a list of such questions, plus others relating to your specific needs, and pose these to each of the prospective advisors. Some people may feel awkward discussing fees and qualifications with a lawyer, for instance, but it is important to establish these matters at the outset before you make a decision to use that person's services. If you decide to hire the individual, it is also a good business practice to follow up the initial meeting with a letter confirming the fees agreed upon and other terms discussed, or request the advisor to do so. The most common selection criteria include qualifications, experience, compatible personality, confidence and competence in area concerned, and fees. Having a comparison of at least three advisors is the ideal approach before you select the one for your needs.

1. Qualifications

Before you entrust an advisor with your work, you will want to know that he or she has the appropriate qualifications. These may include a lawyer's or accountant's professional degree, a university degree in the area of expertise, or some other professional training relative to the area of work.

2. Experience

It is very important to take a look at the advisor's experience in the area where you need assistance. Such factors as the degree of expertise, the number of years' experience as an advisor, and percentage of time spent practising in that area are critically important. The amount of reliance you are going to place on their advice and insights is obviously related to the degree of experience they have in the area. For example, the fact that a lawyer might have been practising law for 10 years does not necessarily mean that the lawyer has a high degree of expertise in the area where you require specific advice. Perhaps only 10% of the practice has been spent in that specific area. An accountant who has had 15 years' experience in small business accounting and tax advice will certainly provide you with a depth of expertise about small business in general. If that accountant also has specialized experience in your industry, this is an additional factor that could assist you. Enquire about the degree of expertise and length of experience in the area of most concern to your business. If you don't ask the question, you won't be given the answer that may make the difference between mediocre and in-depth advice.

3. Compatible Personality

When deciding on an advisor, make certain that you feel comfortable with the individual's personality. If you are going to have an ongoing relationship with the advisor, it is important that you feel comfortable with the degree of communication, the attitude, the approach, the candor, and the commitment to your business success. A healthy respect and rapport will put you more at ease when discussing business matters and thereby enhance your further understanding.

4. Confidence

You must have confidence in your advisor if you are going to rely on the advice to enhance the quality of your decision-making and minimize your risk. After considering the person's qualifications, experience, and personality style, you may feel a strong degree of confidence in the individual. If you do not, don't use the person as an advisor, because there is a very good chance that you will not use him or her as extensively as you should, or when you need to. This in itself could have a serious negative impact on your decision-making.

5. Fees

It is important to feel comfortable with the fee being charged, and the payment terms. Are they fair, competitive, and affordable? Do they match the person's qualifications and experience? The saying "You get what you pay for" is true of fees charged by lawyers, accountants, and consultants. For instance, if you need a good tax accountant to advise you on minimizing taxes, you may have to pay a high hourly rate for the quality of advice that will save you several thousands of dollars. On the other hand, if what you require is the preparation of annual financial statements, perhaps a junior accountant can do the job competently at a more affordable rate. Be certain the rate is within your budget, or you may not fully use the advisor effectively because of the expense. Not using available professional advice when you need it is poor management. At the outset, ask for fee estimates.

6. Comparison

Do not make a decision as to which advisor to use without first checking around. It is a good rule of thumb to see a minimum of three advisors before deciding which advisor is right for you. The more exacting you are in your selection criteria, the more likely it will be that a good match is made, and the more beneficial that advisor will be to your business. It is a competitive market in the advisory business, and you can afford to be extremely selective when choosing advisors to complement your management team.

B. SELECTING A LAWYER

There are numerous ways a lawyer can help you from the time that you have the idea of going into business during the pre-startup phase, right through to the startup. You will need a lawyer during the growth phases as well as during the phases of expanding, diversifying, selling, or winding up of your business. Your lawyer can help you in deciding the proper legal structure of your business, drawing up a partnership or shareholders' agreement, negotiating a management contract, and numerous other types of contracts. Advice can also be given about municipal zoning and licensing requirements, firing employees, suing creditors, Revenue Canada or provincial tax audits, wills, buying a business or a franchise, leases, patent, copyright, trademarks, etc. There are few business decisions that do not involve some legal, financial, or tax implications. It is important to keep that thought in mind through the day-to-day operation of your business. Although your lawyer is trained to give legal advice as to your rights, remedies, and options, it is you who must decide on the action to be taken.

Lawyers in Canada must have a Bachelor of Laws degree (LL.B.) from a recognized Canadian university. A lawyer in Canada is automatically licensed to be a "barrister" and a "solicitor." A barrister is a lawyer who practises courtroom law, and deals in civil and/or criminal legal matters. A solicitor generally does not attend court, and performs services such as drafting or reviewing legal agreements including wills, leases, mortgages, contracts, etc.

1. Methods of Finding Lawyers

(a) Lawyer referral services

Most provinces have a "lawyer referral" program which is usually coordinated through the Canadian Bar Association. Simply look in the Yellow Pages under "Lawyer Referral Services" or contact the Law Society or the Canadian Bar Association. When you call, explain briefly the problem you have, or the type of business law on which you want a legal opinion (e.g., small business, contracts, tax, patents, trademarks, copyright law). The service will give you the name of a lawyer in your geographic area, and you can set up an appointment with the lawyer. A lawyer will give you an interview of up to 30 minutes at a nominal fee (generally around $10 to $25) or for free, depending upon the province or the location. At the end of the interview the lawyer will tell you whether he or she thinks you have a legal problem, what is involved, how long it should take to solve, and about how much it will cost. Then, if you agree to proceed, you may hire the lawyer to help you further at a negotiated fee. If you decide not to hire the lawyer, and wish to consult someone else, or if you are satisfied that you do not require any further help, it won't have cost you any more than the nominal fee.

(b) Referral by friends, relatives, business associates, banker, or accountant

Ask one or more of these sources if they can recommend a lawyer who would be appropriate for your needs within the business context. If someone recommends a lawyer, or a number of lawyers, ask the reason why the person would be helpful for your small business needs, and what the source's own experience has been with that lawyer. A friend or relative might suggest a lawyer, for example, who specializes in an area of law that has nothing to do with business.

(c) The Yellow Pages

In the Yellow Pages under "Lawyers," you may note that some lawyers advertise a preferred interest or designated specialty.

Many lawyers will offer the initial consultation without fee, as this provides them an opportunity to hear what is involved in your situation and to decide if they are interested in taking on the work. It is also an effective "loss leader" marketing technique. You should take advantage of that opportunity to pose the questions you have prepared to determine if the lawyer is well-suited to your needs. It is quite common to have more than one lawyer assist you in your business needs, either for a second opinion, or for advice in a different area of expertise. Patent and trademark law, for instance, is a specialized area in which most lawyers may not have had experience.

2. Preparing for the Meeting

Before going to see your lawyer, make sure that you get all your papers and documents together and put them in order — assuming that you wish to get advice on existing facts. Then, write out all the issues that you want advice on, and all the questions you want to ask. Arrange the sequence of your questions so that the critical matters are dealt with first. It may be helpful to give a copy of your questions to the lawyer who could use that as an agenda for covering the various issues. Thinking about your questions in advance of the meeting will force you to focus on the reasons for seeing the lawyer. You will be satisfied that the meeting was productive when all questions are answered by the end of the interview.

When you talk to the lawyer, stick to the facts and make sure you tell your lawyer all the facts, good and bad. Ask questions if you don't understand the advice you are given, and ask what you can do to minimize costs. A word of caution: It is common for people to be unfocussed, emotional, or overly enthusiastic, depending on the stage of their small business venture. But don't think that the lawyer is indifferent to your needs if he or she does not respond to your feelings; by training and discipline, the lawyer is supposed to be objective, balanced, and dispassionate.

3. Understanding Fees and Disbursements

In many cases a lawyer's fee structure is based on what other lawyers are charging. Although competition in the legal profession is obviously a factor in keeping fees within bounds, there are many circumstances wherein two lawyers will charge a different fee for performing the same routine or specialized service. The most common types of fee arrangements are (1) an hourly bill-out rate of $100 to $200 or more per hour, and (2) a fixed fee for routine services such as incorporation.

In addition to paying your lawyer fees for time spent, you may have to pay for the lawyer's disbursements (out-of-pocket expenses). Disbursements incurred on your behalf by the lawyer would include payments for such things as photocopies, couriers, registry searches, registry agent fees, long-distance telephone calls, fax charges, provincial or federal filing fees, and process serving fees of writs or other documents.

Since you are buying your lawyer's time, the less you use, the less it will cost. On the other hand, it is important that you clearly understand the advice given and what options are available to you.

You can keep your legal fees down by not making unnecessary telephone calls to your lawyer's office. If you must call on routine matters, you may prefer to talk to the lawyer's secretary: his or her response would not necessarily translate into a bill for the time. Be realistic about the matters in dispute or the action you are considering. For example, you don't want to spend $1,000 in legal fees to collect a $500 debt. You may want to go to a small claims court yourself.

C. FORMS OF LEGAL STRUCTURE

One of the first problems you have when starting a small business is deciding which form of legal structure you should choose for your company. This will be necessary before you set up a company bank account, apply for a business licence, or register your company name. Your main alternatives are sole proprietorship, partnership, and corporation. A description of these structures follows, along with advantages and disadvantages of each.

The type of legal structure you decide on will depend upon the type of business you are in, your potential risk and liability, the amount of money needed to start, and what you expect to earn. If your risk and liability is high, the incorporation process will provide protection from disasters. On the other hand, a person starting a home-based business may recognize the advantages of having a sole proprietorship instead. Once you become familiar with the differences between each form, you may wish to consult a lawyer, tax accountant, or other business advisor. The decision is an important one.

1. Sole Proprietorship

A sole proprietorship refers to an individual who owns a business in his or her personal name. The business income and the owner's personal income are considered the same for tax purposes. Therefore, business profits are reported on the owner's personal income tax return, and are based on federal and provincial income or loss schedules. Business expenses and losses are deductible. It is advisable, though, to keep personal and business bank accounts separate. For instance, you should pay yourself a salary from your business account and deposit it into your personal account for your personal needs — food, clothing, lodging, personal savings, etc.

In a proprietorship or partnership, the company continues until the owner ceases to carry on the business or dies. If the business uses a name different from the owner's personal name, the company name (called a *trade style* name) should be registered with the appropriate provincial registry.

(a) Advantages

- It is easy to get started. You don't even need to register with the provincial registry if you are doing business under your personal name. If you have a trade style name, you have to register with the province, for a nominal fee.
- There is minimal government regulation.
- It is relatively easy to roll over into an incorporated company if necessary or desired at some later point.
- There is total control by the owner, and all profits go to the owner.

(b) Disadvantages

- The owner has *unlimited liability*; that is, he or she is personally liable for all debts and obligations of the business.
- It is frequently difficult to raise capital, apart from conventional loans, because of the personal liability and risk.
- Customers and creditors may perceive the proprietorship as having a low level of business sophistication. It may be perceived to be in business for the short rather than the long term.
- Some government loan, subsidy, or guarantee programs are available only to limited companies (corporations).
- Sale of the business could involve having to disclose the owner's personal tax return.
- If the business fails, the owner is not eligible to collect unemployment insurance benefits.
- The death or illness of the owner endangers the survival of the business, because the owner and the business are deemed legally to be one and the same.

2. Partnership

A partnership is a proprietorship with two or more owners. The owners may not necessarily be 50:50 partners; they may have whatever percentage properly reflects their investment and contribution to the partnership. The partners share profits and losses in proportion to their respective percentage interest. While the partnership has to file a tax return, it does not pay any tax. Instead, the partners pay tax on the basis of their portion of the net profit or loss. In a partnership, each partner is personally liable for the full amount of the debts and liabilities of the business. Each of the individuals is authorized to act on behalf of the company, and can bind the partnership legally, except if stated otherwise in a partnership agreement. It is sound business advice not to enter into any partnership arrangement without a written agreement between the partners regarding responsibilities for financing the business, sharing the profits and losses, working in the business, specific duties, and other important considerations. Checklist 3 will help you decide what to include in a partnership agreement. Partnerships are governed by provincial Partnership Act legislation, and the Consumer and Corporate Affairs office of your provincial government will provide the necessary forms to be completed.

(a) Advantages

- It is easy to get started. You don't need to register with the province if you are doing business under your personal name. If you have a trade style name, you have to register with the provincial registry, for a nominal fee.
- There is minimal government regulation.
- It is relatively easy to roll over into an incorporated company if necessary or desired at some later point.
- There is joint responsibility: everything does not rest on your own shoulders.
- There is greater access to money and skills.

(b) Disadvantages

- There is potential conflict of authority.
- There is *unlimited liability*: all partners are individually and collectively liable for all the debts and liabilities of the business. Thus, if one person makes an error in judgement (e.g., ordering too much inventory, or underestimating a fixed price bid), all partners will be exposed.
- There is no continuity at retirement or death.
- Ownership and control must be shared, as well as the profits.
- Most business partnerships that do not survive, experience conflict of egos, power and/or money. The partners may have unrealistic expectations or are making unbalanced efforts/contributions to the business.

3. Corporation (Limited Company)

A corporation is a business which is a legal entity separate from the owner or owners of the business. After being incorporated with the provincial or federal registry, a business must file annual reports, submit regular tax returns, and pay tax on its profits. The owners are called *shareholders* and have no personal liability for the company's debts, unless they are also directors or have signed a personal guarantee. The liability of the company is limited to the assets of the company. The shareholders elect *directors* (usually the shareholders) who are responsible for managing the affairs of the corporation. Directors have some liability to statutory creditors (e.g., Revenue Canada, Workers' Compensation Board, Ministries of the Environment) for debts or liabilities of the company. The profits of the corporation may be retained for reinvestment or distributed to the shareholders in the form of dividends at the discretion of the directors.

It is advisable to obtain legal and tax advice to assist with the preparation of the incorporation documents and shareholders' agreements.

(a) Advantages

- The shareholders are not personally responsible for any of the debts or obligations of the corporation, unless a shareholder has signed a personal guarantee.
- A corporation has more financing options available. It is eligible for government financing incentive programs. It can attract investors and provide better security to lenders in the form of debentures, common shares, convertible shares, and other structures.
- The corporation continues regardless of whether a shareholder dies or retires.
- There are various tax advantages not available to a proprietorship or partnership.
- The tax rate could be lower than for a proprietorship, up to a certain level of income.
- In general terms, a corporation can imply higher prestige, more stability, and greater resources in terms of capital and expertise.
- There is increased stability, in that while shareholders may come and go, the business continues uninterrupted and all contracts of the corporation remain valid.
- Share ownership interest is transferable.
- A corporation is a separate legal entity from an individual. It may sue or be sued in its own name.

(b) Disadvantages

- Corporations are regulated by each province or the federal government. The regulations are more complex than those of the Partnership Act.
- The costs of incorporating are higher — approximately $300 to $500 in legal fees, plus applicable taxes and the lawyer's out-of-pocket disbursements, which are approximately $300 for a simple incorporation.
- The operating losses and tax credits remain within the corporate entity; they are not available to individual shareholders if the corporation is unable to utilize them.

D. PROTECTION OF YOUR IDEAS AND CREATIONS

You may have an innovative idea which has been developed into a product and want to obtain protection from others taking your idea or design. The concept of law that deals with this type of protection is that of *intellectual property*. It refers primarily to patents, copyright, trademarks, and industrial design.

The terms and concepts of intellectual property law are frequently misunderstood by the public. While all of them are rights granted for intellectual creativity, they take different forms. *Patents* are for structure and function, whereas *copyright* is for literary, dramatic, artistic, or musical works. A *trademark* is a word, picture, or symbol, or a combination of these, used to distinguish goods or services sold by one person or organization from the goods and services of others in the marketplace. *Industrial designs* are for the shape, pattern, or ornamentation applied to an industrially produced object.

The laws governing these areas are federal statutes. Legislation is always in a state of flux, so if you are considering making an application under any of the intellectual property statutes, obtain the advice and assistance from professionals well in advance. This is essential to save time, expense, and inconvenience as well as avoid pitfalls. You can obtain names of a registered patent or trademark lawyer from the Yellow Pages under "Patent or Trademark Attorneys."

Legislation governing intellectual property is administered and regulated by Industry Canada. This department has branches in various cities throughout Canada, and you can find the address and phone number in the Blue Pages of your phone book under "Federal Government." Contact this department for general enquiries and to obtain their excellent series of free booklets on intellectual property.

E. REGULATIONS, ZONING, AND LICENSING

In all communities in Canada there are public laws that regulate the operation of a business. These regulations may be set by local, regional, provincial, or federal governments. And in some cases there are private regulations that impact on home business operation. It is important to know the rationale behind these regulations, how the regulations operate, whether you are permitted to operate out of your home and, if not, what your options are.

The remainder of this chapter will discuss the legal aspects relating to the regulation of a business in general and home business in particular. This should give you a much clearer idea of how to attain your home business objectives.

1. Municipal Regulations

Municipal government has the authority to make its own regulations relating to home business operation. These regulations are intended to protect the general public and prevent or minimize public nuisances and misleading business practices. There can be a considerable range of bylaw differences between one community and another in terms of how each deals with the issue of a home-based business. To complicate matters, you may find that some of these regulations may be based upon clearly stated rationale, while others may be antiquated statements designed in and for a different era. Unless challenged or specifically requested to be changed, these regulations may go unnoticed. Such situations may likely be found in smaller communities or areas where major corporations are the primary employers. With the trend for businesses to be operated from home, entrepreneurs and city officials are getting rid of the mothballs and rewriting the bylaws to be more representative of present-day needs of the community.

There are basically two types of regulations which attempt to meet the above objectives: zoning and building regulations.

(a) Zoning regulations
Zoning regulations divide a community into four basic classifications: *residential, commercial, industrial,* and *agricultural.* Each of these areas includes further subcategories such as residential single-family or residential multiple-family. The types of activities that can be carried out in each classification vary by locality. Home-based businesses are usually referred to as "home industries" or "home occupations."

Since municipal government is run by elected officials, the government concerns are naturally a reflection of the concerns of the residents in their particular community. There is no consistency of approach for regulations which relate to home business, because each community may have its own personality or mix which could encourage either a liberal or a conservative attitude toward the regulations. Factors that may impact on city council's decision on the regulations include the rural, urban, or metropolitan nature of the community; the visibility of a community lobby group; the prevalence of, and economic spirit generated by, local entrepreneurs.

Some of the considerations that local government officials take into account when dealing with the issue of home-based business include:

- preserving the economic well-being of commercial areas
- preventing unfair competition to commercial areas
- preserving neighbourhood amenities
- preserving the appearance and character of residential neighbourhoods
- preserving residential property values
- controlling traffic in residential neighbourhoods
- controlling the density of property use in residential neighbourhoods
- protecting residential neighbourhoods from nuisances such as noise and odour
- maintaining the tax base revenue in commercial and residential areas
- fulfilling the perceived needs and expectations of the community
- avoiding criticism or complaints from the community.

In general terms, local governments are becoming more receptive to the growth in numbers of home businesses. Although business owners in commercially zoned areas sometimes perceive that the home business entrepreneur is not paying the same taxes, not meeting the same regulations, and competing unfairly, in many cases the perception is not the reality. The home-based owner may be targetting a different market completely. Another factor is that almost 50% of home businesses eventually move out of the house, which could favourably increase the revenue tax base and overall economic well-being of the community. Encouraging and fostering the home business concept is therefore enlightened self-interest for local governments. It provides employment in the community, either self-employment or hiring of other employees. It provides an incubator for people who by choice or necessity would not be able to start a business except from the "incubator" of the home.

For the above reasons, many local governments are attempting to recognize the reality of home-based business by legitimizing them, classifying them, and licensing them.

Ultimately the elected officials attempt to keep the interests of the community foremost in mind. Some of the common types of local regulations relating to home-based business are as follows. Some, all, or none of these may be applicable in your community.

- Control of nuisances, such as noise, smoke, and odour.
- Control of unsightly garbage or junk.
- Control over employing workers in the home. (There could be a restriction that only family members can work at home.)
- Control of traffic to avoid congestion, noise, or parking problems; restriction on trucks being used in the business.
- Control of signage or advertising on the premises (restriction on number and size, restriction on location, or total restriction).
- Control over types of businesses allowed. (There could be regulations allowing certain businesses and prohibiting others. Some communities distinguish between a business and a profession, and generally allow more flexibility under the "professional" category.)
- Control over the maximum number of customers served at the home at any one time, or possibly restriction against any business-related foot traffic.
- Control over the amount of space that can be used for the business (e.g., not more than 25% of the total residential square-footage).
- Control over retail sales (total or limited restrictions).
- Control over storage of inventory (permitted, restricted, or prohibited).
- Control over manufacturing (permitted, restricted, or prohibited).
- Control over entrance (separate business entrance either required or prohibited).

Many governments require that a business take out a licence to operate. Some smaller communities do not require this. Before issuing a licence, the city may first investigate whether you have complied with the appropriate zoning, health, building, sanitation, and other business bylaws. Some of these regulations are local, but others could also be governed by provincial or federal regulations.

(b) Building regulations
If you are going to make any modifications or additions to your house, you should enquire as to whether a building permit is required. There is generally some flexibility according to the local policy. Depending on the nature, extent, and purpose of the construction or renovation, there could also be provincial or federal regulations which apply. Local building regulations may also involve electrical, fire, health, plumbing, and other types of inspection.

2. How to Determine Whether the Zoning Permits Home Business Operations

With the wide range of zoning restrictions on home business, you may find that there are no restrictions, some restrictions, or a total restriction. Or, you may be able to get a temporary permission while the regulations are under review. Certain steps may be followed to ascertain the zoning issues, and your rights and options.

First of all, determine if your local community has zoning regulations. This is done by contacting your local government office. Speak to someone in the planning department, zoning department, or licensing department, or to the building inspector. You do not necessarily have to give your name and address at this stage, as you are asking for public information to which you are entitled.

Determine how your property is zoned. As mentioned earlier, zoning classifications include residential, commercial, industrial, and agricultural. Locate your property on the official map at your local city hall zoning department. If your home business is in an area zoned *agricultural*, you can be almost certain that you can operate a business, since farmers were the pioneers of "home businesses." Many *commercially* zoned areas permit usage for both businesses and residential — the example of a family living in the back or upstairs of a "mom and pop" business is common — however, some industry zoning restricts any residential use. This can sometimes present problems for those who want to rent and live in a warehouse or other industrial building and operate a home-based business such as an artist's studio. *Residential* zoning, as previously discussed, can be more restrictive of home business operation, or limit the scope and nature of business activities that can be operated at home.

Next you should determine what is allowed and what is not. Since there is a wide range of possible restrictions or latitude, enquire specifically what is and what is not permitted in your zone and for your intended business. Refer back to the discussion on zoning regulations and the common types of restrictions, so that you are conversant with them. Remember, you are entitled to this public information. If you are still unclear as to your rights and options after doing your initial research, speak to a lawyer who is conversant with municipal law.

3. Steps to Take If Your Home Is Not Zoned for a Home Business

(a) Adjust your planned business to meet regulations

After you know specifically what you can and cannot do at home, you may choose to modify your projected operation to comply with the regulations. For example, if you can't have non-family employees working at your home, it may be feasible to have your employees work from their own homes instead. If you can't make retail sales from your home, consider mail-order merchandising or distribute your product through sales representatives or directly through distributors or retail stores.

(b) Establish and maintain good relations with your neighbours

Find out how your neighbours look upon the idea of your working from home. They could be very supportive of your intentions. Your business could be providing a local service which is desired. You could be creating employment for neighbourhood youths. Also, you could be providing a form of security in the neighbourhood if you work in your house during the day. Your neighbours could provide important local support if you want to make special requests to the zoning department, and minimize or neutralize the risk of a neighbour's complaint.

(c) Apply for a use permit which would allow you to use your home as a business

After you have discussed your business plans and intended facilities with the zoning officials, you could be permitted to use the premises for the purpose stated, without the need for a public hearing. Technically speaking, your business can operate, although it is not lawfully permitted. In some cases, if you have such a *non-conforming use* status under the existing bylaw, the right you have could be cancelled automatically if you cease doing business for a certain continuous period of time (e.g., six months) or sell the house. Generally, a non-conforming use status can be revoked at any time if your local government policy changes.

(d) Apply for a variance

You can request the local zoning board, planning board, or appeals board to waive the zoning restrictions in your particular case. A variance normally requires a public hearing. There are several arguments that you may be able to present in order to accomplish your objectives:

- Show that there would be no harm done to the neighbourhood. Attempt to get the written support of your neighbours beforehand, and have them attend the hearing. If there are no objections at the hearing, you could succeed.
- Show that what you intend to do is comparable to a home business which is permitted.
- Show that you would suffer hardship and be deprived of a livelihood if the zoning bylaw was enforced in your circumstance.

Attend several zoning board meetings to see how they are conducted, and note which board members seem to be the most influential. Speak to a lawyer familiar with municipal law, if possible, who can assist in evaluating your situation and planning your appeal.

(e) Lobby to have local zoning regulations amended
Due to the trend toward more understanding and acceptance of the important role of home-based businesses, you may wish to lobby for changes. You could find other home business owners through professional, trade, and civic organizations, the Yellow Pages, or local newspaper advertising. You could form a group to lobby for changes. You may have to educate the community and elected officials about the benefits to the community of home-based businesses, in order to elicit their support. It would be helpful to retain a lawyer to assist in your efforts.

(f) Rent a private mailing address
To resolve the problem of having your home address as your business address, for business image, security or zoning compliance purposes, you could use a mail box rental or mail forwarding service. Packaged office service companies, for example, offer "business identity package" services to those who wish to create the impression that they are operating out of a business address. Mail is delivered to that address and held for you to pick up. Normally the "package" includes a telephone answering service, but this could be an option. Renting an office address in this manner effectively keeps mail, parcels, and visitors from coming to your home or apartment, which may satisfy the wishes of your neighbours. (See Chapter 2.C, "Establishing a Business Image.")

4. What Happens If You Violate Zoning Regulations?

In practical terms, possibly nothing. Many people ignore the local zoning regulations, either because they don't realize that they apply or because they think that no one will find out about it because local officials don't have the time or resources to look for violators. This is not meant as an encouragement to ignore zoning laws, but a simple statement of reality.

There are many ways that officials could find out about zoning violations:

- Unhappy neighbours could complain about traffic congestion, cars parked in front of their homes, or too much noise.
- Spiteful, envious, or feuding neighbours could complain as an expression of their dislike.
- Application for a provincial sales tax licence, a business licence, or a business telephone hookup could alert authorities.
- Advertising in the local newspaper could alert authorities.
- Competitors could complain, anonymously or otherwise.
- Potential customers could make innocent enquiries at City Hall to see if you have a business licence; or, if they are dissatisfied with your service or product, complain to City Hall.

If a complaint was made, you would receive a notice requesting you to stop the violation, and setting out the reasons for the request. You would have the right to appeal the notice and give reasons why an exception should be made. Some reasons for appeal were discussed earlier in the section on variances.

If you ignore the warning, or fail in an appeal, the city can go to civil court and obtain a court order (called an *injunction*) prohibiting you from continuing the violation. You would have to pay some court costs and your own legal fees of course. Local authorities can choose to prosecute the zoning bylaw violation in criminal court. This is very rare, and would only be contemplated if you were a repeat violator or if the City wanted to "send a message" to other home business owners, because of chronic abuses of the zoning regulations, for example. A prosecuted offender, if found guilty, could be fined and/or imprisoned — the latter event being, however, highly unlikely.

5. Provincial, Federal, and Private Regulations

There are provincial government regulations that impact on business in general, and possibly on your home business. These would include matters dealing with sales tax, building codes, employees, safety, health, trade protection, etc. The Business Regulations Checklist (Checklist 2) in Section Four provides a list of other regulations which may be applicable. Also check with your lawyer and provincial government small business department officials for information.

Federal regulations which may affect your home business include: building codes, health, safety, product safety, customs duties, sales tax, trade practices, and payroll deductions. (Also refer to Check-list 2.)

In addition to regulations imposed by the various levels of government, there could also be private regulations. Some of the common ones are:

- **A residential tenancy agreement**   The terms of the written agreement between you and your landlord could forbid operating any business out of the house, apartment, or condominium. If you are in breach of this clause, it could permit the landlord to evict you.

- **Condominium bylaws**   The bylaws of a condominium development, as well as the rules and regulations, could restrict any business activity by owners or renters of the unit. If you are a tenant and in violation, you could be evicted. If you are the owner, you could be fined by the condominium corporation. If the violation continued, the condominium corporation could obtain an injunction restraining you from continuing the violation. You would have to pay court costs, possible damages, and your own legal fees and expenses. Before buying a condominium, therefore, have your lawyer check the "fine print" in this regard.

- **Restrictive covenants**   If you bought a house in a subdivision, it is common for restrictive covenants or building schemes to be registered against the title to the residential property by the developer. There could be a restriction prohibiting any business from being operated from the home, and although local government would permit the operation of a business, private regulations take precedence. Therefore, other property owners would have the right to enforce the restrictive covenant which has the objective of restricting the use of property to strictly residential purposes. If the restrictive covenant was enforced in civil court, you would be out court costs, possible damages, and your own legal costs and expenses.

Before starting out, you should get the facts on zoning regulations to see how they affect you. Get the input and advice from your professional advisors. By taking a positive approach and having a responsible attitude toward your neighbours, potential problems may be avoided.

In practical terms, it obviously depends on the nature of your business as to whether others would be aware of your activities. It also depends on whether you go to clients/customers, or the reverse.

CHAPTER

5

Accounting and Tax

Income taxation in Canada has become increasingly complex. Tax laws and regulations are constantly changing, making it difficult in many respects for the small business owner to keep current on, let alone understand the relevant tax laws. Proper tax planning is critically important to the small business owner. In addition to personal taxes, the taxation of the business and the relationship between the owner and the business must be thoroughly considered in order to maximize all your tax advantages.

Many entrepreneurs feel intimidated and confused by the tax aspects. You should speak to an accountant at the outset to get advice that is customized to your specific needs and circumstances. An initial interview with an accountant is inexpensive and well worth the benefit. You want to make sure that you maximize your net after-tax profit and get all the deductions available.

This chapter will discuss how to select an accountant, recordkeeping matters, taxation issues, and allowable business deductions.

A. SELECTING AN ACCOUNTANT

An accountant's chief concern is to monitor the financial health of your business and reduce the subsequent risks and tax payable. Along with your lawyer, your accountant will complement your "management team" to ensure your business decisions are based on sound advice and good planning. An accountant who is familiar with your type of business can provide much insight and assistance in reviewing your business plan. An accountant can help you to analyze your operations, establish your break-even point, pinpoint problem areas, and assist you in developing solutions. After reviewing your situation, your accountant may make recommendations with regard to reducing the operating costs and improving profitability. The timeliness of the decision to expand your operations or to introduce a new product line is crucial to your success, and an accountant can assist you in your strategic planning. Your accountant can develop information systems that can alert you to problems before they arise. Either manual or computerized systems for accounting and management information and controls may be used.

It is somewhat pointless to enlist the services of an accountant to prepare financial statements without also having the statements discussed with you and interpreted. What do the statements mean? And how should you use the information to modify your day-to-day operations? Your short- and long-term plans should be based on the activity to date, noted improvements or trends, and your sales and operating cost projections.

An accountant can help you from the pre-startup phase through the ongoing operation to the eventual sale or closing down of the business. The services that can be provided are wide-ranging, and include:

- Setting up a manual or computerized bookkeeping system that both the owner and accountant can operate efficiently.
- Setting up systems for the control of cash and the handling of funds.
- Obtaining government grants and other means of raising capital.
- Preparing or evaluating budgets, forecasts, and business plans.
- Assessing your break-even point and improving your profitability.
- Providing advice on issues such as buying or leasing equipment, compensation, and benefit plans.
- Preparing and interpreting financial statements.
- Providing tax- and financial-planning advice.
- Preparing corporate and individual tax returns.
- Assessing risk and insurance planning.
- Providing advice on expanding, buying, or selling a business or franchise.

1. Qualifications

In Canada, anyone can call himself an accountant. One can also adopt the title "public accountant" without any qualifications, experience, regulations, or accountability to a professional association. That is why you have to be very careful when selecting the appropriate accountant for your needs. There are three main designations of qualified professional accountants in Canada: Chartered Accountant (CA), Certified General Accountant (CGA), and Certified Management Accountant (CMA). Accountants with the above designations are governed by provincial statutes. The conduct, professional standards, training, qualifications, professional development, and discipline of these professionals are regulated by their respective institutes or associations. Rely on the advice of an accountant, therefore, only after you have satisfied yourself that the accountant meets the professional qualifications that you require for your business needs.

There are differences in the educational requirements, training, experience, and nature of practice of the accounting designations mentioned above. Some accountants pursue careers in public practice (e.g., serving the needs of the small business owner); others enter positions in industry, education, or government; or specialize in the areas of management, cost, financial, or tax accounting. For further information, contact the professional institute or association for the specific accounting designation, and request an explanatory brochure. You can obtain the contact phone number from the Yellow Pages under "Accountants," or from your local library. The professional governing bodies are referred to as the Institute of Chartered Accountants, the Certified General Accountants' Association, and the Society of Management Accountants.

2. How to Find an Accountant

(a) Referral by business associates, banker, or lawyer

Often a banker, lawyer, or other business associate will be pleased to recommend an accountant who has expertise in small business. Such referrals are valuable, since these individuals are probably aware of your type of business and would recommend an accountant only if they felt he or she was well qualified and has a good track record in assisting small businesses.

(b) Professional associations

The professional institute or association which governs CAs, CGAs, and CMAs may be a source of leads. You can telephone or write the institute or association with a request for the names of three accountants who provide public accounting services to small businesses within your geographic area. It is not uncommon for an initial consultation to be free of charge, but call in advance to confirm this is the case. For marketing and goodwill reasons, it is generally free.

(c) The Yellow Pages
In the Yellow Pages under the heading "Accountants," you will find listings under the categories "Chartered," "Certified General," and "Management."

3. Preparing for the Meeting

Prior to a meeting with your accountant, make a list of your questions and concerns. Put them in writing and list them in order of priority. As noted earlier, you will want to know the person's qualifications, areas of expertise, and method of recordkeeping (for example, is a computerized system used or necessary for your needs?). Ask the accountant what his or her range of experience is in your type of business: tax, small business advice, accessing financing, etc. Ask about fees, how they are determined, how accounts are rendered, and what retainer may be required. Ask who will be working on your file — the accountant, an articling student or junior accountant, or a bookkeeper. It is common for accountants to delegate routine work to junior staff and keep the more intricate matters for their own review.

4. Understanding Fees and Costs

Accountant's fees vary according to experience, specialty, type of service provided, size of firm, and other considerations. They can range from $40 to $150 or more per hour. It is common for an accountant to have different charge-out rates for the various activities performed: bookkeeping, preparation of financial statements, tax consultation, and advice. For example, if an accountant is doing bookkeeping, it will be at a lower rate scale; complex tax advice is charged at the high end of the range. Accountants generally charge for their time plus additional costs such as bookkeeper, secretary, articling student. The bill-out rates for these staff members vary and you should ask exactly what you will be charged.

Accountants will prepare an engagement letter after the interview, if you agree to proceed with the accountant's services. The engagement letter sets out the terms of the agreement between you and the accountant, the nature of services that will be provided, the fee for the accountant's services for various tasks, and the bill-out rate for other staff members. A retainer is usually requested, and when that retainer has been expended, a further retainer may be expected for ongoing work. If you have an incorporated company, it is common for your personal guarantee to be required on the contract letter. This is a guarantee that you will be personally responsible for paying any outstanding fees incurred by the company.

As with your lawyer, a good level of rapport and communication with your accountant will enhance the quality of advice and the effectiveness of your use of that advice. Openly discuss your concerns and questions with your accountant. You may from time to time wish to seek a second opinion on advice you have been given. If you are not satisfied with your accountant for any reason, you should find another.

B. RECORDKEEPING

1. Why Recordkeeping Is Necessary

Records must be kept regardless of how small your business is. In business, records — such as bank deposit books, delivery slips, invoices, receipts, sales slips, contracts, and numerous other documents — are continually generated. It is critically important that systems be developed for recording and filing the various types of records, in order that they can be retrieved and examined quickly and efficiently.

Accurate records should be kept for both external and internal reasons. Some of the external reasons for keeping records are as follows:

- Government regulations. Federal, provincial, and municipal departments and agencies have set rules and regulations relating to the keeping of records for a small business. For example: Statistics Canada requires that information be supplied upon request; and Revenue Canada requires businesses to pay income tax and to remit deductions at source of employee taxes and contributions to unemployment insurance and the Canada Pension Plan. In addition, you need records relating to your GST filings. If an audit is required by Revenue Canada, you will need to produce your records for review.
- Raising financing; attracting potential investors.
- Selling a business.
- Creditor and supplier requirements.
- Insurance company requirements for a loss claim.

Internal reasons for maintaining records include:

- Keeping you better informed about the financial position of your business.
- Making it easier to complete accurate income tax returns with supporting receipts for expenses.
- Providing the basis for evaluating the condition and effectiveness of equipment.
- Reminding you when creditor obligations are due.
- Providing an opportunity for comparing budget goals with historical records and future projections.
- Providing the basis for preparing cash flow and break-even analyses to enable you to improve your cash management position.

The Income Tax Act requires that you keep your records and books in an orderly manner at your place of business or your residence, as this material may be requested at any time by Revenue Canada for review or audit purposes relating to Income Tax or the GST. You are required to maintain business records and supporting documents for at least six years from the end of the last taxation year to which they relate. If you filed your return late for any year, records and supporting documents must be kept for six years from the date you filed that return. Revenue Canada permits computer storage of records, as long as it provides adequate information to verify taxable income.

Some examples of typical financial records are:

- sales journal
- cash receipts journal
- accounts receivable ledger
- accounts payable journal
- cash disbursements journal
- credit purchases journal
- credit sales journal
- payroll journal
- GST journal
- general synoptic ledger.

Some of the non-financial records include documents relating to personnel, equipment, inventory, and production.

2. Recordkeeping Systems and Equipment

The equipment and systems that a small business uses for recordkeeping can range from simple, inexpensive manual procedures to more expensive computer systems. You should request advice from your accountant as to the most efficient recordkeeping system for your type of business. If you are just starting a one-person business out of your home, you may only require a one-write system for cheque writing, a general ledger, and a ledger system for receivables and payables. As your business expands, it may require more specialized ledgers. Here are some of the common systems that you may wish to consider:

- **One-write systems**   This system allows a user to enter a business transaction onto several forms at the same time with the use of carbon paper. This type of system minimizes the number of entries required for each transaction, thereby saving time and reducing the risk of error. For instance, the basic system might combine the business chequebook with the cash disbursements journal and employee earnings record. When the cheque is written, the information is transferred automatically by the carbon paper onto the appropriate journal and record. For further information, look in the Yellow Pages under "Accounting and Bookkeeping Systems."

- **Specialized recordkeeping systems**   One of the systems that you may wish to consider is called a ledgerless system for accounts receivable and accounts payable. This type of system is suitable for a business with a relatively low volume of sales transactions. It enables the business to keep track of its accounts receivable and accounts payable with a simple filing system rather than detailed subsidiary ledgers.

- **Ledgers and journals**   Stationery and office supply stores sell many of the standard ledger and journal record systems as well as binders with preprinted column headings with up to 20 or more columns. Various forms are available to meet the specific needs of small businesses. Specialized recordkeeping systems, designed to meet the needs of businesses within a particular industry, are also available through trade associations.

- **Specialized cash registers**   Computerized cash registers are designed to record sales entries as well as inventory control data. Sales journals and inventory record sheets are automatically generated by the information entered through the cash register.

At a certain stage in the business growth, a computerized system of recordkeeping could be very valuable. All of your accounting functions could be handled on the computer, which could then automatically produce summary statements for you. There are basically two options that you may wish to consider:

- Bookkeeping service bureaus, professional accounting firms, and banks have prepackaged systems available that will process one or all of the basic accounting functions. Fees for services are usually based on the volume of transactions processed and the number of reports that are generated.
- Personal computers are becoming very common in home businesses. Depending on the type of business, it could be far more efficient to buy or lease a personal computer. Many professionally qualified accounting firms specialize in advising small businesses on selection and development of a computer system. Seminars on using computers in small business are also offered by the Federal Business Development Bank and colleges.

C. TAXATION

This section includes a discussion of tax accounting methods, the taxation year, and the tax effects on the legal structure of your business (proprietorship, partnership, or corporation). Allowable business expenses and tax avoidance and evasion are also reviewed.

1. Accounting Methods

Businesses normally use the accrual method of accounting for tax purposes, but may qualify for the cash method. Under the accrual method, income is reported in the year in which it is earned, regardless of when payment is received. Available expenses are deductible in the year in which they are incurred, whether paid or not. The accrual method must be used by business people and professionals when inventory, accounts receivable, and accounts payable are significant factors in determining income, costs, and expenses.

2. Taxation Year

The January 1 to December 31 calendar year is the taxation year for individuals. The income from a business or profession may be reported on the basis of a fiscal year period ending at any time in the calendar year, but must not be longer than 12 months. The fiscal year-end is normally determined by your accountant to be the date which is most beneficial to you in your first taxation year. A short fiscal period may occur in the first year of operation if, for example, you started on January 1, and January 31 was chosen as the fiscal year-end. In this case, income from February to December would not be included in taxable income until the following year. Proper selection of a year-end is therefore a significant consideration in deferring taxes for businesses starting up; here your accountant can advise you. Of course, once you have established a fiscal year-end, you have to keep to that date, unless there are unusual circumstances.

3. Tax Effects on Proprietorships, Partnerships, and Corporations

If you are the *sole proprietor* of your business, your salary and the profits that you earn in your business constitute your personal income and are taxable as such. When you file your personal income tax return at the end of April, you have to complete the form titled "Statement of Income and Expenses," which can be obtained on request from Revenue Canada. It outlines many of the basic sources of income and types of expenses and allowances.

If your business is a *partnership*, all partners are taxed on their salaries and their share of the profits, whether withdrawn or not. The same Statement of Income and Expenses form can also be used for a partnership, the difference being that you must fill out the section of the form which details the percentage share of profit or loss which is being declared.

A *corporation*, which is separate and distinct from the individuals involved in the company, files a corporate tax return.

A corporation in Canada is entitled to a small business tax deduction, assuming various conditions are met, such as being active business income. This deduction, which is approximately one-half the regular tax rate, is designed to help Canadian-controlled private companies accumulate capital for business expansion. Many provinces also allow a provincial tax rate reduction as well as other possible incentives. An active business, as the name implies, is one in which people are actively involved in generating income, rather than passively involved in receiving income.

An individual who is providing his or her employment services for a company through a service corporation is considered by Revenue Canada to be operating a "personal services business." These individuals are usually taxed at full corporate tax rates and therefore do not receive the full benefit of a small business deduction.

Naturally, all these provisions could change at any time, as well as any other incentive programs for tax reduction or tax deferral, so obtain a current opinion from your accountant.

4. Business Expenses

An expense is deductible if its purpose is to earn income, it is not of a capital nature, and it is reasonable in the circumstances. A *capital expense* is an asset which is depreciated over a period of time according to the Capital Cost Allowance (CCA) class. The allowance must not exceed the maximum rate allowable in any year. The rates range from 4% to 100% depreciation in a year. You can obtain a copy of these categories from Revenue Canada upon request.

There are numerous categories of expenses that can be deducted depending on the nature of your business. Your accountant will advise you as to which are deductible and which are not. Also, if some of the expenses are related to personal use, you are required to deduct that portion from the business expense. Reasonable salaries paid to a spouse for services rendered to the business are also deductible. The Statement of Income and Expenses form from Revenue Canada outlines some of the expenses that you may wish to consider. Your accountant may suggest others for which you could be eligible.

Refer to Checklist 4, which is an outline of the home business tax-deductible expenses that you should be familiar with, and discuss with your accountant. As a reminder, be aware of the fact that tax law changes can and do occur from time to time which could affect any of the following deductions.

You may only claim expenses for the business use of a workspace in your home if either:

- The workspace is your principal place of business (for the self-employed aspect of your career); or
- You only use the workspace to earn income from your business, and it is used on a regular basis for meeting clients, customers, or patients.

Also, the expenses you may deduct for the business use of your home generally cannot exceed the income from the business for which you use the workspace. This means that you must not use these expenses to create or increase your business loss. You may carry forward any expenses that are not deductible in the year and deduct them, subject to the same limitation, in the following year.

5. Income Tax

Revenue Canada does not object to a taxpayer openly arranging financial affairs within the framework of the law so as to keep taxes to a minimum. There is a distinction, however, between legitimate tax planning and tax evasion. When attempting to avoid or reduce taxes, be certain to obtain professional tax advice to ensure that your approach is within the bounds of legitimate tax planning. If a taxpayer deliberately conceals income, or attempts to evade the payment of taxes by misrepresentation, conspiracy, or some other means, this will be deemed to be the commitment of an offence and is liable to criminal prosecution. This will result in a severe penalty, a heavy fine, or in some cases a jail sentence. In a proprietorship or partnership, you would be personally liable; in a corporation, the directors and officers of the corporation could be deemed liable.

For further information on the tax issues you have to consider, contact Revenue Canada and ask for the most recent guide entitled "Professional and Business Income." Also, obtain all their other pamphlets and brochures that might be relevant to your needs. You can obtain basic bookkeeping and tax information by attending small business seminars offered by the Federal Business Development Bank, community colleges, and school boards. Books on small business tax matters are also available in the bookstores and public library. Some of these books are referred to in Appendix B. Always make sure the book has Canadian content and data for the current tax year.

There are distinct tax advantages to operating a home-based business. While some business expenses are fully deductible within the same year, others have to depreciate over time. Revenue Canada allows you to go back three years and carry forward up to seven years any legitimate business expenses you incur. You then offset those expenses against income. Remember to get in the habit of keeping receipts for everything. Your accountant can advise you later as to what expenses can be used and in what portion or fashion. You can also carry forward business-related expenses incurred prior to generating income in your business, until you do. Here are the key areas to be reviewed:

• **Home/Apartment**   Revenue Canada states that the area of your home designated as your "business location" must be used exclusively and regularly for business-related purposes. This could include a work area, office area, or storage space. If you do have customers coming to your home, claim a separate reception area and washrooms for business use, if that is the case, or else a portion of "common area" (personal and business) usage for business purposes.

   There are various ways of calculating the percentage of home office use. You can divide the total house or apartment square footage by the overall square footage used for business-related purposes, or calculate the number of rooms used of the total rooms in the house — whatever formula works to your advantage. Don't forget to also take a portion of the "common area" used for business purposes (e.g., the hallways and stairs). Also, don't forget to include any remodelling and decorating costs involved in converting a room. These improvements are considered allowable expenses.

In addition, you can claim a portion of all the house-related expenses for your home office use: mortgage interest and property taxes — or rent — plus insurance, maintenance costs, and utilities (electricity, water, heating, telephone). If your total house expenses are $25,000 per year for all the above, for example, and 25% of the square footage of your house relates to your home office, the deductible expense against business income would be $6,250 per year.

- **Car** If you have one car and use it 50% of the time for business, claim half of all your car-related expenses (e.g., gas, oil, maintenance, insurance, interest on car financing costs) as business expenses. You are supposed to maintain a mileage log book to support your business usage claim. For a jointly used car (personal and business), you may want to consider charging a per-kilometre charge instead. If you have two cars and use one exclusively for business, you can claim 100% of that car's expenses. In addition, be sure to claim depreciation of 30% on your car and deduct the appropriate portion each year from income.

- **Furniture and equipment** Your office furniture, computer hardware, printer, software, etc. and other equipment have to be depreciated over time, using the capital cost allowance formula, which allows for a portion (from 20% to 100% per year) to be deducted each year.

- **Salaries** Salaries paid to your children, spouse, relatives, or others to perform work for your company are also deductible business expenses. However, the amount you pay them should be reasonable in the circumstances.

- **Entertainment** Entertaining existing or potential customers/clients for promotion or prospecting purposes is another deductible expense. You can claim as an expense 80% of the cost of the entertainment or meals, including tips and taxes.

- **Education** Your professional or business education, such as books, seminars, conventions or conferences, provide other opportunities to claim deductions against your business.

- **Trade shows** Any expenses relating to trade shows that you attend for your business purposes are deductible. To find out about upcoming trade shows or conventions, check with your local convention bureau or government small business centres.

- **Travel** If you travel for business-related purposes, you can write off all or a portion of expenses such as airfare, transportation, car rental, hotel, conference or trade show costs, and a portion (currently 80%) of your meal costs.

- **Telephone**   If you have a separate business line, the cost is deductible in full (e.g., monthly service charges, long distance). If you are using your residence phone for business use, deduct the business-related portion of costs. All long-distance charges that are business-related are, of course, totally deductible. Other phone-related costs that you could deduct, in full or in part, include installation costs, telephone equipment, an answering machine, answering service, or voice mail.

- **Remodelling or decorating costs**   These costs include repairs or renovations done to a room to have it function as an office (drywall, painting, carpentry, flooring, plumbing, electrical). If you add an extension to your home to accommodate the office, that expense would be deductible as well.

Remember to obtain tax advice prior to starting your business and on an ongoing basis from a professionally qualified accountant such as a Chartered Accountant or Certified General Accountant. Advice customized to your specific circumstances is essential. The rule of three — that is, having an initial consultation with at least three accountants and ideally the tax expert in the firm — before selecting your advisor, is important. In most cases, the initial consultation is free. Ask in advance before making an appointment. Put your questions in writing so you don't forget any. Ask specific questions about income splitting, fiscal year-end, business structure options, and ways of maximizing deductions and minimizing taxes.

The expenses just discussed are just some of the many tax deductions that may be available to you. As recommended earlier, refer to Checklist 4 in Section Four for a detailed list of possible expense deductions. Remember, you may be able to claim 100% of the cost of the expense or a depreciated amount over time, depending on the item. To clarify what you can deduct and how to do it, speak to your accountant.

If you deal with tax issues in a forthright manner, you will not in any way compromise or taint the principal residence status of your home, as far as Revenue Canada is concerned. In other words, the profit on the sale of your home will not be affected by the fact that you operated a business from home, and deducted expenses. Therefore, you would not have to pay any tax on the proceeds from the sale of your home. Confirm this issue with your accountant.

6. The Goods and Services Tax

This federal tax, which is administered by Revenue Canada, came into being on January 1, 1991. The rationale for the GST was to have it replace the hidden 13.5% sales tax on manufactured goods. The GST is a 7% tax on sales.

You are not obligated to apply for or use a GST registration number if your gross sales do not exceed $30,000 a year. However, you may wish to do so, if you are paying out GST on your purchases and want to get it back.

The basic premise of GST is simple, although there are various unique provisions in certain situations. Basically, there is an input tax credit for GST you paid that you can offset against GST you collect. You either remit the difference if you owe money to Revenue Canada, or request money from Revenue Canada if there is an overage of money owing to you. For further information contact your local Revenue Canada office and obtain the various explanatory publications for small business and the GST.

The GST methods of payment and regulations are changed from time to time, so check with Revenue Canada and your professional accountant for guidance on the current policy and procedures.

A summary of the various options for calculating GST are as follows:

(a) The Simplified Method for Claiming Input Tax Credits
The simplified input tax credit (ITC) method gives small businesses an easier way to calculate input tax credits.

If, in your last fiscal year, your total GST-taxable sales in Canada were $500,000 or less, and your GST-taxable purchases were $2,000,000 or less, you can use the simplified ITC method.

Instead of tracking the GST you paid on each invoice, you multiply the total of your business purchases that are GST-taxable at 7% (including non-refundable provincial sales tax, the GST, tips, and late-payment penalties) by 7, then divide by 107 (7/107), or you can multiply the total by 0.0654.

You cannot use the simplified method to calculate input tax credits on purchases of real property, such as lands and buildings.

Some of the benefits of this type of calculation are:

• you can reduce your paperwork, accounting, and bookkeeping costs;
• you have fewer and simpler calculations;
• your input tax credits are slightly increased, since you apply the factor of 7/107 to amounts that include provincial sales tax, the GST, tips, and late-payment penalties.

(b) The Quick Method of Accounting
The Quick Method gives you a simple way to calculate the amount of net tax you have to remit. It is easy to use, and will reduce the

net tax remittances for some small businesses on average by $300 per year.

If your annual GST-included sales are $200,000 or less, you can use the Quick Method.

With the Quick Method, you collect the GST on your sales in the usual way. To calculate your net tax remittance, multiply the total GST-included sales on which you collected 7% GST by your Quick Method remittance rate and send Revenue Canada that amount. You do not need to keep track of GST paid on day-to-day operating expenses and inventory purchases.

However, you can claim input tax credits in the usual way for all purchases that are eligible for a capital cost allowance under the *Income Tax Act*.

Depending on your type of business, the remittance rate is either 2.5% or 5%. Businesses that provide services (e.g., quick-service food outlets, painting contractors, and auto repair shops) use the 5% remittance rate, while wholesalers and retailers whose cost of goods for resale is 40% or more of total sales, use the 2.5% rate.

You should reduce the rate by 1% on the first $30,000 of your taxable sales in a fiscal year. In other words, you have to remit either 1.5% or 4% on the first $30,000 of taxable sales, and 2.5% or 5% on the balance.

Some of the benefits of this type of calculation are:

- you do not have to keep track of most input tax credits on day-to-day operating expenses and inventory purchases, and
- you can reduce your paperwork, accounting, and bookkeeping costs.

Although many small businesses benefit from using the Quick Method, in certain circumstances it may not be beneficial for you. Carefully examine whether it is suitable for your business, before you elect to use the Quick Method. If you need more information about the Quick Method, contact any Revenue Canada office, and speak to your accountant.

(c) Annual Filing

If your business has annual revenues of $500,000 or less, you can file your GST returns annually instead of quarterly. As an annual filer, you pay four tax instalments based on the lesser of the net tax you paid in the previous year, and an estimate of the current year's net tax. At the end of the year, you file one return that reports your transactions.

If your net tax payable last year was less than $1,500, or you correctly estimate that the current year's net tax will be less than $1,500, it's even simpler. In this case, you only have to send one payment per year with your annual return. If you are expecting a refund, you do not have to make any instalment payments during the year, and you claim your refund when you send in your annual return.

If you base your instalments on an estimate of the current year's net tax, it is important that your estimate be accurate. If you underpay your instalments, you will be subject to penalty and interest.

Some of the benefits of this type of calculation are:

- you only have to complete one GST return a year;
- you have fewer calculations; and
- you have less paperwork to do.

You can change to annual filing at the beginning of your new fiscal year, or prior to that point depending on the circumstance.

CHAPTER

6

Insurance

Operating a business from your home presents areas of risk exposure. It is important to recognize these and the types of insurance policies available for protection against them. If you don't have insurance protection, you could be personally liable for all financial losses. First of all, you should advise your insurance agent that you are operating a business from your home. You will need to have extra coverage to protect you for any risk areas involved directly or indirectly with your business operation.

Because of the higher risk involved with operating a business, the insurance company obviously will be charging you an increased premium on your current auto or home insurance policies. However, it will still be a saving compared to the higher insurance premium you would be required to pay if your business was located in commercial premises. Attempt to use the same insurance broker for all your policies if possible, as you should be able to negotiate better rates, if any flexibility is available. Make sure you receive copies of the extra policy coverage for your file.

You may be unaware of the types of liability you could be exposed to in your home business. Here are a few examples and the type of insurance coverage that would protect you:

- **Case 1** You provide a computer consulting service and a client who relied on your advice subsequently suffers a $100,000 loss.

You are being sued for negligence for the financial loss that your client suffered. (Professional liability/malpractice insurance)

- **Case 2** You operate a day care business, and in the process of transporting children your car is accidentally hit by another car and a child is injured. You are sued as the driver and car owner. (Automobile insurance)
- **Case 3** You operate a catering business, and someone who eats one of your muffins cracks a tooth on a walnut shell. He sues you for dental expenses. (Product liability insurance)
- **Case 4** You operate a tailoring business, and someone who comes to your house slips on the stairs, breaks his leg, and is off work for two months. You are sued. (General liability insurance)
- **Case 5** You have expensive desktop publishing hardware and software in your basement. A fire breaks out, damages your equipment, and destroys all your clients' records. (Fire/business property/business replacement cost insurance)
- **Case 6** You are a tradesman, and while lifting a heavy object you dislocate your back. You are immobilized for three months and cannot perform any work. You are the sole income earner and need income to meet your normal personal expenses. (Disability insurance)

The rest of this chapter will discuss selecting an insurance agent, organizing your insurance program, and types of business and personal insurance.

A. SELECTING AN INSURANCE REPRESENTATIVE

Before you start shopping for insurance, you should recognize the difference between *insurance agents* and *insurance brokers*.

An *insurance agent* is an employee of a particular insurance company which sells life, home, car, or other common types of insurance. The agent sells the insurance plans of primarily one insurance company. In some cases, agents are under an obligation to place a certain volume of insurance with that company in order to remain an agent with that firm. Therefore, it is possible that you might be sold policies that are adequate, but are not the best policies available in the industry.

An *insurance broker*, on the other hand, is not committed to any particular insurance company, and therefore can compare and contrast the different policies, coverage, and premiums from a wide range of companies that offer the type of insurance coverage that you are looking for. Also, insurance brokers can obtain a premium quotation for you and coverage availability from insurance company under-writers if the particular business you have is unique or difficult to cover by other existing policies. If the brokers are using the same insurance base for the best coverage and premiums, then any three brokers, in theory, should recommend the same insurance compa-nies for the various forms of coverage that you are requesting. Ask for brochures describing the main types of insurance and an explanation of each.

When selecting an insurance representative, you should enquire about each candidate's credentials, expertise, and experience. It is important to have confidence in your representative's qualifications and objectivity, and to know that the person is affiliated with a repu-table firm. You can find insurance companies listed in the Yellow Pages, or through friends, business associates, your accountant, or your lawyer.

As in all matters of obtaining professional advice or assistance, you should have a minimum of three competitive, quotes, and an oppor-tunity to evaluate the relative strengths and weaknesses of each.

B. ORGANIZING YOUR INSURANCE PROGRAM

It is important to consider all criteria to determine the best type of insurance for you and your business. Your goal should be adequate coverage. That can be achieved by periodic review of risk, and by keeping your insurance representative informed of any changes in your business that could affect the adequacy or enforceability of your coverage. For example, such changes would be additional equip-ment purchases, extension to your home, or business use of your personal car.

The following advice will help you plan an insurance program:

- Assess your business and identify the likely risk exposure.
- Cover your largest risk(s) first.
- Determine the magnitude of loss that the business can bear without financial difficulty, and use your premium dollar where the protection need is greatest.
- Insure the correct risk.
- Decide which of these three kinds of protection will work best for each risk:
  - Absorbing the risk;
  - Minimizing the risk;
  - Insuring against the risk with commercial insurance.
- Use every means possible to reduce the cost of insurance:

- Negotiate for lower premiums if loss experience is low.
- Increase deductibles as much as you can if you need the protection, but can't afford a low deductible premium.
- Shop around for comparable rates and analyze insurance terms and provisions offered by different insurance companies.
- Avoid duplication of insurance. Have one agent handle all your business insurance.
- Incorporate if necessary to further reduce personal liability.

As your risk exposure changes, a periodic review will save you from insuring matters that are no longer exposed to the same degree of risk. Conversely, you may need to increase limits of liability. Reviews can help avoid overlaps and gaps in coverage, and thereby keep your risk and premiums lower. This is especially important if the business is growing. Reviews can also help you keep current with inflation.

C. TYPES OF INSURANCE

The types of insurance coverages you might need will vary of course, depending on the nature of your business operation. The following brief overview is intended to alert you to the main types of coverage you may wish to consider.

1. General Liability

This type of policy covers losses that you would be liable to pay for causing bodily injury to someone (e.g., in an accident) or damage to the property of others. Make sure that your policy covers all legal fees for your defence and all other, related costs incurred. This type of policy generally covers negligence on your part that accidentally causes injury to clients, customers, employees, or the general public.

2. Business Property

Your current basic homeowners' or apartment owners' policy may void any coverage of business-related assets. Therefore, you should request that coverage be added to include the business assets, or purchase a separate policy. If you own a computer, you may wish to get a special "floater" policy covering risks unique to computer owners. This extra coverage should insure such factors as power-surge damage, as well as fire and theft of software and hardware.

3. Fire

This coverage enables you to replace or rebuild your home as well as replace inventory and equipment. Make sure your policy is a "replacement" policy and covers business use of the premises.

4. Theft

This type of policy covers losses due to robbery, and is generally part of a comprehensive general liability coverage plan.

5. Automobile

Automobile insurance protects against physical damage to the car and bodily injury to the passengers as well as damage to other people's property, car, or passengers. It also includes theft of your car. Make sure that your car is insured for business use. Otherwise, if the facts came out on a claim that it was being used for that purpose, your policy would normally be voided and your claim would be disallowed.

6. Product

A product liability policy offers protection against a lawsuit by a customer or client who used your product and sustained bodily injury or property damage because of it.

7. Disability

If you become permanently or partially disabled, or ill for a short or long period of time, disability insurance coverage pays you a certain amount each month (as set out in the policy). The amount is reduced depending on the extent of partial disability. The waiting period before payments commence will also be set out in the policy.

8. Business Loan

Business loan insurance will cover the balance outstanding of a business bank loan, and is usually arranged through the bank at the time of the loan. In the event of your death, the loan is paid off completely.

9. Malpractice

Malpractice insurance, also referred to as a professional liability insurance, protects you from claims for damages from your clients. This could arise out of negligence or failure on your part to exercise an acceptable degree of professional skill.

10. Errors and Omissions

Errors and omissions coverage protects you against litigation arising from losses incurred by your customers or clients as a result of an error or omission in the information you provided to them.

11. Business Interruption

Business interruption insurance compensates for lost earnings during a temporary cessation of business caused by fire, theft, flood, or some other reason. This policy covers you until you return to normal working conditions. Check to make sure the coverage includes the costs of temporarily renting other premises.

12. Life

Life insurance coverage, if a term life policy, insures a person for a specific period of time or term, and then stops. Term life does not have a cash surrender value or loan value such as is found with a whole-life plan. Term premiums are less expensive than whole-life premiums. If you have a bank loan or personal or business obligations, you should consider term life coverage.

13. Workers' Compensation

If you have employees who, in the course of their daily work, may potentially suffer personal injury, you should make certain that they are covered by workers' compensation insurance. The insurance covers all costs that may occur due to an injury to an employee. If you do not have coverage and your type of business requires it, you could be personally liable for all medical and other disability losses incurred by the employee. *Note*: Some types of work, such as desk-type jobs which have low injury risk, are exempt from workers' compensation regulations.

When starting a business, it is common for people to save on expenses whenever possible. This is a good attitude to have, but when it comes to insurance it is important to be realistic and prudent. You have to weigh the risks and potential personal financial exposure if you have no insurance or inadequate coverage. Look upon insurance premiums as an additional cost of doing business and budget accordingly.

CHAPTER

7

Financing

Based on a recent survey, approximately 60% of the home-based business owners who responded did not borrow money from banks in order to start their businesses. Instead, they relied upon use of their personal funds or money borrowed from family, friends, or relatives. This may be because they had difficulty accessing bank financing, or merely that their startup costs were low and within their own means of financing.

There are many reasons why and stages when a business may need financing. At the outset, funds may be required to do product research, conduct a marketing study, purchase supplies and equipment, patent an invention, or obtain professional advice. It might be necessary to get a home-improvement loan in order to provide suitable space for the business. If you choose to expand the business, additional financing may be required to increase your workspace, inventory, equipment, marketing, etc. You may be extending credit, and require a line of credit to cover your business needs.

This chapter will therefore provide a brief overview of the factors you should be aware of when negotiating a loan. Topics covered will include selecting a banker, types of financing, sources of financing, the credit granting process and why loans are turned down, and granting credit terms. (The term "bank" is used generically to include other lenders such as credit unions and trust companies.)

A. SELECTING A BANKER

When deciding which bank, credit union or trust company to deal with for your business affairs, it is advisable to shop around, especially if you are in need of bank financing. You will find that services and rates vary between branches of the same bank. It is helpful to have a banker who has had experience in your industry sector, if at all possible. As a banker's loan approval limit will vary from branch to branch, you will want a banker who has a loan approval level greater than the amount of money that you need to borrow. It is much easier to sell one person on the merits of your loan application than to have it screened at a head office branch by people you have never met. Another advantage of dealing with a banker with extensive experience is that generally you can negotiate a better rate of interest. Shop around for the bank and branch that will negotiate the most favourable package.

(a) One of the most effective ways of selecting a banker is through a referral from your accountant or lawyer. If they spend a high percentage of their time on small business matters, they may be aware of specific bankers who understand the needs of small business owners, or who have had experience in your industry sector.

(b) If you are a member of a trade or professional association, you could ask the members what bank they would recommend, what banker, and why. In this way, you may find a banker who is familiar with your industry sector.

(c) Contact a commercial banking centre (or equivalent) of the major chartered banks in your area, and ask the manager which senior loans officer in that branch has expertise in your industry sector. Then set up a meeting with that person.

(d) Banking with the branch that your family has been dealing with for many years could add credibility to your own business relationship and loan application in terms of the track record and reputation.

When putting together a loan proposal, you should consider eliciting the assistance of your accountant and lawyer to ensure that it is complete. Once you have negotiated a favourable loan package and have it confirmed in writing by the bank, proceed to transfer your accounts to the new bank.

Ideally, you should start getting to know your banker before you need to request financing. Take the opportunity to introduce yourself the next time you are in the bank. A few casual comments about your new venture could be followed up with a request for a brief discussion at the banker's convenience. At that meeting you might provide a sample of or a brochure on your product, and discuss in general your overall business plan. Keep the banker informed on a casual basis of your progress. By taking the initiative to develop a first-name relationship with your banker, you have paved the way for a future loan request. Most people only approach a banker when their businesses fall upon tough times or they are in need of money. Therefore, the banker has to decide whether they are a high risk without having had the opportunity to know them personally. If you establish a favourable relationship with a banker who is subsequently transferred to another branch, it may be prudent to move your account to that branch if it is within your geographic area.

It is possible at some point that your relationship with your banker may not be satisfactory. This could be because the person with whom you had an excellent relationship was transferred to another branch outside your geographic area, and the replacement did not have a relationship of the same quality with you. Possibly a new manager has come into the branch, has reassessed your file, and wants to have additional security or charge a higher interest rate, or wants to reduce your line of credit. Another factor could be that the head office of your bank has looked at certain types of industry profiles and has seen that there is a high failure rate or other problems in the industry that could impact on your business. As a consequence of this, a policy could have been adopted that no further loans be given to businesses within that industry sector. Still another reason could be that the service you have been getting is not sufficient for your needs, or the branch is not sophisticated enough to meet your expanding requirements. Whatever the reason, if you are not happy with your banker, explore other options.

A banker can assist you in numerous ways, but the effectiveness of that assistance is based on the experience that the banker has had in the lending business and the knowledge the banker has of your industry sector. Your banker can assist you in setting up the various financial arrangements for different types of loans. Many other banking services are available that can assist you in all phases of your business during the growth and diversification stages and for special needs. For example:

- operating loans
- term loans for plant expansion or renovation, purchase of machinery, equipment, land, and buildings
- interim financing
- term deposits
- current accounts
- retirement savings plans
- factoring services

- VISA or MasterCard merchant accounts
- VISA or MasterCard expense accounts
- money transfers
- credit information
- leasing services.

Once you have obtained your loan, your banking relationship of course does not end. It is an ongoing one until your loan is repaid. If you establish and nurture a good working relationship with the branch manager, it will assist you greatly in the long-term relationship. Some tips on maintaining a good relationship are as follows:

- If you run into unexpected problems, don't hide that fact from the lender. After you have determined reasonable solutions that may be available, inform the lender. If you cause the lender to have unpleasant surprises such as NSF cheques, stalling on loan payments, late loan payments, or unapproved overdrafts, this will certainly impair your relationship. It could very well cause your loan to be called.
- Establish a reputation for integrity by conducting your banking affairs in a consistent and realistic manner.
- Adhere to the policy set by the bank with regard to terms and conditions of the loan agreement.
- If your bank requests financial data, provide it without unreasonable delay.
- Invite the banker to visit your place of business, if appropriate, and explain your operating procedures and future plans.
- Be confident in your approach and be prepared to negotiate the terms by having done your planning in advance, after consultation with your professional advisors.
- Schedule regular meeting sessions with your banker to provide a progress report on your business plan. If you request these meetings as a courtesy, rather than as a further attempt to get more money, it will increase the banker's confidence in you when you do need the money.

Remember, if you are not satisfied with the initial negotiating terms proposed by the bank, or if the relationship is unsatisfactory, consider other lenders. The money lending business is highly competitive.

B. TYPES OF FINANCING

The two basic types of financing are debt and equity financing.

1. Debt Financing

A debt is a loan, and the lender will charge interest on the money you have borrowed and expect to be paid back on the terms negotiated. Most debt financing is paid back in monthly payments of principal and interest. Therefore, you should include that in your business plan. Some of the common forms of debt financing are as follows:

(a) Demand loan

A demand loan is basically a shorter-term or operating loan. It is technically due and payable upon "demand," but this usually occurs only when an account is not operated satisfactorily, or if the business appears to be faltering. In practical terms, though the loan is negotiated for specific periods, its duration can be anywhere from 30 days to one year. Another common characteristic is a fluctuating interest rate based on the prime rate set by the Bank of Canada. Thus, your rate could be anywhere from prime plus 2% on up, depending on your overall circumstances and how well you negotiate.

(b) Line of credit

In effect, this is an overdraft protection rather than an outright loan. You negotiate with the bank the maximum amount of credit that you need for general operating purposes. The loan interest rate fluctuates similarly to the demand loan. The line of credit is supposed to "revolve"; that is, move in a cyclical fashion every month, as cash flows in and out of your account. The bank generally secures a line of credit with your accounts receivable, along with other security.

Many home business owners may require a small line of credit of up to $5,000, for example, You can generally get this type of personal line of credit (as opposed to business line of credit) just on the strength of your signature, without additional security, if you have a good personal track record at your bank, credit union, or trust company. You may then want to use your personal line of credit to lend money to your business operation.

(c) Term loan

A term loan is generally used when you want to borrow money for a period of from one to five years. The payments are generally the same, so you can budget over the term of the loan. The interest rate is frequently fixed, but at a higher rate than a demand loan. In many respects it can be similar to a mortgage.

(d) Trade credit or supplier financing

Trade credit financing is a popular form of financing for a small business. The supplier generally negotiates the terms of payment to be from 30 to 90 days from receipt of goods or date of invoice. Interest does not accrue unless you have not complied with the payment terms. At the outset you may have to pay within a 30-day or shorter period; after you establish a credit history, however, you should attempt to negotiate a longer period before payment. This could save you considerable interest charges on your line of credit or considerable drain on your personal financial resources.

(e) Credit cards

Some home business owners with modest financial needs for their business use the funds available from their credit card to "lend" money to the business. As a short-term measure it could be an effective approach, but over the long term the interest rate on credit card charges and cash withdrawals can be considerably higher than those of a commercial loan or personal line of credit.

(f) Secondary mortgage financing

You may want to take out a second or third mortgage on your home, or a first mortgage if you have clear title, for your business needs. You could take out $5,000 or $10,000 for example, with complete repayment over a three- or five-year period, with equal monthly payments for principal and interest at a fixed interest rate.

2. Equity Financing

Equity is the money that you put into your own business. This money may come from your own financial resources, or from friends or relatives. Equity financing generally means the money does not have to be repaid by the business. For example, a relative investing into the business may want 10% of the business in exchange. As mentioned before, most home businesses initially get their financing by equity rather than debt funds.

If you are operating as an incorporated company, though, for tax reasons you may want to show your investment in the business as a loan. That way the money can be paid back to you by the business when the company can afford to do so. The money would not be subject to tax, as it is a repayment of your loan. Your accountant will be able to advise you further regarding the tax aspects.

C. SOURCES OF FINANCING

Although most people think of the obvious sources when they need funds for their businesses, there are actually numerous sources of financing available. In fact, there are well over a hundred ways of obtaining financing or credit for a business venture. Some of these ways are conventional, while others are creative. The traditional sources of financing are your bank, your credit union, your trust company, or the Federal Business Development Bank.

When starting out, though, it may be necessary to find other sources of financing until you establish a track record and the credibility of your business. Many successful business owners can attest to having had "lean" years when starting out, and having to use a conservative and realistic approach in attaining their financial goals.

A cost-saving approach most small business owners use first is modifying their lifestyles. This may mean making personal sacrifices in their entertainment and living expenses. Developing and maintaining a personal cost-of-living budget will be helpful (see Sample 3). Converting your personal assets such as home equity, stocks and bonds, or an extra vehicle into cash often can provide the base you need to get started.

After reviewing your personal financial situation, you may wish to look to family, friends, and associates as possible investors. If your accountant has considerable expertise with small business accounts, he or she may be able to suggest ways of increasing your cash flow. Refer to Checklist 5, "Creative Sources of Financing or Money Saving."

Also, be sure to read *Raising Money: The Canadian Guide to Successful Business Financing* by Douglas Gray and Brian Nattrass. (See Appendix B.)

D. THE CREDIT GRANTING PROCESS

To assist you in negotiating with the lender, it is important that you understand the process involved in the granting of loans. Factors involved include meeting with the lender and the request for money; review of the criteria used by the lender for approving funds; an agreement between the borrower and the lender regarding terms and amounts of money, security, and other factors; and signing of the necessary security required before the funds are advanced.

It is best to set up an initial appointment to discuss the lender's policies without necessarily going into the details of your proposal. During the interview you can discuss in general terms such questions as what type of collateral might be required, limitations the bank might have on types of business loans you are considering, the type of reporting information you may be required to make, and any other information the bank needs. This will prepare you for the type of information needed in your loan proposal. The loans officer may give you a loan application form to complete.

Once you start negotiating with the financial institution, you must sell the lender on the merits of your business proposal. As in all sales presentations, consider the needs and expectations of the other party

— in this case, the loans officer. A loans officer will be interested in the following:

- Your familiarity with the business concept and the realities of the marketplace, as reflected in your business plan (discussed in Chapter 2).
- Your ability to service and pay back the debt with sufficient surplus to cover contingencies, including interest charges, so that you eventually repay the debt in full. This would be demonstrated in your cash flow forecast and projected income statements.
- Your ability to provide security to the bank for the loan.
- Your level of commitment, as shown by your equity in the business or cash investment in the particular asset being purchased.
- Your secondary source of repayment, including security in the event of default or other problem, and other sources of income.
- Your reasons why the money is needed and how long you need it for, and how much you need.
- Your track record and integrity, as shown in your personal credit history, your business plan, and business results or past business experience.
- Your businesslike approach. (During the loan interview, remember that you are doing business the same as when you are with a customer. Don't be subservient, overly familiar, or too aggressive. Remember, a lender is in business for the same reason you are — to make a profit, and to minimize or eliminate bad debts.)
- Your judgement in supplying information. (Be sensible with the number of documents you provide at the outset. You do not want to overwhelm the loans officer with material. For example, if the amount requested is small, an introductory page and summary of your business plan provide a good enough basic loan submission, although you should have all the other documents prepared and available in case they are requested.)
- Your personal appearance. (You should present yourself in a manner that projects self-confidence and success.)
- Your consideration in allowing sufficient lead time for approval. (The lender needs a reasonable time to assess your proposal. Also, the loan may have to be reviewed at another level within the financial institution.)
- Your credit rating. (It's a good idea to review your credit rating periodically, as there may be errors or blemishes to correct in your file. Note your positive and negative points, so you can discuss these when raised by the lender.)

If your request for financing is approved, find out everything you need to know about the conditions, terms, payment methods, interest rates, security requirements, and any other fees to be paid — assuming you have not already negotiated these factors. No commitment to accept the financing should be made until all this information is provided and understood and its impact on the proposed business analyzed. You may wish to ask your accountant and lawyer to assist you in the loan application in advance and to review the bank's approval.

In summary, remember that you are trying to convince the lender of three important factors:

- That your loan application is for a worthwhile purpose and the funds are sufficient to accomplish your business objectives.
- That you have the ability, integrity, and commitment to make your business a viable one, and the management skills or access to those skills to make it a profitable one.
- That the loan can be repaid out of the normal operational activities of the business on a realistic cash flow basis, and the bank will not have to sell the assets that you have pledged as security.

E. WHY LOANS ARE TURNED DOWN

If your request for financing is not approved, find out why. Use the lender's experience to your advantage. Lenders handle many requests for financing, and have experience in the financial aspects of many businesses, even if they do not have direct business management experience. If there is something wrong with the financial proposal, see if it can be corrected and then reapply. Otherwise, use this knowledge when approaching other potential lenders, or on future occasions when seeking funds.

Some of the reasons for a loan rejection are as follows:

- **Outside bank policy** The type of loan you want may be outside the bank's lending policy for any number of reasons.
- **Business idea considered risky or unsound** A lender's judgement is generally based on past performance of other businesses similar to the one you are proposing.
- **Insufficient collateral** A lender must satisfy itself that there are sufficient assets pledged to meet the outstanding debt if your business does not succeed financially. If you are just starting a business, a lender generally requires you to pledge personal assets such as your home, car, or other securities. If you are borrowing funds under a corporate name, your personal guarantee will gen-

erally be requested, and in some cases your spouse's guarantee as well, depending upon the circumstances. In the lender's opinion, you may not have the full amount of security required for the size of loan you are requesting.

- **Perceived lack of financial commitment** Lenders are reluctant to approve loan financing for business ventures if you are not fully committed. The lender does not want to have to foreclose or repossess and then sell assets to collect its money. It will therefore want to know how much personal capital you have made available to the business venture in order to assess your commitment to repay the loan.
- **Poor business plan** A lender could reject your loan application if you have not prepared a detailed and sound business plan or if you do not understand its significance.
- **Purpose of loan not explained or unacceptable** It is important that the specific use of the funds being borrowed be outlined in detail. The amount of funds being requested should be reasonable and appropriate. For example, it could be considered unreasonable for you to calculate a large draw or salary from your business in the first six months. Again, if you intend to use the loan to pay off past debts or financial obligations, it may not be approved, since the funds would not be directly generating cash flow for your new business venture.

Now that you know the factors that institutional lenders take into account when considering a loan application, evaluate your own business proposal on those criteria. Rework and rewrite aspects of your plan to strengthen the points addressed.

F. EXTENDING CREDIT TO YOUR CUSTOMERS

You should be creative and thorough in the way you plan to structure your accounts with customers and suppliers. Look at ways to reserve as much of your financing for operating capital.

Cautiously look at extending credit to customers and clients. If you are supplying to businesses or wholesalers, you may be expected to grant credit, as that might be standard practice in the industry. If you are dealing directly with consumers, there are definite advantages to accepting credit cards such as VISA, MasterCard, and American Express. You will pay a fee for using the credit card company's service, which varies depending on the volume and the institution issuing the card. By accepting credit cards, though, you minimize the risk of receiving bad cheques. In addition, you provide extra convenience to your customers, which facilitates and encourages impulse purchases.

If you do provide credit to regular customers, it is important to maintain strict control on the amounts outstanding and the period of time the debts are outstanding. See Checklist 6, "Credit and Collection Procedures." Assess granting credit in the same manner as discussed earlier in this chapter from a lender's perspective.

There are ways of minimizing the risk of bad debts, although not all of the following will be applicable to every business:

- Getting the full amount in advance (e.g., mail order, COD).
- Obtaining an advance deposit or retainer.
- Receiving prepaid disbursements (out-of-pocket expenses).
- Third-party billing long-distance phone or fax charges to your client's phone number.
- Requesting progress payments for major projects lasting several months.
- Billing on time.
- Monitoring payment trends of customers.
- Following up promptly on all outstanding accounts.
- Obtaining personal guarantees of the principals of a corporation.

Finally, before extending credit to your customers, obtain the advice of your accountant and lawyer.

CHAPTER
8

Marketing

Marketing is an essential part of any business operation. Every business obviously needs customers in order to succeed. Marketing means understanding your customers and their needs. Marketing is also the process of selling what the market (your customers) wants to buy, not what you want to sell. The function of marketing is comprehensive and includes such factors as researching, pricing, advertising, promoting, and selling. In addition, if you are a manufacturer or distributor, it would include such activities as product design, packaging, and labelling.

This chapter discusses some of the key areas that should help you in attaining your objectives. Topics covered include identifying your market, the marketing process, product, pricing for profit, place (location), promotion, low-cost advertising, and getting the product to your customers.

A. IDENTIFYING YOUR MARKET

In order to identify your market, first you will have to classify your product or service. Is it perceived by customers as a basic need (food, shelter, clothing) or a luxury item? It is usually only after people's basic survival needs are met that their remaining funds ("disposable" income) are available for optional luxury items. Another consideration is whether people are likely to make an "impulse" decision to buy your product.

Once you have classified what you're selling, you begin targeting the market you're selling to — that is, who potentially wants or needs your product or service — and direct your marketing to them. To be successful at marketing you must thoroughly understand your potential market. This includes understanding the demographic aspects (age, income levels, employment, class) and the psychographic aspects (interests, attitudes, lifestyles, activities) of the customers you wish to attract to your business. For instance, are your customers fashion-conscious? Upwardly mobile? Traditional? You might find it useful to consider customer types. Is your market individual consumers, specific types of businesses, industries, institutions, or governments?

Geography might be a determining factor. If you are a service such as a hair salon, you may only be interested in targeting your surrounding neighbourhood. But, if you want to appeal to an élite clientele to buy your exclusive glassware products, your geographic market segment will have to be based on a much larger area — perhaps the entire city, province, or country.

Try to discover what your potential customers have in common. Don't forget that users of your product or service may be fulfilling totally different needs — for personal or business use, or as a gift item. You may choose to service a variety of customer needs, using different marketing strategies to appeal to each. Or, if a small segment of your target market accounts for the majority of your sales, you may wish to concentrate all of your marketing efforts on that one segment.

A lot of what you need to know about your industry and its customers has already been researched by others and is available to you. One of the most valuable sources of demographic and psychographic data is Statistics Canada. It publishes the results of surveys on a wide diversity of subjects, from single and family population densities to how the elderly are spending their money, what Canadians are eating, earning, or buying, and what they're doing with their spare time.

Basic market information can be found in the *Survey of Markets*, published annually by the *Financial Post*. It includes data on population, households, disposable income, and retail sales in a variety of geographic breakdowns. It also publishes a listing of current research studies. The business reference section of your public library will have both general and specialized business directories.

You may choose to identify your market through a customer questionnaire or survey. However, in order to get accurate and usable information, the survey must be carefully designed. Keep it short and simple. This will encourage your customers to fill it out. Design the questions so that the customer gives you the specific information you need in a format that will make compiling and comparing the data easy. For instance, use a multiple-choice category format. Ensure the categories are meaningful and will influence how you will advertise. Your questions may include: Sex? Age category? Marital status? Number of children and ages? Does your spouse work? What is the combined family income range? How frequently do you dine out monthly? How frequently do you entertain in your home? What hobbies, favourite sports, reading habits do you have? You may also ask which of your products or services your customers enjoy the most, and what other products they would like to see offered. The answers to your questionnaire should give you a profile of your typical customer. Be certain to keep the names and addresses of your survey respondents to use as a customer mailing list.

Once you know who you want to reach, your task is to find the advertising and promotion vehicles that will appeal to them. For instance, if your survey determined that a number of your customers enjoy reading magazines, you may decide to test an ad in a popular monthly magazine. Or you may write an article for publication on a one-time or regular basis. Promotion and advertising techniques are discussed later in this chapter.

B. THE MARKETING PROCESS

Marketing objectives will be a paramount consideration when determining the volume and production goals for your business. Like the business plan, the marketing plan is a written action plan. It helps you determine the various factors and steps involved in performing the marketing function. The marketing plan must be coordinated with all the other business decisions outlined in your business plan (discussed in Chapter 2) and involved in the running of the business. These would include such factors as:

- financial decisions
- inventory decisions
- buying decisions
- decisions relating to bookkeeping and accounting systems
- production decisions if you are a manufacturer
- distribution decisions
- decisions about the location of your present home office or future business

- pricing decisions
- decisions on how to deal with competitors, and how to place your company in a unique position to attract customers
- layout and display decisions for retailers
- decisions on means of communicating to the public, including advertising and promotion
- decisions on personal selling.

Whatever marketing approaches you decide to try, learn as much about them as you can in advance. Most people have had no experience in dealing with marketing concepts unless through previous sales experience or a family business.

From a marketing perspective, the successful small business owner achieves maximum profit by providing the right product at the right price in the right place and with the right amount of promotion. Marketing decisions are therefore centred around these four Ps (product, price, place, promotion), among others. Poor decisions regarding any one of the four could easily lead to business failure.

C. PRODUCT

The term *product* frequently refers to a service as well as a tangible product, although in practical terms they are different concepts. While product marketing has much in common with service marketing, the strategy may have to be varied, since services are "performed" and "consumed," while products are "manufactured" and "possessed." Services also differ from products in that services are intangible, which makes it difficult for the consumer to inspect them before purchase. You may have to rely on the testimonials of previous customers to help attest to your service quality. Services cannot be displayed, inventoried, or standardized. In most cases, the quality of a service performed differs according to the person providing the service. Therefore, if an owner needs to hire staff to handle an expanding volume of business, careful training and supervision is necessary to ensure quality control.

A product must be developed to satisfy consumer needs. Product strategy includes decisions about its uses, quality, features, brand name, style, packaging, guarantees, design, and options. You will have to identify its unique customer appeal.

You should be thoroughly familiar with the product or service, the industry, and what similar products and services are available. Have you had previous experience or training in the area? Identify your market niche. To have a successful product or service, you will have to emphasize the benefits to your customers: that it is bigger, more compact, better, faster, lasts longer, etc. Ensuring a consistently high quality is paramount, along with taking a personal interest in servicing your customers' needs.

D. PRICING FOR PROFIT

Pricing a product or service is not an easy undertaking, and requires much thought as well as computation. Its importance cannot be overemphasized, however, since incorrect pricing is a major cause of business failure. If all the costs of the business are not reflected in the product or service price, the business could lose money and fail. There is rarely an exact "right" price, but rather an acceptable price range within which you will want to work. Avoid the two common mistakes made by many new business owners: charging too much and charging too little. Use several approaches to arrive at a cost and "test" the price. If your ego is too much involved, your price may be too high. On the other hand, if you have the attitude that "This is just a little something I do in my spare time" or "Anybody could do this," then your price may be too low.

Four main factors will help you decide what to charge for your product or service: (1) your direct and indirect costs; (2) the profit you want to make; (3) your market research data on competitors' prices; and (4) the urgency of the market demand. Below, a procedure is presented for setting a fair price for a product or service, but you may wish to modify it on the basis of your specific situation and other formulas that you have reviewed.

1. Typical Product Pricing Formula

(a) Material costs

Figure the total cost of the raw materials you have to use to make up a single item. For some products (such as large furniture items), it may be easy to determine a per-item cost. However, with items produced in volume, it may be easier to obtain a per-item cost by dividing the material cost of a batch of items by the number of items eventually produced.

(b) Labour costs

Figure what you pay to employees to produce the item (whether or not you have employees now). You must assign a wage figure, even if you are the only one producing the item. Take the weekly salary you pay someone to produce the weekly volume of items and divide it by the number of items. Add this figure to your material costs.

(c) Overhead
This refers to expenses like rent, gas and electricity, business telephone calls, packaging and shipping supplies, delivery and freight charges, cleaning, insurance, office supplies, postage, repairs, and maintenance. The accuracy of your costing depends on your estimating logical amounts for all categories of expenses. Since you will be working from home, figure a portion of your total rent or mortgage payment (in proportion to your workspace and storage areas), or assign a reasonable, competitive rent figure for the same amount and type of space. List all overhead expense items and total them. Divide the total overhead figure by the number of items per month (or time period you used above). This amount will be your overhead per item.

Materials Cost + Labour Costs + Overhead Expenses =
Cost per Item

(d) Profit/competition/market demand
Include an amount added to the cost of each item so you won't end up just breaking even or making an employee's wage. Check your competition and see what they are charging. (Retailers generally double the wholesale price.) If your product is a little better than the competition, charge a little more. Refer to the "Competition Checklist" (Checklist 7) in Section Four. If your product is comparable, price it similarly. Remember, you will receive the profit from each sale, in addition to the salary figure. Add the profit figure you have chosen to the total cost per item to get your total price per item.

Cost per Item + Profit = Total Price per Item

2. Typical Service Pricing Formula

(a) Overhead expenses
As detailed above, calculate all the costs related to operating your business from home to arrive at a total cost per month. Divide this by the average number of hours worked per month to arrive at your hourly expense.

(b) Hourly wage
Decide on a wage that you will pay yourself, taking into consideration your background, training, and special expertise in your field. Compare this to industry averages.

(c) Hourly profit
Add a factor to your hourly wage to provide a profit margin. Check your competition and the market demand.

$$\text{Hourly Overhead Expense + Hourly Wage + Profit =}$$
$$\text{Total Price per Hour}$$

Remember, the main purpose in operating a business is to make a profit. Don't undersell your product or service just because "I'd be knitting sweaters anyway" or "I'm just starting out" or "I work out of my home." If you have a new, rare, handmade product or personalized service, the demand may be so high that customers are willing to pay a little more.

It is important to note that pricing must be continually evaluated, as material costs will increase due to inflation. Your prices should reflect these increases.

E. LOCATION

When determining the location of your home-based business, different factors will have to be considered, according to whether you are operating a retail, a service, or a manufacturing business. Will your customers be coming to you? Will you be delivering the product or service to your customers? Will municipal bylaws permit you to operate the type of business from the location you select?

For a retail business, where the customer comes to you, your three most important marketing decisions are location, location, and location! You will have to make sure that your business is well situated in a high-traffic location within your target market area. Good signage will provide you with the advantage of walk-by business. It must have easy access by car and public transportation and convenient parking.

You should also look at space and cost considerations, such as: Is the space at home suitable? Is it large enough? Is there room for expansion in the future? And what will it cost me to renovate or prepare my space for storage needs, retail space, and service areas?

While the location of your business is also important for service and manufacturing operations, the major considerations are likely to be the cost and ease of getting your product or service to the customer, since, for the most part, you will be delivering the product or service to your customer. You must consider the distribution methods you will use. What will it cost you to deliver directly to your customers, wholesalers, or agents? Ensure that such costs are factored into your pricing. Will the location of your business be within the pickup and delivery area of your suppliers? Other considerations for the location of your service or manufacturing business will include the availability of warehouse storage space within your proximate area, and a location for servicing and repairing products or equipment.

F. PROMOTION

For most homeowners, money for marketing is limited. You will be interested to learn, then, that some of the most effective marketing techniques are free or inexpensive and fall under the category of *publicity* or *promotion*. It is particularly important, therefore, to be aware of various techniques to create public awareness of your product or service. The following strategies are the most common ones, though not all of the examples would necessarily be appropriate for your type of business, or compatible with your style or personality. The first strategy discussed, the media release, is covered in considerable detail, whereas the other methods are just highlighted.

1. Media Releases and Exposure

Media or news releases can be an extremely effective means of obtaining publicity — that is, if you do the release correctly. Most small business owners haven't the remotest idea how to prepare a release, and therefore do not use the technique, or use it incorrectly. The secret is to create a media release which is newsworthy, interesting, and topical. Keep in mind that reporters and newscasters are constantly searching for material that could be of interest to their readers, listeners, or viewers. Some days they may have little material, while other days may be packed with late-breaking news. If your timing is right, your release could be used as a "filler" on an otherwise light newsday. When submitting releases, be certain to allow sufficient lead time in order to enhance the likelihood of your release being used.

The term "media" refers to the communication vehicles of print (newspapers, magazines, newsletters), radio, and television. When deciding where to send a media release, do your research to target the correct persons within the medium in question — whether publishers, general editors, section editors, journalists, reporters, freelance writers, syndicated columnists, book reviewers, news broadcasters, program directors, talk show hosts, or researchers.

The following resources may help you to locate the various media and best person in each category to send the release to:

- Look in the Yellow Pages under "Radio," "Television," "Newspapers," and "Magazines." Stop by newsstands and visit libraries to become aware of publications in your area of business interest.
- Check with your public library for *Canadian Advertising and Rates Data* (CARD), a directory listing all the media in Canada. Also check directories that list various trade publications and newsletters in Canada and the U.S.

- Contact the media concerned and enquire about the name of the editor, talk-show host, program director, or news director, as well as address, postal code, etc.
- Check the print media and gather names of reporters, writers, or columnists who write about subjects which could encompass your business area. And be aware of TV or radio news stories that you could "piggyback" on.

You may want to send the release to several key people within the same newspaper, radio, television, or magazine organization. For example, you may believe the subject matter of your media release would be relevant not only to a newspaper's business section, but also its lifestyles section and its seniors section. Usually each section has a separate editor — though a community newspaper which is published once or twice a week, for example, may just have a general editor.

Before you start preparing a release, there are a number of initial steps you have to take. You have to ask yourself what benefit you hope to get from the exercise. Do you want local, regional, provincial, national, or international publicity? It will obviously make a difference in terms of your media contacts and the content of the release. Do you want to generate a telephone or letter response from prospective clients or customers? Your objective could be to stimulate sales orders, attract potential investors, or obtain consulting contracts, freelance work, or speaking engagements. Do you want just to make the public aware of your product, so that they will look for it in specialty or general retail stores?

To prepare a good release you should follow these general recommendations:

- Make it clear and easily readable.
- Use short sentences and simple English.
- Make sure it is grammatically correct with accurate spelling.
- Avoid flowery phrases, exaggerated or superlative statements, and other hype. Remember, this is a news release and not a sales letter.
- Use 1½ inch margins all around, and have it typed on white paper, on your business letterhead, or on specially designed news release letterhead.
- Have it photocopied or printed; quality of reproduction is paramount to portray a "professional" image.
- If referring to yourself in the release, which is a common technique, always use the third person: "she" or "he" rather than "I." This will make it sound like someone else has written about you,

which is a desirable impression to create, and makes it easier to quote yourself Readers tend to believe what they read as being credible and accurate because it appeared in print, and publicity legitimizes information, but this is undermined if the first person is used.

- Keep the release to one page ideally, and not more than two pages, or it might not be read. Keep in mind that the reader of the release is time-pressured and has to select from many releases received every day. If the release goes onto a second page, print "more" in the lower right-hand corner of the first page, and attach a second page. Never print your releases on both sides of the same sheet.
- You may wish to attach a separate, biographical media release to your general release. The biography should read like an article and show why "the person being quoted" and your business are interesting. The more finished the appearance of your media, re-lease and/or biography, the more likely a busy reporter or editor will use it — in some cases verbatim or with very little editing.
- You may also wish to consider attaching a photograph (ideally, professionally taken) to your release, depicting either yourself or the item being profiled. It should be black-and-white and have good resolution. If it does go into the newspaper or magazine, it will add a graphic impact and more human interest to the article.

There are several basic elements to a media release, as described below, concerning the format, layout, and content. An example of a typical media release is shown in Sample 6.

(a) "MEDIA RELEASE" or "NEWS RELEASE" Put these words in capitals at the very top and centred. Don't use the term "press release," if you intend to send it to media other than "the press" (newspapers).

(b) Date Place the date of the release at the top left corner.

(c) Contact person Put the name of the person who is the source of the release at the top left or right side of the page, so that he or she can be contacted for more information. Include the person's position/title, address, and phone number with area code.

(d) Release date Put the date on which the media is to release the information. Generally, one states, "FOR IMMEDIATE RELEASE" in capital letters. This line should be placed on the right side of the page, just above the headline.

(e) Headline This is centred on the page and typed in capital letters. It summarizes the content of the media release, so that the reader can quickly see what it is all about, and decide if he wants to read further. It should, therefore, be an attention-grabber. Editors generally write their own headlines for actual publication, however.

(f) Basic facts   The first paragraph of your release should state the key facts and information you want the media to know. It should cover the "who, what, when, why, where, and how" aspects of your story. It is important to have a "news peg" in this first paragraph — something to give the editors a reason to publish it, or radio or TV broadcaster a reason to comment on it. If you can't cover all the basic facts in the first paragraph, finish in the second.

(g) Important details   You will want to add some details other than those covered in the "Basic Facts" section, in order to encourage the media to consider a feature story rather than just a brief announcement. You may cover the benefits of the product or service or why it is unique, pitfalls to avoid, tips to save money or make money, or quotes from yourself (in the third person, remember).

(h) Supplementary information   In this part of the release, which could be the third or fourth paragraph, you provide information which adds colour to a feature story. For example, simple questions consumers could ask themselves; discussion of the trends or implications involved; the impact on the community such as increased employment, or an export market created; or an award received.

(i) Further information   Many releases don't include this line, but it could be an appropriate one for your type of home business operation, especially if the purpose of your release is to obtain a direct and quantifiable response from the public. The last line or short last paragraph should have your business name, your address and phone number, and a list of the free promotional material that is available upon request. Alternatively, the line may simply state that the product is now available in retail outlets (state type).

Although this "Further Information" line is a form of advertising, editors will generally include it if they think it will benefit the readers or audience to have it noted.

(j) The closing   End the release by putting "End" or "-30-" centred after your last paragraph.

If you feel unsure about writing your own biography and media release, you can refer to books, some of which are referred to in Appendix B, "Recommended Reading," or pay a freelance writer to prepare the material for you.

2. Media Interviews

Your news releases, or discussions with decision-makers at local newspapers, magazines, radio, or TV, could result in interviews. You could have news articles which profile you and your business, or appearances on TV or radio talk shows or feature programs. Over time, you could attempt to cultivate a relationship with the media, so that they perceive you to be an expert or credible authority. From time to time they may want to interview or quote you on matters relating to your area of "expertise."

If you have a specific event occurring, you should attempt to encourage media coverage of it. For example, an upcoming craft show could be considered newsworthy to the media in your local community. TV, radio, or newspaper coverage of the event would give you widespread publicity at no cost.

3. Cable TV Opportunities

In addition to being interviewed on your local cable station, you may want to obtain positive public exposure in other ways. One way is to give a free gift of a product you sell or a service you provide to a local TV benefit auction. Obviously you have to weigh your actual cost against your perceived return, in terms of publicity value or increased clients, customers, or sales.

Another idea would be for you to produce your own local cable show in your specialty area. It could be an ongoing weekly half-hour show or a two-, four-, or eight-part series. For example, if you are a property inspector, you may want to host a regular phone interview program on renovating old homes; if you are a doctor, physiotherapist, or chiropractor, you may want to host a regular series on health subjects or a specialty program on dealing with back pain; or if you are a craftsperson, you may want to host a program on painting or making pottery.

You will not get paid for producing a local cable program. It is a trade: you do the organization of the program, and the cable station provides the facilities and does the taping. But in addition to increasing your skill and self-confidence, such a program will provide your business with exposure and credibility.

4. Teaching Courses and Seminars

Teaching adult education classes is an effective way to make business contacts, meet prospective clients, obtain public exposure, and enhance your reputation as an expert. In addition to your being paid, teaching also has the fringe benefit of keeping you current on your area of interest. There are many opportunities to teach a course, or a one- or two-day seminar. Contact the continuing or adult education program coordinators of school boards, colleges, and universities in your area. Also consider YM-YWCAs, community recreational centres, seniors' organizations or centres, churches, and other groups that you perceive would be appropriate educational vehicles for your program.

5. Speaking

Trade, professional, or community groups or associations regularly look for speakers for breakfast, lunch, or dinner meetings as well as conferences or conventions. In most cases you will not receive a fee, as these organizations normally obtain speakers for free. In the case of conferences or conventions, though, there are sometimes opportunities to get paid for your presentation. Check in the Yellow Pages under "Associations" or in one of various directories of associations available in your public library, and contact the program coordinators for the groups or associations that you think might be interested.

If you are in a personal services business, speaking on subjects related to your business is an effective marketing technique. This is particularly true for businesses such as consulting, counselling, real estate, child care, financial advising, and any of the "traditional" professions such as law, medicine, or dentistry. People naturally want to have a relationship of confidence and trust with such professionals, and by giving speeches you have a chance to create that bonding and perception which may result in subsequent business.

6. Writing an Article

Writing is a classic technique for building credibility and exposure, and establishing yourself as an expert in your field. Considering the large number of publications available, it should not be difficult to have an article published in a magazine or newsletter that potential customers would read.

You may already be aware of most of the publications in your area of interest or general publications that could be appropriate. Check with your local library and newsstands for other publications that might interest you. Also consider writing a regular column, perhaps monthly or more or less frequently, in your community newspaper or other publication. Most of these types of articles tend to be from 500 to 1,500 words in length. After contacting the editor of the publication, send your piece along with a picture of yourself and brief biographical profile. Add your name, address, and telephone number to be included at the end of the article. In most cases you won't get paid — unless you are a freelance writer of course — but in some cases you will be able to obtain free advertising space in exchange. In any event, make sure you receive credit in the form of a byline if possible, as well as a brief biography and contact information.

7. Writing a Book

Having a book, pamphlet, or workbook published is another marketing technique to establish yourself as an expert, as well as produce ongoing income. You can either self-publish or find a publisher for your book. Attempt to evaluate the cost/benefit ratio of the exercise, in terms of your time, money, and resources. And you have to look at the indirect benefit in terms of credibility; for example, you could use your books as promotional items, include them as incentives for people to buy your service or product, sell them at seminars or presentations, or use them as a tool to get appearances on TV or radio programs.

8. Newsletters

If you know your business area well, and see that there is a niche in the market for a newsletter, you may find filling this need to be a good marketing option. The newsletter could come out monthly, bimonthly, quarterly, or semiannually. It could be from two to 12 pages in length, and be distributed either free as a promotion device or by paid circulation. The newsletter should have tips, news, and ideas and possibly a question-and-answer column. Check to see if your competitors use a newsletter and see how it can be improved. Review the various directories of newsletters in your public library.

9. Contact Networks

A high percentage of the clientele of many home-based businesses is acquired through a contact network which can provide much referral business: relatives, friends, neighbours, business associates and acquaintances, past and present customers, employees, and your accountant, lawyer, and banker.

Joining select associations or clubs could also foster exposure and sources of new business. There are many types of clubs and associations: professional, trade, business, community, fraternal, religious, and charitable. There are also organizations set up which are specifically designed for networking. Developing a contact network is one of the most inexpensive and effective ways of increasing your business credibility and exposure.

G. LOW-COST ADVERTISING

Advertising makes potential buyers aware of your product or service, and hopefully induces them to buy. Another benefit of advertising is that it could expose you to retailers, wholesalers, or distributors who may approach you with bulk orders. Also, repeated ads in trade-related publications creates an impression that your business is credible and stable. You probably already know which publications target your market within your area. Otherwise, check with your newsstands and public library for further ideas. Here are some tips for low-cost (or no-cost) advertising strategies.

1. Word of Mouth

It is a cliché but an accurate one: word of mouth is the best form of advertising. The more people promote your product or service because they know you or are satisfied customers, the more sales you are going to make. Personal testimonials are very persuasive and credible. Attempt to cultivate positive and respectful customer relations at all times. Remember, the customer is always right, even when the customer is wrong. One dissatisfied customer can taint your goodwill to many other people. You should therefore deal with any customer complaints in a prompt and efficient manner.

2. Business Cards and Stationery

Creating a positive image with your business cards and stationery was covered earlier. The initial impression should be a positive one. Your cards and stationery should also reflect the type of business you are in, and what you do. This could be reflected by your business name and/or brief description under it. For example "residential and commercial property inspection."

3. Signs

Signs are an inexpensive form of advertising. Subject to your local zoning regulations and the type of house and business you have, you could place a tasteful and professionally prepared sign on your lawn, on a fencepost, or somewhere on your house. You can also place a sign on a window of your car (both sides) so that it is seen by pedestrians and other car drivers. The sign should reflect the image you want to project.

4. Brochures and Posters

Brochures and posters can be very effective and relatively inexpensive. Some of the advertising uses of a brochure are leaving it with a prospective client; distributing it at a seminar, presentation, or other distribution location; sending it as part of a direct mail campaign; and mailing it after a written or phone request for further information. A poster can mention upcoming shows or seminars that you have or other products or services. They can be placed at major traffic areas for your target market such as store windows, etc. Always obtain competitive quotes on printing, as prices can vary considerably.

5. Flyers and Tear-off Ads

Flyers and tear-off ads are a simple and inexpensive technique to use if your market is restricted to a certain geographic area. For a tear-off ad, the advertisement would be typed on a sheet of paper with tear-off tabs at the bottom of it, with your name and phone number on each tab. If you have a typing/résumé service, for example, you could place an ad on the bulletin boards in key locations of local universities, colleges, and institutes to elicit students who needed term papers typed. Or, if large layoffs had recently been announced in your community, you could place flyers on all the cars in the employee parking lot announcing your résumé service.

6. Catalogues

Catalogues tend to be more expensive to produce and distribute because of the cost of the photography, artwork, typesetting, paper, and postage. Also, the pricing in catalogues can become dated quickly and therefore need to be published regularly. The benefit of a catalogue, though, is that your customer would have your menu of product selections for easy access. An alternative is to have your product accepted by an established catalogue company which covers your target market.

7. Computer Bulletin Boards

Local and national computer bulletin boards provide advertising opportunities. These boards provide information via the computer keyboard and list services of referral networks. People can phone the network, using a computer and modem, to view the listing of the services they need. Each of the businesses listed on the service pays a fee. If you want further information about local boards, make enquiries at computer user group meetings and computer stores. If you want to use a national system, you need to subscribe to the service and pay a fee based on time.

8. Trade and Professional Directories

Many directories are available which are annually published and accept paid display ads. Some publications charge for a listing and others do not. If you carefully select your directory, you could accurately hit your target market. Check your library for directories related to your business.

9. The Yellow Pages

Determine if this form of advertising is appropriate and cost-effective for your type of business. For both product- and service-type businesses it could be a practical and effective method for you, as potential customers may look to the Yellow Pages first. Check to see if your competitors are listed. The telephone company provides one free Yellow Page listing under one category if you have a business line. You have to pay extra for additional listings and other features, such as bolding, capitals, colour, and box ads.

10. Classified and Display Ads

You may want to consider advertising in the classified sections of newspapers, magazines, or newsletters targeted to your market. Display advertising can be expensive and is not appropriate for everyone, although it can be very effective if properly targeted. A larger ad does not always bring in a greater response. You may want to test the market by placing classified ads in selected magazines, and tracking the response. You may then want to test a display ad in those magazines that produced a good response.

11. Drop Shipping

Publishers of magazines, catalogues, or newsletters are sometimes willing to act as distributors and sell your product by a *drop ship* arrangement. In this situation, the publisher displays or lists your product, takes orders by phone or mail, generally by credit card, and retains an agreed-on percentage of the revenue plus the cost of mailing of the publication. You are then sent the balance by cheque, along with the names and addresses of the people who ordered the product. It is then your responsibility to ship the product directly to the buyers, whose names can now be used for your mailing list.

12. Direct Mail

Direct mail is a popular and effective method of selling certain types of products or service. You can develop a mailing list by building up your own and/or buying a mailing list. You can locate the names of mailing list companies by looking in the Yellow Pages under "Mailing Lists." Also check with your library for a publication entitled *Direct Mail List Rates and Data*. Keep a list of your past customers and everyone who asks for information about your business by phone, letter, or in person. Check with your local Canada Post office for free information and advice on direct mail.

13. Trade Shows

Trade shows can be an effective way to reach potential customers. A trade show is usually marketed to the consumer (end users) or the industry (retailers, wholesalers). At many of the trade shows you not only sell products, but also generate potential customers or business contacts such as retailers, wholesalers, distributors, manufacturers' representatives, and buying agents (e.g., for retail chains). Exhibiting is a good way to test a new product, do informal surveys, and build your mailing list by collecting business cards or names.

It is also common for booth exhibitors to conduct a seminar or speak at the trade show. This technique creates exposure and credibility and provides you with the additional opportunity of explaining, demonstrating, or displaying your products.

Attend some trade shows in your field before exhibiting. Afterward ask exhibitors if the trade show has been successful, in terms of the number of sales, leads, or contacts, and the reputation and success of the promoter in advertising and marketing the trade show. Would they take a booth in that same trade show again? Also ask exhibitors if they would be interested in sharing booth space in the future, selling your product at their booth, or adding your product line to theirs.

Be careful in selecting trade shows. You could waste a lot of time and money exhibiting at a show that is poorly promoted or attended. Check out the reputation of the promotion company by making enquiries of people in the industry and the Better Business Bureau. To find out all trade shows scheduled across Canada, contact your public library and look at the most recent annual trade show directory for Canada. There is also a similar annual directory for the U.S. available in most libraries.

14. Special Promotions

You may wish to attract the interest of your target market, by advertising such promotions as senior, student, or family discounts, free trial offers, "two for one" sales, and raffles.

H. GETTING YOUR PRODUCT TO YOUR CUSTOMER

No matter how good your product is, it cannot benefit anyone unless it is available for the customer to purchase. The goal of any distribution system is to get your product to your target market in a timely and convenient fashion, so that it is easy for the customer to buy. There are four main methods of distributing your product: retailing, wholesaling, consigning, and agents or representatives.

1. Retailing

This method involves personal selling; that is, face-to-face meetings with consumers or commercial or institutional buyers of your product. Retailing is the most direct means of selling your product, and could create a higher gross profit for you as it eliminates commissions or fees paid to wholesalers or agents. The drawback, of course, is that you have to do the selling yourself or hire salespeople. That involves time, expense, and, to some people, discomfort — discomfort in wearing the different hats of owner and salesperson.

Here are some of the ways of selling directly to consumers:

- retail shop or studio in your home
- door-to-door sales and in-home demonstrations
- street vending
- public market
- home parties
- trade shows, fairs, festivals, flea markets.

You could also consider selling directly to buyers for business, institutions, or government. Provincial and federal governments and their Crown corporations have a policy of trying "Canadian first." In practical terms, though, you would have to have the production capacity to meet the large volume and consistency of quality requirements of large organizations.

2. Wholesaling

Wholesaling is an ideal distribution method if you would prefer not to direct-sell. You would have the capacity to expand the volume of production and therefore the potential volume of sales. This is an indirect method of selling to the consumer, and involves either selling directly to a retail outlet or through a wholesaler who in turn sells to retailers. Some retailers will only deal with wholesalers and do not want to deal directly with the producers. Also, wholesalers will not generally buy unless a demand for the product has been demonstrated. This is because wholesalers expend the time and money to sell the product by means of sales calls, trade shows, trade advertising, special distribution programs, and direct mail promotions. The drawback of wholesaling, of course, is that you receive less money for your product than by selling it directly, as the wholesaler has to add a markup.

The main forms of wholesaling include:

- retail outlets (department stores, craft, hobby, gift shops, etc.)
- merchandise marts
- premium sales
- mail-order catalogue sales
- institutional buyers
- foreign markets.

3. Consigning

This approach involves selling the goods through a retailer. It is frequently used by people who can't sell through a wholesaler, or who want to provide greater distribution and exposure of the product. If it is a new product with an unknown demand, retailers may be reluctant to buy your products, but may be willing to display them on consignment.

In a consignment situation, you remain the owner of all the consigned goods and only receive payment after they are sold. The retailer retains a percentage of the selling price as a commission or fee. However, this could tie up your funds and present cash flow problems. The retailer has no obligation to pay you until the goods are sold and can return the goods to you at any time. Another drawback to consignment is that you have no way of controlling or being reimbursed for damage to the product by shoppers. But despite these limitations, it is an option you may need to consider in order to get some exposure and create a product demand.

Another variation of consignment is *rack jobbing*. In this approach, the retailer provides you with floor or shelf space to display your "rack" of goods free of charge. The "rack," or point-of-purchase display unit, is either supplied by you or by the retailer. You then pay the retailer a commission on sales.

4. Agents, Brokers, and Manufacturers' Representatives

These people are independent, self-employed contractors working as commissioned salespersons. Their role is to act as a liaison between retailers or wholesalers and you, represent your interests, and promote the sale of your product. The advantages of using agents, brokers, etc. include the following: it saves you money since you do not have to hire employees; they only get paid if they perform; it frees you up to spend more time on your other business matters, since customers are located for you; it provides you with the opportunity for business growth and increased sales; and it enables you to access new territories or obtain contracts because of their connections and experience in the industry.

An *agent* is a person who acts for you in your business capacity. An example would be a booking agent who tries to book a professional speaker into trade shows or conventions. An agent for your product could have either an exclusive or a non-exclusive relationship with you. An exclusive agent could be more committed to expending time selling your product or service, but of course there is always a risk and limitation in "putting all your eggs in one basket."

A *broker* could act as an agent for both sides of the business, depending on the nature of the product or service. For example, a training broker could be retained by a speaker to sell corporate training programs. Conversely, a corporation could retain a training broker to search out, evaluate, and recommend training programs appropriate to the defined needs of the organization.

A *manufacturers' representative* is an agent who represents similar product lines from different businesses.

There are several ways of locating agents, brokers, or representatives: look in the Yellow Pages under "Brokers" or "Manufacturing Agents and Representatives"; look in trade magazines for ads; ask others in the industry whom they would recommend; go to a merchandise mart and speak to representatives or wholesalers; and attend trade shows.

Always make sure your business arrangement is covered in writing in advance, after you have concluded your negotiations. Don't forget to scan the market before deciding. You don't want to have any misunderstandings, with the stress or loss of goodwill and money which could result. According to the nature of the relationship, cover such matters (as applicable) as commission; each party's responsibilities; authority; exclusive or non-exclusive; duration; sales territory; and policies concerning credit, down payment, retainer, discounts, billings, warranties, returns, shipping, packaging, and advertising. To be on the safe side and for peace of mind, if the agreement was supplied to you, have your lawyer look it over before you sign. Otherwise, develop your own agreement and show it to your lawyer for comment. Never base business relationships on a "handshake." The stakes are too high and you will likely regret it.

To be successful, you will have to become the marketing manager along with your other business roles. The information and assistance you need is readily available, so take the time and be resourceful in seeking it. Read pertinent books and articles (refer to Appendix B for books on product or service marketing for small business); attend an adult education class or Federal Business Development Bank (FBDB) seminar; contact the FBDB CASE (Counselling Assistance for Small Enterprise) counselling program or a provincial small business centre; or hire a marketing consultant. Talk to other, successful entrepreneurs whenever you have the opportunity. Effective marketing is an ongoing concern of every successful business. Be certain to repeat the techniques that work, modify or discontinue those that no longer produce results, and continually test new markets.

Review *Marketing Your Product*, 2nd Edition, by Douglas A. Gray and Donald Cyr (see Appendix B).

CHAPTER

9

Time and Stress Management

Time is a precious and limited resource. When operating a business there are numerous demands placed on your time and you will want to make the most efficient use of it. In your business plan you have outlined a number of your goals and objectives, and you will need an action plan to keep you on track. Effective time management means organizing your day so that you accomplish your goals and objectives within the time frames you have established. You may not be able to complete all of your tasks; some will have to be deferred until the next day, and some will have to be delegated to others. To be a good manager, you must be able to set priorities and decide which tasks should be delegated and which ones should not.

When you become overburdened with a heavy workload and fatigued from working long hours, there is usually a buildup of negative stress. It is commonly viewed that stress is a bad thing, and dangerous to our health. On the contrary, most people work most effectively while under a tolerable amount of stress. And the absence of any stress in one's life usually leads to severe depression and low self-esteem. It is necessary, therefore, to distinguish between *positive stress*, which is a motivator, and *negative stress*, which endangers your personal and business health.

A. POSITIVE STRESS

Positive stress can be defined as the stress of pleasure, challenge, and fulfillment. All activities involve stress, from a game of tennis to writing a business proposal. In fact, the motivating factors that influence a person to start a business — risk, drive, challenge, fulfillment — can be viewed as positive stressors. A person with a high degree of self-confidence will usually have a correspondingly high degree of positive stress. A sense of being in control enables a person to handle minor setbacks within the stride of day-to-day activities. Stress is a very individual reaction. An activity such as making a presentation at a business meeting will affect people differently. One person will display confidence and enthusiasm, while another will become extremely nervous and perhaps nauseated. What we want is the right amount of stress for the right length of time — at a level that is best suited for us. To know what this level is, we should look at circumstances where we have gone beyond this level and which led to *distress*.

B. NEGATIVE STRESS

When the activities that bring us positive stress are insufficient, excessive, or inappropriate, then frustration, discomfort, disease, or psychosomatic illness (negative stress) may result. Negative stress is typically referred to as a loss of control. By examining your own behaviour in previous circumstances where you have been under a great deal of pressure, you may be able to identify characteristics that you are not particularly proud of. Examples may include impatience, curt answers, raised voice, or excessive gestures. Often in hindsight we can clearly see how the situation could have been handled quite differently if we had regained control before allowing an emotional response. Looking deeper into the root of the situation, you may be able to attribute the cause of your negative behaviour to: being late for a deadline or appointment, a missed opportunity, too heavy a workload, fatigue, feeling out of control, someone else's mistake, or being treated unfairly.

The purpose of delving into past experiences is not to relive them and burden ourselves with guilt, which is a type of self-induced negative stress. Rather, we should learn to recognize the circumstances that typically lead to such negative stress buildup for us. Then, when we see ourselves failing into the same trap, we can take measures to alter the outcome of the situation. For instance, a person who has an extremely heavy workload and is frustrated by always being behind schedule should practice effective time management techniques, delegate responsibilities to others or hire part-time staff, and reduce his or her expectations of what can be reasonably accomplished in a normal workday. Or, the person who feels he or she is being treated unfairly may decide to take an assertiveness training course to build self-confidence and composure when faced with difficult situations. The person who feels out of control should recognize the danger of no one being at the helm of the ship.

As individuals, we all react to stressful situations in different ways. Some people are able to conceal their expressions of negative emotions, but carry them inside and start to feel a mounting pressure. Often this type of individual will suffer from hypertension, insomnia, headaches, ulcers, and other physical signs of the negative stress. If your body starts to show symptoms of stress, it is necessary to take an honest and objective look at your personal and business life. Make a list of all your frustrations. This can sometimes best be done with another person who knows you and your business well: a spouse, partner, or business advisor. It may also mean that you are neglecting your physical health. A healthy diet and regular exercise are necessary to keep your mind alert and your body fit to handle a challenging and longer workday. You must take action to reduce the negative stress.

As mentioned, operating a business can be stressful, and this can sometimes be compounded by working alone at home. In order to stay motivated to work and maximize your coping skills under stress, try some of these coping techniques:

- Avoid undesirable influences and suggestions that can bring you down.
- Avoid negative, destructive, or critical people or situations.
- Read books that contain positive and optimistic advice.
- Call a friend or business associate who understands your situation. It can assist your morale greatly to hear words of encouragement.
- Keep a diary of your accomplishments and reread it from time to time for positive reinforcement and encouragement. (If you completed the questions in Chapter 1 on self-assessment, you should have many positive thoughts in terms of what you have going for you.)
- Associate with enthusiastic and inspiring people. Communicate with them by phone, by mail, or in person.
- Consider setbacks as profitable learning experiences.
- Join trade or networking associations and participate as regularly as you feel comfortable.

• Pat yourself on the back frequently.

Your business success depends upon a positive and optimistic attitude. Try to counter any negative situation with a positive one. A decisive, take-charge attitude will help you to recognize that you always have choices, even if it is only a choice not to continue an activity.

C. TIME MANAGEMENT TECHNIQUES

Like any other valuable resource, time can be managed. The better it is managed, the more productive and profitable your business will be. All the other acquired skills you possess will lose much of their effectiveness if you are disorganized. As you probably will not have the time to attend to all the matters requiring your attention, you must ensure that the important tasks get done. Be certain to attend to the activities which generate continued profitability and future growth. By using some of the following proven techniques, your efficiency, productivity, and satisfaction will be increased considerably.

1. Set Priorities

Based on the goals you have established for your business, set your priorities in terms of high, medium, and low priorities. Write them down. High-priority items are those that are vital to the business, have a deadline affixed to them, and usually need your personal attention. Medium-priority tasks are necessary to the business, but may not require your immediate attention; perhaps some of these tasks could be delegated. Low-priority items may be postponed to a more convenient time, or not done at all.

It is not sufficient to know in your mind what has to be done. Making a list of your "to do" jobs enables you to plan your day effectively. A daytimer or similar day calendar system is a useful tool. At the end of each day, list and classify the next day's jobs into A, B, and C priorities. The A items are those you must accomplish today. B items may be accomplished today, or could be dealt with tomorrow as an A-priority job. The C items may be used as "filler" jobs at the end of your day, or at a time when your concentration is not sufficient to handle an A- or B-priority job. Examples of A-priority jobs are writing paycheques or paying bills; drafting a proposal for a bid on a large contract which closes in three days' time; telephoning the airlines to make a flight reservation on the last day of the discount rate period (may be a B priority if you can delegate it to someone else to do as their A priority). As each job is completed, cross it off your list. At the end of the day, those items not crossed off the list must be carried over to the next day, along with any new jobs that might have arisen. At the end of each week, list those items which need to be accomplished the following week.

Keeping a "to do" list provides a source of satisfaction and feeling of progress as items are crossed off the list. It can also alleviate the stress that results from trying to remember everything that has to be done.

Dealing with the high-priority items *first* is a particularly effective time management technique. By handling a critical task early in your day, you have the reward of feeling a sense of relief and accomplishment. Often this provides additional motivation and drive to maintain the productivity momentum. If there are unexpected interruptions, or minor problems arise, you are able to devote attention to them knowing that you have already dealt with your top-priority item. If, on the other hand, you defer your high-priority item until the afternoon, chances are that problems will arise that prevent you from getting to that task. As there can be a daily stream of unexpected interruptions, some people operate day after day in this time trap, never getting to those critical tasks.

In order to accomplish your high-priority tasks, it will be necessary to have a block of uninterrupted time. Ask your telephone answering service to hold all calls for the first hour of each day. Schedule other blocks of time that are necessary to fully complete a priority task.

Avoid procrastination. If one of your critical tasks doesn't have a built-in deadline, set one. In this way you will ensure that it gets to the top of your priority list. Perhaps you are having trouble starting a major project because it appears to be massive and you don't know where to begin. It is helpful to divide the major project into manageable stages. For instance, when preparing a bank loan proposal, one day's task may be to make a list of all the items you will include in your proposal. The other stages will be preparing each of the items on your list: sales projection charts, net worth statement, marketing concept, and loan rationale. By handling this large project in bite-sized pieces, it is conceivable that the task could be accomplished within a week.

2. Schedule Your Activities

Especially in a home-based business it will be necessary to have a schedule to follow to help your motivation and keep you on track with your business plan. Often home-based entrepreneurs experience a feeling of isolation and lack of motivation when working on their own at home. The absence of the stimulus of having others working along with you may cause you to be unfocussed in your approach. Keeping a schedule and planning your daily activities will help you to avoid this trap.

Constant interruptions can cause delays in accomplishing your goals. The main sources of interruptions may be personal telephone calls, drop-in visits from friends and relatives, and distractions from children and mounting household chores that may be calling out to you. A sense of self-control and personal discipline will help you to overcome these temptations to waver from your business efforts.

Using a daybook or diary will help you keep track of your appointments and things to do. If you make a habit of writing everything in your diary as soon as you become aware of an event, you will avoid double-booking appointments or forgetting them. You may decide to schedule your appointments for the afternoon whenever possible, to allow your morning to be a free block of time during which you can accomplish items on your "to do" list. When scheduling your workday, allow yourself some flexibility and leeway, as things don't always go according to plan. Allow sufficient time so that each task can be carried out in a thorough, unhurried manner.

3. Be Organized

Having an up-to-date and efficient filing system will enable you to find your files quickly. On the other hand, keeping every piece of paper that comes across your desk in an escalating stack, or in overstuffed files, only creates frustration and delay when trying to locate a piece of information. Of course you will need to keep a copy of your important correspondence, proposals, and bookkeeping records. But filing space is expensive. Before filing a piece of paper you need to ask yourself, "Will I ever have to refer back to this? Can I get another copy of this if sometime in the future I need to refer to it?" For example, keeping a copy of equipment suppliers' brochures and price lists is usually unnecessary. Chances are that when you decide to purchase that type of equipment, the brochure and price list will be out of date, and a newer model of equipment will be available. Another example may be copies of newsletters, agendas, and minutes of meetings of the professional association of which you are a member. Unless you are on the executive committee or have a specific need to refer to such dated material, it can consume a lot of file space and never be referred to after it has been filed.

There is much to be said for the person who is able to keep a tidy workspace. While many defend their cluttered desks by saying, "I know exactly where everything is," it is not shown how much time is wasted shuffling papers. The hidden time waster is the distraction created by a cluttered work area. Instead of having a clear train of thought when working on the critical priority items, a casual glance at the clutter may trigger numerous reminders of things that must be done. This could create unnecessary delays in completing the immediate task, as well as cause extra stress and feeling of being overwhelmed.

Being prepared for meetings and appointments saves time otherwise spent in prolonged discussions. Before the meeting you should review your file, make notes, prepare an agenda, *and stick to it*. Anticipating potential problems will enable you have an action plan ready to implement, rather than merely reacting to events as they occur.

4. Delegate

If your home-based business grows and you decide to employ staff, it will be necessary for you to delegate some of your responsibilities. At times it will appear easier to do it yourself than to explain the process to someone else, train, and supervise him, and check that it has been done right. You are quite right — at least for the first time and perhaps the second time. However, once you have trained someone in how to handle the task, your time can be spent elsewhere. Nor should you waste time in excessive supervision of the person. It is necessary that your employees have sufficient scope and authority to make decisions within the responsibility of the task. Delegating the authority builds staff morale, competence, and motivation.

Learn to say no. You may receive a request, for example, to participate in a community activity that will require taking time from your business day. Knowing your daily workload and having the ability to say no is important to your time management.

5. Be Decisive

Preciseness in identifying problems and decisiveness in the actions to be taken will save time in your workday. Similarly to the technique used with large or insurmountable tasks, by breaking a problem down into different parts, you can see more clearly the root of the problem. To resolve it, then, list the various alternatives and rate the degree of effectiveness of each. Practising this technique will help you to develop the ability to go through this process quickly in your mind. This will enhance your effectiveness in resolving small problems before they escalate into big ones.

The art of speaking and writing concisely is a time saver for you and the people you deal with. It will also foster improved communication between you and your customers, and any employees.

D. AVOID TIME WASTERS

- **Too many telephone calls** Bunch your calls before lunch or toward the end of the day when people are less likely to chat.
- **Overscheduling/too many things to do** Concentrate on important items and disregard trivia. Use your diary to plan your day and prepare a priority list of tasks. Learn to say no. Delegate.
- **Junk mail** Avoid spending time reading or filing brochures and pamphlets. Put junk mail in the wastebasket.
- **Too much paper** Deal with each piece of paper only once. If it is junk mail, throw it out. If it is for the file, file it immediately. If it requires a response, a handwritten response or a telephone call may suffice. If you have staff, delegate routine matters to them. By handling your morning mail in this manner, you will avoid tomorrow's task of dealing with the paperwork you set aside today.
- **Reading reports/trade magazines** Learn to skim or speed-read. Skip to the summary or recommendations of articles. Review the table of contents and read only those articles of specific interest. Skip to the highlighted sections or main points; usually the essence is given in the first two paragraphs.
- **Unexpected visitors** Keep the visit brief. Conduct stand-up meetings. Once someone is settled into a comfortable chair with a coffee in hand, a good portion of your day could disappear. Arrange to meet the person for lunch or after work for an extended discussion, if this seems necessary or desirable.
- **Scheduled meetings** Be certain they start and end on time, and follow the agenda. Keep on topic. Ensure that a summary is given, noting any action to be taken after the meeting and by whom.
- **Lack of communication** State clearly what is expected when assigning work. If the work is submitted in an unfinished manner, rather than correcting it yourself (also known as upward delegation), return it in a tactful manner with an explanation of the finishing touches required. This will also help the employee's personal growth and understanding of the business. Encourage staff to ask questions if they are uncertain — remember, dumb questions are easier to handle than dumb mistakes!
- **Perfectionism** Striving for excellence is healthy, gratifying, and attainable. However, aiming for perfection is frustrating, neurotic, and a waste of time.
- **Fatigue** If you find you are unable to work productively owing to fatigue, take time to relax and refresh yourself. Stretch, take a break from what you are doing, take a short walk. You will find

that when you have returned, so has your energy and concentration. Eat regularly but sparingly, and avoid alcohol.

E. MAINTAINING A TIME LOG

A helpful tool to demonstrate how effectively or poorly you are managing your time is to keep a daily time log for a random week. This in itself is a time-consuming task, as it means you need to record minute by minute how you spend your time. It will include the telephone calls you make, those you receive, the tasks you accomplish on your priority list, the interruptions you receive, what you read, what you write, and so on. A sample time log is shown in Sample 7. After completing a week of such logs, you need to review them and assess the portion of your day which is spent productively. The logs will also show the time wasters which repeatedly get in the way of your accomplishments. Once you have this information, you are better able to plan your day and to block out interruptions. For example, you may set aside an hour or two of uninterrupted time during which you work on your priority tasks. If you have staff, you may train them on the procedures for handling certain tasks, thereby delegating the responsibility to them.

From time to time you may choose to repeat the time log exercise to check back on your degree of success in time management. As situations change, new time wasters may appear. Deal with them. Sample 8 shows a weekly time-use analysis which may be helpful in summarizing your completed daily time logs. By rating yourself on your use of time management techniques, you will identify your strong and weak areas. Asking yourself questions such as "What else could I delegate?" and "How can I reduce or eliminate specific time wasters?" will help you to focus on developing good habits. The weekly time-use analysis is an effective planning and management tool. Write it in your diary and do it!

If you recognize that you need to work on time and stress management, there are many sources of assistance. The FBDB and other institutions offer a range of half-day and full-day seminars on such topics as time management, staff productivity, communication skills, and effective customer relations. Commercial stationery stores frequently carry time log systems for use by you and your staff. Day-Timers of Canada has a comprehensive selection of products. Make use of the resources available to help you manage your stress and time, and be certain there is always someone in control at the helm of your ship!

CHAPTER

10

Dealing with Growth

To grow or not to grow? At some point the day may come when the owner of a healthy business thinks about expanding and moving the business away from the home. A decision must be made as to whether it is more financially viable to grow larger or to stay the present size.

Perhaps your business has grown so much that there is little room left in the house, and you are starting to feel cramped and disorganized. For some, the decision is easy because working from home was only a stepping stone on the road to another goal. For others, working at home is a valued way of life and they have no desire to change. For many people, though, deciding whether to move out or stay at home is not an easy choice. When faced with the option, the majority of home-based business owners feel pulled between the comfort, convenience, flexibility, and financial benefits of working at home and the opportunities for expansion, greater challenge, and increased income by moving out of the home.

Growing larger will probably mean a longer workday, increased stress, additional expense, more debt, increased bookkeeping, higher inventory and supply costs, increased product or service line, the need to hire employees, expansion into new markets, and more demands on your personal and family life. In addition, operating a larger enterprise requires greater management skills and operational systems.

How will you know if and when it is time to move out? The answer is, you will clearly see the signs that it is a time for a change; you will not be able to ignore them. At this stage you need to carefully review and rewrite your business plan. Consider it from three perspectives: (1) if you stayed the same size, (2) if you expanded the business within your home, and (3) if you expanded the business by moving out of your home. Factors you should consider include:

- **Your personal and business goals**   Have they been met fully in your home enterprise? Have your goals changed? How will they be affected by moving away from home?
- **Sales potential**   Have you reached your maximum potential sales for a home-based operation? Will moving to a new location enable you to double or triple production? Compare your maximum sales potential in dollar figures.
- **Space**   Is lack of space limiting your growth? How much additional space is required for working area, client visits, storage of materials, supplies, and inventory?
- **Time**   Do you at present do all the work yourself? Are there aspects that can be delegated to staff without risking the quality of service and personal attention to detail? Have you weighed the benefits of adding staff along with the cost of salaries and benefits, extra work space, hiring and training skills required, etc.?
- **Paperwork**   Is your present system of invoicing, receivables and payables, and bookkeeping well managed? Can it withstand the impact of expansion? Might computerization be necessary?
- **Changing roles**   With expansion, will you be more of a manager than a salesperson or a doer? Does this fit your talents and ambitions?
- **Additional financing**   How much additional financing will you need for the expansion and ongoing operating costs? Consider salaries, materials, renovations, rent, marketing, and advertising costs. Will you have easy access to such financing?

A. STAYING THE SAME SIZE

When you consider the reason why a lot of home-based businesses get started, it is easy to understand why, when given the option, many entrepreneurs prefer to remain as a small, home-based operation. The comfort, convenience, and flexibility of the home-based lifestyle is reason in itself. If the business is meeting these and your financial needs, then truly you may have the best of both worlds — so why spoil it? Besides, it is a misperception to assume that expansion and extra profit go hand-in-hand.

B. EXPANDING THE BUSINESS WITHIN YOUR HOME

On the basis of your financial projections, you may have decided that expanding the operation within your home will increase your profitability. By hiring additional help for certain aspects of the business you may be able to double your production while only marginally increasing your overhead costs. Perhaps by increasing and improving your workspace, you will be able to work more efficiently and with a greater degree of satisfaction. You many consider some of the following options, which will have varying impacts on the amount of increased help, money, space, and paperwork required.

(a) Adding to Your Home

There are many creative ways of modifying unused space in your existing house to convert it into additional space for your business. You may also want to make additions to your house or construct a separate structure on your property for your business needs.

(b) Renting Storage or Warehouse Space

Renting storage or warehouse space may be an option for you if you have an occasional or permanent need for more space. There are numerous mini-storage areas that you can rent month to month if you do not have storage capacity at your home or apartment.

(c) Moving to a Bigger House

You may wish to build, buy, or lease a larger place to live to accommodate your growing business needs. This could provide you with the added or specialized space for your projected business requirements and enable you to continue working from home.

(d) Hiring Employees to Work from Their Homes

This is a very easy way of expanding as quickly as you need to, but keeping the costs to a minimum. Naturally it depends on the nature of your business as to whether this is a viable option. The 19th-century cottage industries were a classic example where pieceworkers could work from their homes. Commissioned salespeople, software development or programming, computer inputting or research, telemarketing, house cleaning, or temporary relief personnel are other examples.

(e) Contracting Work to Other Businesses

Rather than have to rent office space or move your business to a warehouse, you may wish to subcontract out some of the extra work for temporary or occasional projects. This is commonly done by consultants. Rather than moving a small-scale manufacturing or distribution company out of your home, you may wish to negotiate a contract to have certain parts of the process performed by others.

C. MOVING OUT OF YOUR HOME

If you have decided that your best option is to move the business to commercial space (office, retail, warehouse), then be prepared for major changes. Your daily schedule, the manner in which you market and sell your product, and the way you personally view the business will be different. It may seem a bit overwhelming and scary at first, and rightly so, because your risks are that much greater. As you did with your initial business plan, you need to take one step at a time and work through each phase thoroughly and methodically on paper. Work closely with your professional advisors, especially in your dealings with a landlord regarding leasing space and with your banker regarding accessing financing. Remember, at this stage your business management skills will play a large role in the future success of your business. A lack of management skills is, in fact, one of the major reasons why businesses fail. If you have not already done so, you may need to enroll in some business-management-related courses and to do some additional study and research based on the nature and size of your business. This book is intended to address the issues of a home-based operation only. A recommended title for your business success outside of the home is our *The Complete Canadian Small Business Guide,* 2nd Edition (McGraw-Hill Ryerson), which extensively covers the various aspects of business management.

(a) Renting a Packaged Office

If your business is operated within an office environment, the most economical route is to rent office space in a shared office facility called a *packaged office* (also referred to as an executive suite or business centre). You can rent on a month-to-month basis or a longer term such as six months or one year. For a fixed monthly fee, you can obtain the following features in a packaged office: a fully furnished office, a central receptionist, a reception area, a boardroom, a telephone answering service, access to support secretarial and word-processing services, and use of fax, telex, photocopier, and other office equipment. Besides the flexibility of short- or long-term leases, you have no staff, furniture, or equipment costs, and no administrative or setup time is required. Because the services, equipment, and furniture are already in place, it is actually an instant office. Much time and money is therefore saved from having to shop around and select and purchase equipment that may only be used minimally. This leaves 100% of your time to devote to your business matters. Look in the Yellow Pages under "Offices for Rent."

(b) Subletting Space from Another Company

Many companies downsize to save on costs, depending on the economy, increased rent, etc., so there may be numerous opportunities available to sublet suitable office, retail, or warehouse space. The subletting company may also be willing to share staff; for example the receptionist, who could answer your phone line for you. The main advantage to subletting is that most of the responsibility for the entire leased space lies with the person from whom you sublet. The main disadvantage, though, is that the person who holds the lease may decide not to continue at that location, and then you would be forced to search for another location for your business.

(c) Leasing Space

When choosing suitable leased space, your options include office, warehouse, retail store, and shopping mall outlet. The deciding factors will be location, affordability, and risk. The lease may require a large deposit, personal guarantee, and long-term commitment. You should recognize, however, that lease clauses can be modified or removed through astute negotiating techniques. It is prudent never to sign a lease (or similar contract) without first having it reviewed by your lawyer.

In summary, your detailed revised business plan showing your three options will give you. a clear picture of the financial viability of each option. While you will be able to generate increased sales, will the added costs result in increased profits? Will the additional time, risk, and stress be worth the effort? Review your revised plan with your professional advisors and get their input. Talk to others who have expanded in a similar way to hear their perspectives. Again, by doing your plans for expansion on paper first in the form of a business plan, you will avoid the risk of expanding too quickly. Your decision, instead, will be founded on extensive financial calculations and expert advice.

CHAPTER

11

Reasons for Success and Failure in Business

To be successful, it is helpful for you to understand the reasons why others were not. The bad news is that the overall statistics of small business failures are very high. In fact, there is about a 75% failure rate over a five-year period from business commencement. The rate for home-based business failures is lower because the initial and ongoing risk is usually lower.

A. REASONS FOR BUSINESS FAILURE

The reasons for business failure are many. The entrepreneur's personal limitations are the primary reason. This includes, in order of priority, lack of personal qualifications to run a business, lack of experience in the line of business, lack of training, and unbalanced experience. These limitations lead to the following more specific reasons.

1. Money Mismanagement

Money mismanagement is a common reason for business failure. Here are some of the typical problems home businesses encounter: insufficient funds to meet startup and operating expense needs; cash flow problems; too much debt; not enough money to grow; charging low rates that lead to little or no profit; inadequate financial planning;

poor credit and collection practices; and inadequate bookkeeping. Many entrepreneurs "bleed" the business by taking more money from the business than it can afford. It is important to save some of the earnings as a buffer for unexpected business expenses or to reinvest in the business.

2. Poor Marketing

Many entrepreneurs simply don't know who their prospective customers are. They have not done their marketing research — have not identified their market, segmented it, or actively promoted on an ongoing basis. You may have a great product or service, but if the message does not get out, the business will suffer accordingly. Preparing and following a written marketing plan is necessary.

3. Mistaking a Business for a Hobby

Many people enjoy what they are doing, but never consider it more than a hobby. The object of operating a business, of course, is to earn a salary, recover all your expenses, and make a profit.

4. Failure to Evaluate Themselves Realistically

The failure to make a frank assessment of personal strengths and weaknesses, needs, and desires is a common mistake. You may find that your business requires skills that you do not possess, such as goal setting, decision-making, and selling. Objective feedback from your family, friends, relatives, and business associates is necessary.

5. Failure to Set and Revise Goals

Goals or objectives are not determined, or they are ineffective because they are not measurable, specific, or realistic. Preparing a business plan is an essential part of goal-setting. Failure to reassess goals can create serious problems. Various direct and indirect factors can affect your goals and require them to be modified in order to remain viable and effective. For example, unexpected problems could occur such as the illness of the owner, new competition, overly ambitious timetables, supplier delays, increase in lending rates, or loss of a major client. Revising goals will ensure your business continues to grow despite unexpected obstacles. Reviewing the targets you have met can provide an important sense of accomplishment, self-confidence, and motivation to continue.

6. Not Being Suited for a Home-Based Business

A person could otherwise have good business potential but cannot adjust to the unique features of operating a business out of the home, such as self-discipline to establish a regular work routine, or ability to separate family life and work.

7. Lack of Commitment

Personal motivation and desire to stick with the objective, regardless of the normal ups and downs, is essential. Some people give up their commitment too easily if the goal is not attained quickly and without difficulty.

B. REASONS FOR BUSINESS SUCCESS

By now you probably have a good idea of the factors that contribute to entrepreneurial success. Reflect on the reasons for failure described above and set out to do the opposite. Review the chapter on the characteristics of successful entrepreneurs and your personal assessment, then ask yourself how close you are and be honest with yourself. Attempt to follow the tips outlined throughout this book and avoid the classic pitfalls. Seek and obtain quality input from your professional advisors and from those people who matter most.

There are many other ways to achieve business success. Learn about philosophies and techniques for personal success, motivation, goal-setting, and time management through books, magazines, seminars, and cassette tapes. Read about people who have been successful. Network with other business owners and cultivate relationships with successful entrepreneurs. Identify role models and try to learn from them.

Your interest in this book shows a desire for knowledge and to achieve success. The dream is the first step to achieving the reality. Best wishes on your entrepreneurial endeavours!

SELECTING A HOME-BASED BUSINESS

There are literally hundreds of types of businesses that could be easily operated from the home. No list would ever be complete, as technology, trends, and people's needs are constantly changing, making some businesses obsolete while opening up new opportunities for others never tried before. The business you choose to operate will largely depend on the lifestyle that you wish to create for yourself. It should also be based upon your business motivation, personal skills and attributes, background of experience or technical knowledge, and financial expectations. If you have other responsibilities that consume your time, some businesses may be ideal for a part-time venture. Others may prove to be more lucrative with a healthy profit margin when full-time effort is devoted. To ensure that you maintain your commitment and enthusiasm for the business after the novelty has worn off, you should be certain that your motivational and personal needs will be met. Earlier sections in this book have dealt with self-assessment and business preparedness to help you identify your specific lifestyle needs and wants.

CHAPTER

12

Identifying Ideas and Opportunities

RECOGNIZING TRENDS

Trends are creating growth markets throughout Canada and the United States for certain types of businesses. Some of these trends are experienced nationally and internationally, while others are felt only on a provincial, regional, or local level. A trend is an event which lasts a minimum of a decade. A fad, on the other hand, is short-lived and may last for possibly only a few months.

There are several ways of learning what opportunities lie in future trends. One way is to read business-oriented newspapers and magazines. The national Canadian newspapers are the *Globe and Mail* (Report on Business), the *Financial Post*, and the *Financial Times*. Of course, read your local newspaper to keep current on local trends. National business-oriented magazines in Canada are *Profit Home Business, Profit, Opportunities Canada* and *Canadian Business*. There are also provincial and local business magazines at your local newsstand and public library.

In addition, you can become aware of many trends before they reach Canada by reading American business magazines and newspapers. Some of the recommended magazines include *Entrepreneur, Income Opportunities, Small Business Opportunities, Home Office Computing, Venture*, and *Inc*.

Other ways to anticipate or be aware of trends is to subscribe to trade magazines or newsletters in your field of interest, and attend association or business networking meetings. Speak to suppliers and customers to find out which products and services are in greatest demand. There are several books on the subject of trend projections which you may find interesting. Some suggested ones are *Megatrends 2000* by John Naisbett; *The Third Wave* by Alvin Toffler; and *The Popcorn Report* by Faith Popcorn.

Some examples of current trends for the 1990s which could impact on the business you are considering include:

- **An increase in leisure time**   Due to shorter work weeks, flexible workdays, compressed work schedules, and people working at home (employed or self-employed), people have more time available for leisure activities. This will result in increased travel, adult education, and self-development courses, and an overall interest in recreation.

- **General aging of the population**   Studies show that by the year 2000 approximately 20% of the population will be over 65 years of age. This will create an interest in travel (especially group or package tours), products for the aged, retirement and investment planning, and assistance in home renovations and repairs. Downsizing from a home to a condominium or townhouse and an increase in retirement homes in a warmer climate will occur. We can expect to see an increase in sales of recreational vehicles (mobile homes) and any products to do with security (fire, medical, burglary, etc.).

- **Born in the '60s**   The post-baby-boom generation is ensuring that products and services for children will be in demand, especially by parents with a high disposable income, and therefore have higher expectations of quality and uniqueness in the products they buy. As older homes are sold by the senior population (for the reasons referred to in the earlier point) to young families, there will be an increase in the home renovation business.

- **Baby boomers**   Baby boomers have an appreciation of nature and the outdoors, in terms of their adventure trips and leisure activities, perhaps as an antidote to the pressures of urban living. An increase in personalized services such as investment and consulting advice will be in demand. In the case of two-income families, with or without children, demand for services and products (child care, house cleaning, etc.) which make life easier will increase.

- **An increase in health concerns**   As the majority of the population is aging, there is an increased interest in looking good, feeling good, and being healthy. This takes the form of participation in fitness and recreation, the purchase of cosmetics, and a desire to learn about the aging process through courses and books and other publications. In addition, an increased awareness of the need for healthy eating habits is also occurring. This takes the form of better attention to diet, in meals at restaurants and in food preparation.

Especially with a product or service trend, being in the right place at the right time could result in huge financial rewards through uniqueness and volume sales. A word of caution, though: the trick to succeeding with business trends is much like the sport of surfing. You must get in at the start of the swell, ride it through its buildup, and get out while riding at its peak. To stay in a trend beyond its lifespan may turn the business into a financial disaster.

FINDING BUSINESS OPPORTUNITIES

There is a distinction between an idea and an opportunity. Many people have good business ideas, but the idea may not be a viable business opportunity with potential for success. Careful research, evaluation, and preparation of a business plan will separate the real opportunities from casual ideas. There are many innovative techniques for finding business ideas and opportunities. But before you start your search, make sure that you have completed the self-assessment discussed in Chapter 1, which will help you to find opportunities suited to your lifestyle needs. Here are some sources of information:

- **Books**   There are numerous books available which detail business opportunities that can be started with minimal financing (i.e., about $500 to $1,000). A listing of these is given in Appendix B, "Recommended Reading." Check with your public library and local bookstores to see if these books are available.
- **Magazines and newspapers**   The key magazines and newspapers that you should be aware of are referred to in the discussion on identifying business trends. National magazines which are oriented more towards the home-based business are *Profit Home Business, Entrepreneur, Income Opportunities, Small Business Opportunities*, and *Home Office Computing*.
- **Trade and business associations**   Almost every type of business has a professional or trade association which you may wish to check into. The association could be local, provincial, national, or international in scope. Check in the Yellow Pages under "Associations" for ones that interest you. In addition, check with your local library for directories that list associations in Canada and the United States. The main directories are:

- *Directory of Associations in Canada*
- *Encyclopedia of Associations*
- **Trade publications and newsletters**   There are thousands of trade publications covering every type of business interest. Check with the business resource librarian at your local library and ask to see the various directories of trade publications in Canada and the United States, such as:
  - *Gale Directory of Publications*
  - *Business Periodicals Index*
  - *Canadian Advertising Rates & Data*
  - *Canadian Almanac & Directory*
  - *Canadian Business Periodicals Index*
  - *Gale's Encyclopedia of Business Information Sources*
  - *Standard Rates and Data*
  - *Ulrich's International Periodicals Directory*
- **Foreign trade publications**   There are many foreign trade publications which list import and export opportunities. Check with your local library or provincial government small business resource centre.
- **Public libraries**   Your public library is an invaluable source of business ideas, opportunities, and information. The business reference librarian will help you gain access to an extensive range of information relevant to your business interest. Many public libraries, depending on the size of the community, have a full range of business-related books, catalogues, directories, trade publications, magazines, and newspapers.
- **The Yellow Pages**   These telephone directories list many products and services relating to small business. Turn to the cross-referenced index and methodically work your way through the listings. Look for the types of businesses that supply products or services that interest you. For example, if you are interested in gardening, you would look up all the cross-referenced classifications associated with gardening. That would include florists, nurseries, and landscape architects.
- **Trade shows/conventions**   Trade shows can be an excellent way to examine the products and services of many of your potential competitors. You will have an opportunity to meet distributors and sales representatives, learn of product and market trends, and identify potential products or services for your business venture. You will find trade show information in the trade magazines servicing your particular field. Also look at the annual directories

that publish a listing of trade shows in Canada and the United States. The main directories which can be found in your public library and/or provincial government resource centre are *Canadian Industry Shows and Exhibitions, U.S.A. Trade Shows and Exhibits Schedule, Trade Shows Worldwide*, and *International Trade Fairs and Conferences Directory*.

Conventions also offer an excellent opportunity to stimulate creative thinking. At a convention you are exposed to speakers, panelists, films, and displays. You also have an opportunity to exchange ideas with other people.

- **Seminars/courses**   There are many seminars, workshops, and courses available on small business, including home-based business, offered through government agencies (the FBDB and provincial government small business departments), school board and community college adult-education programs, and enterprise development centres. Contact these agencies or organizations and ask to be put on their mailing list for upcoming programs. Seminars offer an excellent opportunity to meet other people with interests similar to yours.

- **Franchises/licences**   There are many home business franchises available. Some of the types of businesses include bookkeeping/accounting, interior design, house cleaning, and lawn maintenance. Statistically the survival rate of franchises is very high. The reason tends to be because of the formalized and tested business plan and support systems offered by the franchisor, including training, advertising, and promotion, computer and/or other management and administrative systems, and ongoing monitoring of performance.

Licensing means having the right to distribute or manufacture a product within agreed-upon stipulations. The owner of the licence retains ownership of all product or service rights, then receives a royalty or fixed fee from the licensee.

There are good and bad franchises and licences, and any potential investor should be cautious. Obtain the advice of your banker, lawyer, and accountant before committing yourself to any contractual arrangement. Check the reputation of the franchisor through the Canadian Franchise Association (Toronto) and the Better Business Bureau. To obtain information about home-based franchises and licences, refer to the publication *Opportunities Canada*. This excellent publication is updated and released twice yearly, and is Canada's only directory of franchises and distributorships. It is published by Prestige Promotions of Toronto. This company also conducts franchise and business opportunity seminars throughout Canada. Contact them for further information.

You may also wish to refer to the *Franchise Annual*. This publication by Info Press Inc. gives an information profile of over 4,000 franchise and licence companies throughout Canada, the United States, and other countries. The *Franchise Yearbook* is published by *Entrepreneur* magazine and is a directory of franchises in Canada and the United States. It can be obtained at newsstands or your public library. The Canadian Franchise Association has a kit of information available for prospective franchisees, including a booklet entitled *Investigate before Investing*. Also see *The Complete Canadian Franchise Guide* by Douglas A. Gray and Norm Friend (see Appendix B).

- **Examination of existing products or services for improvement**
  There are many products in great demand, but few people know about them because of ineffective marketing. Investigate products that you think have a possibility of success. Find out the marketing methods that were used. You might be able to obtain that product's distribution rights at a low price. There are innovative ways of modifying or repackaging an existing product to appeal to new markets. For example, there could be an industrial version of a consumer product, or vice versa. There could also be foreign market possibilities that have never been explored. For example, if a product is seasonal, you could locate a country in the southern hemisphere which has opposite seasons. By exporting your product during your own off-season, you would be able to produce and sell the product throughout the year.

  Look for modifications to a product or service that would improve its marketability and profit. Ask yourself the following questions:

How can I:

- Make it safer, cleaner, slower, or faster?
- Make it at home and save overhead expense?
- Contract out to have other people make the product or perform the service out of their homes?
- Make it more convenient or inexpensive?
- Cut costs of material and labour?
- Combine it with or add it onto other products or services?
- Make it easier to package, store, or transport?
- Condense or enlarge its size?
- Make it easier to use?
- Make it less expensive to replace, repair, or reuse?

- Make it more attractive and appealing?
- Make it lighter, stronger, adjustable, thinner, or foldable?
- Make it quieter or louder?
- Minimize its potential hazards?
- Add new features?
- Improve its availability or distribution?
- Improve its production?
- Improve its design?
- Improve its marketing?
- Improve it in other ways?

- **Distributors**   If you are interested in selling or distributing a product, contact the manufacturer to enquire if a sales territory is available in your area. There may be an opening, or possibly a dissatisfaction with one of the present distributors who may not be effectively performing in the territory. Distributors and wholesalers have an extensive knowledge of the strong and weak points of existing products, and the types of product improvements that are needed by their customers. Distributors can be located in the Yellow Pages, *Opportunities Canada*, the classified ad section of business newspapers and magazines, and through business opportunity trade shows.

- **Travel and hobbies**   Whenever you travel, look for business ideas and opportunities. Many services and products may not have been introduced into Canada. You may be able to negotiate exclusive or non-exclusive Canadian distribution rights for a product. Alternatively, you may wish to duplicate, with modification and improvements, the product or service. This is assuming that your efforts don't infringe upon any legal rights that the originator of the product or service might have. Think of the areas relating to your hobbies or leisure activities where you believe a need exists. You might be able to devise creative ways of meeting those needs.

In summary, when you are looking for potentially profitable opportunities, it is helpful to review some of the main categories of business opportunities:

- Providing an information or consulting service.
- Identifying new opportunities arising from your current business.
- Becoming an agent, supplier, or distributor for someone else's service or product.
- Taking existing local products to new markets within Canada.

- Transferring concepts from one industry to another.
- Buying an existing business or franchise.
- Imitating successful services or products.
- Becoming an agent or distributor for a product imported into Canada.
- Inventing a new product.
- Capitalizing on a growth trend.
- Solving someone else's problem.
- Rebuilding, repairing, or adding to an existing product or service.
- Identifying specific target groups and customizing services or products for their needs.
- Exporting Canadian products to other countries.
- Finding productive uses for waste materials.
- Catering to a market that is no longer being serviced.
- Replacing imported products.
- Targeting a small portion of a large market.

Creativity is an important attribute in successfully operating a business and will ensure that you are always alert for new opportunities, new products, new techniques, etc. Creativity is useful when you are at the idea-generation stage of selecting a business, and every other stage through the lifespan of your business. For example, you will need to be creative when searching out a suitable name for your business, sources of financing, potential customers, low-cost raw materials, etc.

Many people find "brainstorming" an effective means of generating creative ideas. This is how it works. A small group of people (usually from 3 to 7) meets in a round-table discussion-group format with the objective of generating ideas in the categories listed above. One person records on a flip chart or chalkboard all ideas suggested. Some ideas may sound impractical, zany, or impossible, but the task is to list as many ideas as possible without being judgemental as to their appropriateness. In this way inhibitions are removed and ideas are free-flowing. Relax and have fun with it!

Once the ideas have stopped flowing (you may have anywhere from 30 to 80 suggestions), you start the task of evaluating each of them for their merits. With the assistance of your group members, discuss each of the suggestions. You may find that parts of an idea may be workable in specific situations. Others may not work under any circumstances. Eliminate those ideas that would be impossible. Once you have identified those that are most workable, attach a priority ranking to indicate which ones you should try first.

An exercise such as brainstorming may assist you in shortlisting the businesses which have the most potential. The following section will help you to develop a list of factors to use in the evaluation process.

EVALUATING BUSINESS OPPORTUNITIES

Creativity goes hand-in-hand with evaluation. One should not exist without the other. If you have a lot of creative ideas, but do not evaluate them, you could be destined for failure from the outset. Many business failures are the result of starting into business too quickly without prior research, evaluation, and planning — usually because of excitement, enthusiasm, and over-optimism. On the other hand, if you only evaluate a few initial ideas, you may overlook untapped opportunities for true success and fulfillment in your business venture.

Reflect on the business ideas that have appealed to you at this point. Think about the personality traits required to succeed in that type of business. Do these match up with your own personal skills, talents, interests, and aptitudes, as identified in Chapter 1?

Develop a set of criteria on which you can evaluate and rate each of your business ideas. Your criteria will be based upon many factors including your lifestyle needs, financial status and needs, personal needs, business needs, background experience, etc. For instance, if your reason for going into a home-based business is that you want to supplement the family income while caring for your preschool children, factors that will influence your decision will include:

- Can the hours worked be modified to suit the children's schedule?
- Is the business still viable if only handled on a part-time basis until the children reach school age when more time may be available?
- Will travel be necessary to pick up or deliver products?
- Will you be able to use a telephone answering service or machine to take calls when you are not available to the business?

You may find the following evaluation format useful, a copy of which is shown in Sample 9, "Evaluating Business Ideas." Start off by listing at the top of a sheet of paper your financial, lifestyle, personal, and business needs. List down the left-hand side of the page the various factors that will influence your decision. Once you have filled the page, make a sufficient number of photocopies of this form so that you can use one for each of the business ideas that you wish to evaluate. Then start to complete the centre column of the form with answers to each of your evaluation factors. Some responses may be considered to be favourable (pro), while others may present some difficulties for you (con). In the far right-hand column indicate whether the factor has a pro, con, or neutral influence. You may need to do some preliminary research to fill in some of the answers.

Once you have completed this process for each of your business ideas, compare the businesses to identify which ones may be most profitable and appropriate for your specific needs. You will begin to see clearly how some business ideas may show great prospects, while others may involve a lot of hard work but little reward after your diligent efforts. You are now one step closer to making your final decision. Your final step is, of course, developing a full business plan as discussed in Chapter 2, and as shown in Sample 2, "Business Plan Format." Review your completed business plan(s) with your spouse, lawyer, accountant, business associates, and friends for their input and advice.

AVOIDING WORK-AT-HOME SCHEMES AND SCAMS

It is estimated that billions of dollars a year are bilked out of innocent and naive victims throughout North America by work-at-home scheme and scam promotions. While some schemes are not technically illegal, often they are unprofitable. In almost all cases, the promotion is full of hype and tantalizing claims of money to be made with relatively little effort. These promotions are usually aimed at the elderly, the disabled, the retired, the unemployed, and spouses trying to supplement family incomes.

Classified advertising fraud is big business. While the media have an ethical responsibility to inquire about the legitimacy of the money-making offer before accepting the advertisement for publication, in most cases due to indifference, time constraints, or lack of resources, this control procedure is not carried out. Some examples of ad headings to be wary of — and ones that frequently appear in the "Help Wanted" and "Business Opportunities" sections of newspapers and magazines — are: "Earn $1,000s a week in mail order"; "Agents and distributors wanted"; "Work two hours daily at home and make big money"; "$400 for every 1,000 envelopes you stuff and mail"; and "Wanted: Homemakers to earn $1,000 a month minimum for part-time work". If you have reason to be concerned, contact your local Better Business Bureau, or write the BBB in the location of the promoter and ask whether there have been any complaints about the firm in question. You can find out the address from your local library or BBB. In addition, you can contact your provincial consumer protection department and make enquiries about whether there have been any complaints. Note, however, that even if there are no complaints, you still have to be vigilant.

You should be particularly skeptical and cautious in responding to any work-at-home "opportunities" if:

- Personal testimonials are used, but the persons are never identified, making it difficult to check their claims. Frequently, just initials are given, and no city is listed. Even if you could check, the persons could be part of the setup (friends, associates, etc.).
- Money is required for instructions or merchandise before you are told how the plan operates.
- Money is sought before a start can be made in the at-home business.
- The promotional material says that there is a huge demand and/or guaranteed markets for the product or service.
- There is no mention of the total cost involved.
- You are told that no experience is necessary.
- Promises are made that a lot of money can be earned with very little work or on a part-time basis.
- The promoter agrees to buy back the merchandise at higher than retail selling price. The catch may be: "If the work is up to standard"; in this case subjective and arbitrary criteria may be applied.
- The promoter operates from a post office box as a mailing address.

Here are some of the types of schemes that you should avoid:

1. Distributing Mail-Order Catalogues or Circulars

In this scheme you buy and distribute the promoter's imprinted mail-order catalogues and circulars advertising various products. The products could range from self-help books to household items. When an order comes in you will receive a percentage of the sale.

The catch is the hidden costs involved. The catalogues or circulars are usually sold to you for a fee. Also, the ad copy is supplied for a fee. There are other costs which can mount rapidly, especially to the unsophisticated business person. You will have to place and pay for all the ads in newspapers or magazines or direct mail. You will have to pay for the envelopes and postage to mail them. In addition, mailing lists have to be developed or bought. Research studies show that few inexperienced individuals can learn enough about the mail-order business before their capital, enthusiasm, and patience run out.

2. Envelope Stuffing

Promoters of this scheme usually advertise that they will tell you how to earn money by stuffing envelopes at home. A small fee plus a self-addressed, stamped envelope is usually requested for this information. When you receive the brochure there is usually a more detailed pitch that asks you to send more money to obtain the "complete program" so that "you can start making money right away." When you send in the larger amount of money (usually $15 to $25 or more), you receive a more detailed brochure or booklet telling you how to pull off the same scam by renting out a postal mail box, placing a similar ad, and waiting for the money. In short, the work-at-home participant is supposed to recruit others for the same business of offering a work-at-home plan.

When you think about it, home-business envelope stuffing is not a viable or credible concept in this age of computerized and sophisticated mass production techniques such as automatic sorting, stuffing, and mailing machines. It hardly seems probable that stuffing envelopes at home is a cost-efficient "business opportunity." Unfortunately, many people obviously react to the prospect of making easy money, rather than reflecting on the illogic and incongruity of the promoter's advertising pitch.

3. Piecework

In this scheme, you usually have to invest hundreds of dollars in instructions and materials and many hours of your time to produce items for a company that has promised to buy them. Examples of such offers are, to name a few, making aprons, baby booties, and plastic signs. The attractive feature, of course, is having one "guaranteed" purchaser, so that you would not have to do any additional selling. However, once you have purchased the supplies and instructional material, the company may decide not to pay you on the grounds that your work does not meet certain "standards." You would then be left with the equipment and supplies, and would have to find customers for the items you have already made. The prime consideration in any work-at-home assembly scheme is the cost/benefit ratio — your expense and time in relation to your profit. Frequently, the earnings claims are highly exaggerated and the investment risk too great.

If you should have a dispute with a work-at-home scheme promoter, it could be very difficult to get your money back or prove your case, regardless of the "guarantee" or "refund" promises. This may be because the company is out-of-province or outside Canada, and the legal costs of attempting to right the wrong could be considerably more than your original loss. It is a case of "Let the buyer beware." Even if you should "win" your claim, trying to enforce the judgement could be a futile exercise.

So remember, when looking at classified ads, "If it sounds too good to be true, chances are it is." In short, the work-at-home scheme could be a scam.

The next two chapters deal with *service-type* and *product-type* businesses. Your choice of business will be considerably narrowed down once you decide whether you prefer to operate a service- or a product-type business. For each category some general considerations are given to help you to visualize yourself operating in one or the other; this is followed by overviews of several common home-based businesses. These overviews, 20 in all, are intended to provide you with a framework for the start of a business plan, and to galvanize you into acting on possible business opportunities. Remember, you should not start any business before you work through a complete business plan to fully test out its viability and your suitability as owner.

CHAPTER

13

Service Businesses

Service-related businesses by far represent the fastest-growing business sector in Canada. This increasing trend means that personal and business services are used by virtually everyone — individuals, small businesses, large corporations, and government. If you consider the number of service businesses that you use through the course of a week, you can start to appreciate the vast opportunities in this field. A good number of these businesses can be easily operated from your home without special zoning requirements. Although you may be technically operating from your home, a good portion of your time may be spent at your client's place of business, or at other locations to research and collect data or meet with clients and suppliers.

Generally speaking, service businesses are easy to start, require little financial investment, have minimal risk, and may never require the hiring of employees. Many people start their service businesses on a part-time basis to test the market demand, while still working at another job. Others find offering a service from home an ideal way to maintain their business contacts, utilize their skills, and earn an income while providing quality time to raising and nurturing a young family.

When offering a service, you are in fact selling your time and talents. Your clients will choose to use your services over someone else's because of your personality, communication skills, personalized attention to detail, quality work and thoroughness, flexibility in meeting deadlines, or probably a combination of these factors. Maintaining such standards will help you to build a loyal client base. It is understandable, therefore, why many people who have a busy and successful service business prefer to turn away additional work rather than hire employees. They fear that the personal touch and quality which has helped to build their business will be lost in the business expansion. It stands to reason, then, that to offer a successful service business you must know what sets your service apart from the others, and then you must ensure that those standards are maintained on a regular basis. However, because this business is tied to your own personal identity, there is generally no accumulated goodwill or inherent value to your business that could be sold to another party. While you may want to "sell" your client contacts to another party, there is no guarantee that your clients will continue or want to do business with that party.

Many services can be offered to individuals as well as businesses, and when starting out you will want to consider all avenues of prospective clients. You should look carefully, though, at your qualifications, time schedule, and location to decide whether you will direct your marketing more to one than the other. Several suggested service businesses are profiled with some startup and marketing considerations. There are many more to choose from; the businesses profiled are ones that generally do not require any specific expertise or prior long-term training in a profession (such as architecture, accounting, law, etc.). Also, they require minimal initial financing and have good profit potential.

1. SERVICES TO BUSINESSES

With the downsizing of companies and the changed utilization of staff because of the introduction of computerized systems, many opportunities exist for home-based businesses to provide services to these same companies. It is a much smaller cost factor for a business to contract out to a freelancer, for instance, than it is to have a full-time staff member perform the same services. Full-time staff need to be trained, require space and equipment to perform their work, and are paid benefits including vacation pay. In addition, staff could end up being paid for other, non-productive time. Freelance or "on contract" workers can generally produce the same or better results within a shorter period of time at a lesser overall cost. Price is not usually a large factor for businesses, although it will of course be a consideration. Most business clients readily recognize that it costs more to get quality work.

Business clients will demand high quality and professionalism in the product, your advertising, and your image. Strict adherence to time schedules will also be important. Your background experience may be the best indicator to help you decide whether you will cater to individuals or businesses. If you have been in the workforce providing a service similar to the one you are operating as a business, you will be very familiar with business expectations, pressures, deadlines, and decision delays. This will help you to adapt and respond to your clients' needs.

The image you set for your business must be consistent with the clients you will serve. Ensure your letterhead stationery and business cards reflect professionalism. Your telephone should be answered in a businesslike manner. If you are unable to take telephone calls during certain times of the day, have a telephone answering machine with a brief and professional message, or enlist the services of a telephone answering service company. If clients will be coming to your home, ensure your "office" is in a separate area of your home and is kept in a neat and orderly fashion, free of children's toys or household appliances. You want to create the impression that you take your business seriously and work in an efficient and productive manner while in your home surroundings.

There is an extensive list of services that could be offered to businesses. In this section we have selected and profiled six types to give you an example of the startup and followthrough considerations. They are: (a) bookkeeping, (b) consulting, (c) desktop publishing, (d) publicity agent, (e) telephone answering service, and (f) videotaping service. Other types that you may consider are:

Ad writing	Indexer	Property manager
Booking agency	Information	Public speaker
Business and financial	broker	Seminar leader
broker	Interior decorator	Seminar promoter
Calligraphy	Janitorial/	Telemarketing
Cartoonist	maintenance	Trade show organizer
Clipping service	Limousine service	Trainer
Collection agency	Mailing list	Translator
Computer	compilation	Typing/word
programming	Meeting and	processing
Conducting market	convention planner	Writing grants,
surveys	Notary public	proposals, manuals
Data researcher	Photography	Writing résumés
Delivery service	Proofreading and	
Graphic designer	editing	

(a) BOOKKEEPING

The Concept: Owing to the fact that most small- and medium-sized companies do not employ a full-time bookkeeper, and that the owners of these firms are either incapable or too busy to do the work themselves, many opportunities exist for a self-employed bookkeeper to develop a full client load. By contracting out the bookkeeping work, the owners can rely on having up-to-date records and regular monthly statements. This will help them manage their businesses better, especially in the areas of payroll, inventory, cash flow, accounts receivable and payable, and break-even analysis. Your clients will appreciate it if you take the time to interpret the various accounting statements and to give any advice for improvement of the business operation. Although you may not be completing all the formal financial statements and tax returns for corporations, your doing all that is required to that point will save on your client's accounting fees which are charged at a substantially higher rate.

Income tax preparation service for the company and its employees can add a new dimension and substantially increase your income. Depending upon your time schedule, your service could remain small on a part-time basis, or you could handle a large number of accounts and hire part-time assistants to help you.

Money Matters: Once you have furnished your home office, the overhead costs of advertising and stationery are minimal. Your service can be charged at an hourly rate of between $15 to $30, depending upon your experience and certification. If you can estimate the amount of time required to handle a particular account, you may prefer to charge a fixed monthly rate for doing the payroll, for instance. As long as you do accurate work and charge a reasonable fee, your clients are likely to stay with you, providing long-term, predictable income.

Your Background: If you have had any bookkeeping or accounting experience, you are probably qualified to perform this service, especially if you are acquainted with more than one bookkeeping system. Taking an accounting or bookkeeping course may be helpful to you. You should have an aptitude for working with figures, making neat entries, balancing books, organizing and reorganizing, noting debits and credits, adjusting accounts, and calculating percentages. You should be accurate, reliable, and strictly confidential about your client accounts.

What You Will Need: You will need a desk, filing cabinet, calculator, printed forms, ledgers, and stationery. If you are offering computerized as well as manual bookkeeping, you will need a personal computer with bookkeeping software. Bedford is a popular and uncomplicated system; ACCPAC is also used, though to a lesser extent and for more involved applications. There are also many other excellent programs available.

The Plan: In doing your research, you should acquaint yourself with the different systems and methods used by bookkeeping services in your area. Ask about their rates on an hourly or monthly basis. Decide on the system you will use and the rates you will charge. Your services might include writing cheques, completing journal entries, preparing bank reconciliations, remitting government sales taxes and source deductions, and preparing regular financial statements and annual tax returns.

From there it is a matter of advertising your services and building your clientele. The Yellow Pages is a source of ongoing leads, and a small classified ad in your local newspaper may produce results. You may choose to target certain types of businesses in your area by sending a personalized letter introducing your services or by making "cold" calls. Excellent references from satisfied clients will help you win the trust and confidence of prospective clients. Assure your prospects that you conduct your business in a highly ethical and confidential manner, and if that is your policy, that you do not take on work from businesses that would be in direct competition.

You will need to keep careful records of your time and disbursements for billing purposes. There will be times when it is more convenient to work at your client's office, especially when initially setting up systems. However, once an efficient system is operating, it should be possible to do all the work in your home office. On a weekly or monthly basis (depending on the nature of the assignment), you would pick up from the client the necessary records which could include invoices, statements, receipts, deposit and cheque books, and other documents. Then, from your home office, you would record the necessary data and return the documents. You may prefer to use a courier service to save on travel time and expense. Since corporations have fiscal year-ends at varying times, you can set your schedule accordingly with your deadlines spread throughout the year.

Publications

Mobile Bookkeeping Service (Start-up Business Guide X1332). Irvine, CA: Entrepreneur Magazine.

Cornish, Clive G. *Basic Accounting for the Small Business: Simple, Foolproof Techniques for Keeping Your Books and Staying Out of Trouble*. Vancouver, B.C.: International Self-Counsel Press, 1987.

Denney, Robert W. *Marketing Accounting Services*. New York, NY: Van Nostrand Reinhold, 1983.

Fox, Jack. *Starting and Building Your Own Accounting Business*. New York, NY: John Wiley & Sons, 1984.

Walgenbach, Paul et al. *Principles of Accounting*. San Diego, CA: Harcourt Brace Jovanovich, 1988.

(b) CONSULTING

The Concept: Literally billions of dollars are spent annually by governments, businesses, and professionals who hire consultants. The objectivity of an outside expert's opinion often carries more weight than inside staff judgement, thereby creating numerous opportunities for consulting assignments. Consultants are also hired for special projects and troubleshooting. Here are some of the most common services provided by consultants: labour relations; marketing research; public relations; computer selection; business management; employee selection, training, and relocation; office design; efficiency; technical report writing. There is a market in almost any field for specialized knowledge that can help an organization make money, save time, improve productivity, or reduce costs. Your success will depend upon the success you are able to help your clients achieve.

Once you have positioned yourself as a recognized authority in your area, other avenues may present themselves, such as writing articles for trade journals, and public speaking at workshops and conferences or in-house training seminars.

Money Matters: Consulting fees can vary widely according to your credentials and experience, the size of your client's organization, and the magnitude of the problem. Also, the amount of time required is a factor. A daily rate can range from $300 to $2,000, with the average being about $600 to $800. Or, a fixed price may be given if you can predict with some degree of certainty the amount of time you will need to spend. Your startup costs will be about $1,000 to $2,000 for a desk, filing cabinet, calculator, telephone answering machine, business cards, and letterhead. Depending upon the nature of your consulting business, you may require other pieces of equipment, such as a personal computer and fax machine.

Your Background: You must have expertise in some subject area, and almost any area has potential. You should be creative so that you can apply your knowledge to each new set of circumstances. You should be well organized and allocate your time wisely, as in this business, time is money. Good communication skills will help you to foster and maintain good client relations.

What You Will Need: Your business cards and letterhead should present a professional style and image consistent with your area of expertise. Few other amenities are required other than a quiet workspace that is conductive to writing and reviewing data. Basic desk accessories may include a personal computer, telephone, calculator, fax machine, and reference material.

The Plan: Many consultants choose to start their consulting businesses on a part-time basis while they still have a regular income to survive on. It may take three to six months to build a sufficient client base. Offering your services on a subcontracting basis to overburdened consulting firms may be a means of starting out.

Decide on the fee you will charge and how it will be determined. Your options will include an hourly rate, daily rate, fixed price, percentage of net savings, or a combination of these. Be certain to build in overhead and miscellaneous costs. If the assignment extends over a period of time, you should submit interim billings, perhaps at the end of each phase. As you gain experience and your business expands, your fees should be increased. Refer to other consultants' fee schedules and be competitive without underselling yourself.

Prepare a brochure which identifies the services you offer and resulting benefits. List your areas of expertise and professional accomplishments. Be certain it is professionally typeset and printed on quality paper. Determine the exact areas in which you are able to provide advice and assistance, and contact those who might be potential customers. Marketing a consulting business means selling yourself. You may decide to do a direct mail campaign to firms that may require your services. This personalized letter and brochure should be followed up with a telephone call to explore any areas of interest. Your daily newspaper may be a source of leads with reports on staff cutbacks, implementation of new government legislation for corporations to comply with, company relocations and mergers, etc.

Explain what you can do for your client in terms of greater efficiency, increased profits, decreased costs, expanded production, improved quality, or time savings. Prepare a written proposal which outlines the services you will perform, within the specific timeframe, and the fee arrangements. Once you have a signed contract, you will need to identify the problem, gather all available information, analyze the data, list possible solutions, and select the most viable solution to the problem.

While much of the work can be done at your home, you may have to spend some time at your client's place of business in order to collect data. Upon completion of your study, prepare a written report that identifies the problem, states various feasible solutions, and recommends a particular course of action. Of course you would need to provide any statistics, studies conducted, and other data that support your findings. Care should be taken to present your initial proposal and the final report in a neat and professionally printed format. Once you have completed your assignment and rendered the final invoice, you may offer your services on an "on call" followup basis to provide periodic checks.

Associations

Canadian Association of Management Consultants, #303-45 Charles Street East, Toronto, Ont. M4Y 1S2.

Independent Computer Consultants Association, #400-1190 Melville Street, Vancouver, B.C. V6E 3W1.

Publications

Cohen, William A. *How to Make It Big as a Consultant*. New York, NY: AMACOM, 1985.

Gray, Douglas A. *Start and Run a Profitable Consulting Business*, 3rd edition. Vancouver, B.C.: International Self-Counsel Press, 1993.

Holtz, Herman. *How to Succeed as an Independent Consultant*. New York, NY: John Wiley & Sons, 1983.

Kelley, Robert E. *Consulting: The Complete Guide to a Profitable Career*. New York, NY: Charles Scribner's Sons, 1981.

Smith, Brian R. *The Country Consultant*. New York, NY: Kennedy & Kennedy Inc., 1982.

Tepper, Ron. *Become a Top Consultant: How the Experts Do It*. New York, NY: John Wiley & Sons, 1985.

(c) DESKTOP PUBLISHING

The Concept: With a computerized desktop publishing (DTP) system, professional-quality publications can now be designed, typed, and edited by one person. For most applications, this type of publishing can replace the expensive typesetting method and the use of highly trained graphic artists. Computer technology allows graphics to be stored in memory and reproduced alongside columns of text through a laser printer. Opportunities are endless for producing low-cost newsletters, catalogues, flyers, menus, books, directories, corporate annual reports, and magazines. As a diversification, you may decide to offer your services on a consultancy basis to those larger firms that prefer to do their own DTP in-house. You could assist with hardware and software selection, training, and document formatting for their initial applications, and provide backup support.

Money Matters: Unless you already own a computer, it will cost you from $5,000 to $10,000 or more for your computer hardware, software, and furnishings. Ongoing costs will include advertising and supplies such as paper, disks, and toner. You may charge from $20 to $30 or more per page, or $40 to $60 or more per hour depending upon the degree of complexity of the publication.

A recent survey by the Association of Electronic Cottagers listed the ten most popular and profitable computer-related businesses. Most of those businesses surveyed offered more than one type of service, thereby increasing their market and earnings. The survey findings are listed here:

Services Offered	Startup Costs (Basic)	Income Range (Full Time)
Computer consulting	$3,000+	$30,000 to $100,000
Typesetting	$3,000+	$30,000 to $100,000
Bookkeeping	$3,000 to $5,000	$25,000 to $40,000
Writing for profit	$1,000+	$30,000 to $45,000
Data entry and processing	$100 to $1,000	$15,000 to $20,000
Information research and brokering	$10,000	$40,000 to $65,000
Word processing	$1,000 to $3,000	$25,000 to $40,000
Custom programming	$3,000+	$30,000 to $100,000
Desktop publishing	$5,000 to $10,000+	$40,000 to $600,000
Mailing list services	$1,000	$20,000 to $25,000

Your Background: A good command of the English language, and typing, layout, and design abilities are what you will need to operate a quality desktop publishing business. If you are not computer-literate, a course on the subject and hands-on practice will get you started within a few months.

What You Will Need: Your home office will require a computer desk, a chair, and of course computer hardware, desktop publishing software, and a laser printer. If you have decided on an Apple or Macintosh computer, your software options include: PageMaker, ImageWriter II, MacWrite, MacPaint, Ready-Set-Go, and QuarkXpress. The Ventura and PageMaker software are favoured by users of IBM-compatible computers. Leased equipment and a good service contract are options you may wish to consider.

The Plan: You will need to spend some time reviewing the market for the computer hardware and software that you will use. As this is a rapidly expanding and highly competitive industry, you will find that prices are continually dropping on hardware and software that is getting easier to use and offers more sophisticated options. Talking to people who operate DTP systems will give you some unbiased opinions about equipment that salespeople are not inclined to offer. They will also be able to give you some tips on how to price your services.

As soon as you have practised on your DTP system and feel ready to handle client work, you will need to spread the word. A Yellow Pages ad under the categories of "Typesetting," "Word Processing," and "Graphic Designs" will bring you leads. Take samples of your work to the local printer and suggest an arrangement whereby the printer will receive a 10% to 20% commission on any work referred to you. Rather than giving a commission, you might promise to refer to the printer all your clients needing printing services. The printer may be willing to display samples of your work and business cards in the front counter area. You may target lawyers and realtors by offering to design their legal forms. Restaurateurs are constantly updating menus, posting daily specials, and mailing out flyers. If you prepare the newsletter for a professional business association, suggest that you include a small ad on your services to bring in leads from members.

Clients will want to know an approximate cost of the job beforehand, so you will need to become familiar with estimating. You may set either a per-page or an hourly rate. Many prefer the hourly-rate system, as each page will take varying lengths of time to complete. At the outset you should avoid giving a definite quotation, or at least build in a contingency factor for the unexpected. Factors that will affect the cost include the total number of pages of the end product, the condition of the original you will be working from (handwriting may be illegible), the number and complexity of the graphics to be inserted, the number of author revisions required, and the deadline imposed. You may set a surcharge for "rush" work.

Scheduling work and meeting deadlines will become easier and less stressful when you allow for the unexpected. You may decide to hire a fast and accurate typist part-time to handle assignments for you that contain a lot of text such as newsletters, catalogues, directories, and other publications. In this way you will have more time to focus on the more intricate work of graphics and final layout. Part-time typists may be willing to work from their own homes on their own computers, and then send to you by courier the completed work and disks. You can further increase your productivity by purchasing a small fax machine for sending draft copy ready for proofing to your clients' offices. This will save you and your client time and money.

Many people offering DTP services limit their accounts receivable and bad debt problems by requesting a 50% deposit and the balance upon delivery of the completed work.

Associations

Association of Electronic Cottagers, P.O. Box 1738, Davis, CA 95617.

Canadian Information Processing Society, 243 College Street, 5th Floor, Toronto, Ont. M5T 2Y1.

National Association of Desktop Publishers, P.O. Box 508, Kenmore Station, Boston, MA 02215.

World Computer Graphics Association, #399-2033 M. Street N.W., Washington, DC 20036.

Publications

CIPS Review. Canadian Information Processing Society, 243 College Street, 5th Floor, Toronto, Ont. M5T 2Y1 (bimonthly).

Desktop Publishing (Start-up Business Guide XI 288). Irvine, CA: Entrepreneur Magazine.

Dunn Report (Electronic publishing and prepress systems news and views). Dunn Technology Inc., 1855 E. Vista Way, No. 1, Vista, CA 92084 (monthly).

Publish! PCN Communications Inc., 501 Second Street, San Francisco, CA 94107 (monthly).

Small Press Guide to Computers in Publishing. Westport, CT: Meckler Corp., 1987.

Bove, Tony et al. *The Art of Desktop Publishing*, 2nd ed. New York, NY: Bantam, 1987.

Cavuoto, James. *Print It! A Desktop Publishing Guide to Reports, Resumes, Newsletters, Directories, Business Forms and More*. Reading, MA: Addison-Wesley, 1988.

Hewson, David. *Introduction to Desktop Publishing: A Guide to Buying and Using a Desktop Publishing System*. San Francisco, CA: Chronicle Books, 1988.

Kieper, Michael L. *The Illustrated Handbook of Desktop Publishing and Typesetting*. Blue Ridge Summit, PA: TAB Books, 1987.

(d) PUBLICITY AGENT

The Concept: A publicity agent carries a client's message to the media or directly to the public. Many authors, artists, musicians, and others are unaware of how to properly market their products and talents to achieve recognition and financial rewards. Since it is difficult for an "unknown" to break into the business, an agent can help them achieve the success they may otherwise never attain. They are therefore only too willing to pay a publicity agent for getting them into the spotlight. The more success you achieve for your clients, the faster the word will spread about your promotional abilities, which in turn will accelerate your business growth.

Money Matters: Minimal costs are required for startup once you have furnished your home office with a desk, chair, filing cabinet, and telephone. Your earning potential, on the other hand, is unlimited once you establish your reputation, build your client base, and learn how to be selective with your opportunities. Some assignments will be more lucrative than others. Situations where direct sales and revenues will result will lend themselves to a commission fee structure of 10% to 20%. Other occasions where the client wishes you to use your expertise and contacts to line up a number of media interviews may instead be charged on a time-expended basis at a rate of $50 to $75 or more per hour. Of course, your disbursements such as travel, long-distance phone calls, meals, courier, and mailing costs are billable to your client.

Your Background: Since this is a business of finding clients and meeting their promotional needs, you will need to be resourceful on all accounts. You will need to know your market area and be creative, enthusiastic, and aggressive. Persuasion and communication skills will make the difference between a mediocre and a successful business. Media representatives are constantly being hounded for interviews, and you will have to be able to cut through their objections, red tape, and prime-time pressures. Having some inside knowledge of the media will assist you in landing radio, TV, and print interviews for your clients.

What You Will Need: The basic office furniture, an all-important telephone, telephone answering machine (or preferably a telephone answering service), and directories of contacts will get you established. Once your client list builds, a fax machine will become a necessity in sending out media releases. Also, a personal computer will assist you with maintaining mailing lists, typing correspondence and biographical data, and sourcing contacts.

The Plan: Your first step, of course, is to select a field in which you have (or can readily attain) special expertise and source of contacts. Some examples include seminar or workshop leaders, politicians, keynote speakers at conferences, authors of self-published works, small publishing houses, artists, musicians, and craftspeople. Do your research to ensure a need exists in your area. Study the major markets and lesser-known ones. Subscribe to trade publications. While you are researching, which will be a major part of your startup preparation and an ongoing activity, you will need to brush up on marketing professional services and negotiating skills. A journalism background may help you relate to your media contacts and to understand their needs. Know which publications lean toward which stories.

Attending trade shows, and placing ads in trade publications and in the Yellow Pages under "Public Relations" and/or "Publicity," will be your main source of client contacts. Direct mail may also produce qualified leads.

You must be able to develop many media contacts who have confidence in your ability to consistently present interesting subjects worthy of their consideration. You will need to write copy for media releases, prepare biographical summaries on our clients, send out media packages, and follow up to arrange interviews. The itinerary that you arrange may include luncheon or dinner meeting speeches to university, business groups, or trade associations; radio, TV, press interviews including talk shows and phone-in programs; autograph sessions for the public such as book signings, etc.; seminar and conference presentations.

You will need to juggle and coordinate appointments, and confirm them just prior to the interviews to ensure there haven't been late cancellations. Prepare your client with a typed itinerary with clearly marked dates, times, locations, and contact people. Specify the length of each interview, whether it is live or taped, and the interviewer's special interest or "slant." If your client is not experienced with media interviews, you may want to accompany him or her and provide constructive feedback and encouragement after each interview.

Be certain to project a professional image with all your client and media contacts. Respect the fact that those in the media are constantly being pressed by deadlines, late cancellations, and the need for interesting "fillers." You can befriend your media contacts by being flexible and making certain your clients arrive for interviews well prepared and on time.

Associations

Canadian Information and Image Management Society, 86 Wilson Street, Oakville, Ont. L6K 3G5.

Canadian Public Relations Society Inc., #720-220 Laurier Avenue W., Ottawa, Ont. KIP 5Z9.

International Association of Business Communicators, 60 Dickson Avenue, Toronto, Ont. M4L 1N6.

Publications

Advertising Age (International newspaper of marketing), Crain Communications Inc., 1400 Woodbridge, Detroit, MI 48207 (2 issues per week).

CPRS National Newsletter. Canadian Public Relations Society Inc., #720-220 Laurier Avenue W., Ottawa, Ont. K1P 5Z9 (bimonthly).

Marketing. Maclean Hunter Ltd., 777 Bay Street, Toronto, Ont. M5W 1A7 (weekly).

PR Reporter. PR Publishing Co. Inc., Box 600, Dudley House, Exeter, NH 03833 (Newsletter of public relations, public affairs, and communications) (weekly).

PR Strategies. PR Strategies Publishing Co., 1851A Lawrence Avenue E., Scarborough, Ont. M1R 2Y3 (monthly).

Public Relations Agency (Start-up Business Guide X1324). Irvine, CA: Entrepreneur Magazine.

Dilenschneider, Robert L. and Dan J. Forrestal. *Public Relations Handbook*. Chicago, IL: The Dartnell Corporation, 1989.

Garbett, Thomas. *How to Build a Corporation's Identity and Effectively Project Its Image*. Lexington, MA: Lexington Books, 1988.

McLaughlin, Paul. *Asking Questions: The Art of the Media Interview*. Vancouver, B.C.: International Self-Counsel Press, 1986.

Michels, Gloria. *How to Make Yourself (or Anyone Else) Famous: The Secrets of a Professional Publicist*. New York, NY: Cross Gates Pub., 1988.

Parkhurst, William. *How to Get Publicity*. New York, NY: Times Books (Random House), 1985.

Smith, Ruth Q. *Starting a Public Relations Firm*. Nashville, TN: Business of Your Own Publishers, 1988.

Tedone, David. *Practical Publicity*. Boston, MA: Harvard Common Press, 1983.

(e) TELEPHONE ANSWERING SERVICE

The Concept: Business owners are well aware of the importance of having a friendly and efficient-sounding voice on the other end of the phone when their customers and prospective customers call. That is why many small business owners who do not have their own office staff contract with a telephone answering service company rather than having a recorded message on an answering machine. Further, there is a need for small telephone answering service companies to provide the personalized service that the large firms cannot (or do not) provide because of the sheer volume of clients and calls being channeled through their computerized phone systems. While there is also a demand for 24-hour service, by catering to the needs of daytime businesses you will be able to shut the door to your home office after a busy seven- or eight-hour day.

Money Matters: A one-person operation can comfortably handle a 60-line switchboard which would bring in $3,600 per month when charging a monthly rate of $60. Additional revenue of $200 per month could be earned by offering a wake-up service at a minimum of $20 per month. Your overhead costs of telephone equipment and advertising could be kept to $600 per month or less.

Your Background: If you are reliable, have a cheery disposition, and enjoy talking to people, this type of work can produce benefits without your ever having to leave home. In fact, the downside is that you *can't* leave home unless you have someone to mind the phones.

What You Will Need: Check the zoning in your neighbourhood to ensure it will allow some commercial activity. Even if City Hall doesn't require you to check, the telephone company may insist on it. Check also that the telephone company can provide you with the number of line connections that you plan to offer. Try to get this confirmed in writing in case a question arises later. You will need a telephone unit with the required number of lines, a desk and chair, and forms for message-taking. If you have young children in the home, you will want to ensure that the little ones do not share your workspace!

The Plan: Your initial research will include finding out as much as you can about telephone systems, the various types of connections possible, installation, and monthly costs. If your home is located near a switching station for the telephone company, is zoned for commercial use, and is within the telephone exchange area of a number of businesses, then everything may be in your favour to offer this service from your home. An ad in the Yellow Pages under "Telephone Answering Service" is certain to bring in a regular flow of prospects, especially if you specify the "personalized" nature of your service. You may decide to target certain businesses in your area, especially owner-operator and home-based businesses.

Telephone connections may be of three types: a dedicated line, an off-premise extension, or a shared time. A *dedicated line* is hooked up to your system only. With an *off-premise extension* the line rings both at your client's home or place of business and on your system. You allow the phone to ring up to three times before answering, to let your client take the call. If, however, the phone continues to ring, you answer and say the client has stepped out of the office. When the client plans to be out for any length of time, you may ask him or her to advise you, so that you don't have to wait even for the three rings. For both the dedicated line and the off-premise extension, the telephone company will have to visit your premises to install the line.

If you decide to offer *shared-line* answering service, the telephone company will bill you monthly for the cost of a business telephone number. You in turn can "rent" the telephone number to various clients, thereby saving them the installation and monthly costs of a telephone line. Of course, this would work only for clients with a low volume of calls and for those who don't need their phone answered with their company name. If you carry up to 10 clients on the shared line, and charge them $10 per month more because you pay the telephone bill, you could earn $700 per month for one shared line, less the cost of the monthly phone bill ($25 to $50).

Measured line and *call forwarding* hookups are available in some areas which can save money for your clients. If you become familiar with the types of hookups and resultant costs, you will be able to confidently recommend to your clients the most appropriate method. They will appreciate your cutting through the telephone company's red tape for them. There are many voice mail options as well.

Of course, you will need to identify the lines on your telephone system to act as "cues" on how to answer each line. Keep a file card handy on each client with pertinent information that may need to be referred to or relayed to callers. You will probably opt for a computerized system of recording messages. Voice mail for message retrieval is a popular option. Billing is on a monthly basis, paid in advance. At the outset you should collect one month's deposit and postdated monthly cheques, if possible.

Associations

Association of Telemessaging Services International, #500-320 King Street, Alexandria, VA 22314.

Publications

Telephone Answering Service (Start-up Business Guide XI 148). Irvine, CA: Entrepreneur Magazine.

Telephone Secretary. Association of Telemessaging Services Inc., #500-320 King Street, Alexandria, VA 22314.

(f) VIDEOTAPING SERVICE

The Concept: There is a steadily increasing trend towards the use of videotapes by businesses as an aid in training, promoting, public relations, and prescreening products or services. Trade associations may want to have conference or workshop presentations recorded on videotape for sale to those unable to attend. There is also a market with individuals who may want to preserve on tape special events such as weddings, graduations, christenings, bar mitzvahs, etc. If you are creative and sales-oriented, you will be able to come up with video opportunities that potential clients haven't thought of before. A good reputation will reward you with a waiting list of business clients who are willing to pay a premium for your professional work.

Money Matters: A minimum of $2,000 will be required for the purchase of equipment, and ongoing expenses will include tapes, transportation, and rental of editing studio time. You may charge $500 for a 45-minute wedding video or $5,000 for a professional two- to three-minute product sales video.

Your Background: You will need to have some technical ability for operating the videotaping and editing equipment. A night school course or working part-time as an assistant may offer the instruction you need. A steady hand and a creative and artistic eye are also necessary. A good sense of marketing and one-on-one communication skills will assist you in explaining your services, understanding your client's needs, and closing the deal.

What You Will Need: You will need a video camera and videocassette recorder (VCR) or a combined unit called a "camcorder." Since the cost of editing equipment is quite high, at the outset you may consider renting editing time from a local studio for about $30 to $50 per hour.

The Plan: Contact videotaping services in your area to find out what services they offer and what they charge. Set your fee accordingly, taking into consideration the high overhead costs of equipment, repairs, tape, studio rental time, and transportation. Decide on a fair monthly income for yourself and add anticipated costs of tapes, travel expense, and advertising. Factor in an amount sufficient to recoup your equipment investment over a one- to two-year period. Add 25% of the total of these to cover contingencies, startup, and expansion. To arrive at your hourly rate, divide this by the number of hours you expect to work.

In addition to becoming knowledgeable about the equipment and which camera will produce the professional quality you require, you will need to produce a few practice videos at no charge so you can demonstrate a sample of your work. You may be able to arrange a tradeoff with a company such as a caterer, florist, or public relations firm. In exchange for producing a free videotape of their services, they may be willing to refer prospective contacts to you.

Business clients are more likely to bring you repeat business, although at the outset you will want to take on work from a variety of sources to build your revenue and make best use of rented studio time. Some examples of projects you may take on include new product demos, sales training videos, seminar and workshop presentations, video school yearbooks, civic ceremonies, sports events, weddings, graduations, retirement parties, reunions, and taping of valuables for insurance purposes.

Display ads in trade publications and local newspapers may produce leads. Have a brochure which describes your services, and carry a listing in the Yellow Pages. Personal contact, however, is the best means of promotion, as you may need to do some educating and convincing in order to get the job. You may have to conceive the idea and then sell the benefits to your client to secure the contract. You may also have to assist with writing the script.

Your camera should be simple to operate, especially the zoom lens and loading features. Ensure your equipment is not cumbersome (including lights) so that you can move around easily. You will need to arrange the props and lighting, tape the event, and do the editing, which may include dubbing in voice-overs, music, captions, and graphics. You may be able to earn additional revenue by selling duplicates of your tapes. If you send the tape to an outside lab with sophisticated equipment, you can get better copies.

Associations

Association of Independent Video and Filmmakers, 625 Broadway, 9th Floor, New York, NY 10012.

Publications

The Independent. Association of Independent Video and Filmmakers, 625 Broadway, 9th floor, New York, NY 10012 (10 issues per year).

Photo Video. Maclean Hunter Ltd., 777 Bay Street, Toronto, Ont. M5W 1A7 (9 issues per year).

Videography Magazine. 50 W. 23rd Street, New York, NY 10010.

Video Scene. Calder Publications (1980) Ltd., #102-224 Merton Street, Toronto, Ont. M4S 1A6 (6 issues per year).

Videotaping Service (Start-up Business Guide XI 204). Irvine, CA: Entrepreneur Magazine.

Cohen, Daniel and Susan Cohen. *How to Get Started in Video*. New York, NY: Franklin Watts (Grolier), 1986.

Dollin, Stuart. *How to Make Movies with Your Video Camera*. New York, NY: Putnam's Sons, 1985.

Gayeski, Diane M. *Corporate and Instructional Video: Design and Production*. Englewood Cliffs, NJ: Prentice Hall, 1986.

Hehner, Barbara (ed.). *Making It: The Business of Film and Television Production in Canada*. Toronto, Ont.: Doubleday, 1987.

Jacobs, Bob. *How to Be an Independent Video Producer*. White Plains, NY: Knowledge Industry Publications, 1986.

Schmidt, Rick. *How to Make Money with Your Video Camera*. New York, NY: New American Library, 1988.

Schwarz, Ted. *How to Make Money with Your Video Camera*. Englewood Cliffs, NJ: Prentice Hall, 1986.

2. SERVICES TO INDIVIDUALS

The time has passed when one spouse was the "breadwinner" while the other stayed at home to care for young children and look after the household needs. Today's economic situation has changed all of this, and most families now depend on two incomes to maintain a certain standard of living. It is also a fact of human nature that as we earn more money and have a greater "disposable income," we elevate our standard of living and "wants." These wants generally include more free time and more-comfortable surroundings. Time is therefore becoming a precious commodity. People would rather pay someone else to do household chores, for instance, in order to have more quality time to spend with friends and family.

This trend toward more free time helps to create hundreds of new opportunities for service businesses that offer individuals this benefit. As stated earlier, you are selling your time and talents when providing a service. Individuals are inclined to be more price-conscious than are businesses, because they most often are able to do the work themselves, but prefer not to. A pleasant personality, enthusiastic attitude, and willingness to provide quality work is a winning combination when selling to individuals. You need to be well liked by your customers and have their complete confidence in your service and reliability. The tradeoff, of course, is a contented, repeat customer who will be happy to recommend your service to friends and associates. Besides being free, word-of-mouth referrals are the best type of advertising any business could hope for.

In contrast to providing services to businesses, the professional business image requirement is somewhat more relaxed when serving individuals. Although you will be expected to be professional and businesslike in your dealings with customers, most likely they will be less concerned about the presence of a certain image or the surroundings in which you work. Because of this, you will be able to take greater liberties in your advertising approach. A neatly handwritten flyer regarding your house painting service, for example, may result in a response as good as or better than that of a professionally typeset brochure. In fact, if the brochure is a costly item to produce, you may be implying that your fees are high, too. Many people will not pick up the phone to find out.

To assist you in identifying the type of business which may be most appealing to you, we have provided a cursory look at six personal services businesses. They are (a) bed and breakfast inn, (b) carpet cleaning, (c) child care centre, (d) dressmaking and alterations, (e) painting contractor, and (f) tutoring or special instruction. Below is a selection from the ever-expanding list of other services that could be offered to individuals.

Aesthetics and skin care	Home inspection service	Repairing vinyl
Automobile repairs	Interior decorator	Shopping service
Cake decorating	Landscaping and gardening	Sports referee
Catering	Laundry service	Swimming pool maintenance
Children's party planner	Mail service	Tax preparer
Cleaning fireplaces and chimneys	Musician	Tree service
Closet organizer	Pet care and grooming	Tuning pianos and organs
Disk jockey	Real estate appraiser	Videotaping special occasions
Fashion and colours consultant	Real estate salesperson	Washing windows
Furniture refinishing	Repairing old clocks, radios, TVs	Wedding planning service
Handyman		

(a) BED AND BREAKFAST INN

The Concept: "Bed and breakfast" (B & B) accommodations are an increasing trend in North America, although they have been popular in Europe for many years. Many travellers prefer the homey surroundings offered by B & B hosts and the opportunity to socialize with interesting people in the communities they are visiting. Rooms that are reasonably priced and include a full breakfast are a favourable alternative to the rising cost of hotel rooms. Tourists by far make up the main users of B & B accommodations. If your inn attracts business travellers because of its proximity to a city, you will be able to increase your Monday through Friday occupancy rate. You need not be restricted to the traditional B & B inn decor: possibilities for conversions, or interesting surroundings, may be offered by farmhouses, lighthouses, yachts, etc. During off-season months for tourists, you may choose to offer the rooms to other types of boarders, such as university students, at a monthly rate.

Money Matters: The costs for startup are minimal if no major improvements or modifications are needed on your home. You will need to budget for supplies and promotion and periodic replacement of worn and torn linens. The amount that you charge will depend on the volume of the tourist trade and economic climate in your area. You may be able to offer three or four rooms within a range of $35 to $85 per night for double occupancy, although this could be substantially more if your home is quite elegant, the local hotel rates are much higher, or there is a high demand in your area. You will be able to charge a number of fringe-benefit writeoffs to the business besides the obvious overhead, utility, and food costs, such as dining at local restaurants and visiting area attractions, as you will want to make recommendations to your guests. Also, if you stay at competitors' B & B locations when you take your own vacation, this may be considered "research" and therefore tax-deductible.

Your Background: Operating a B & B inn is a lifestyle commitment. You must be flexible and enjoy meeting and talking to people. Doing several loads of laundry and vacuuming daily as well as cooking early-morning breakfasts is all part of the lifestyle choice. You must be a bookkeeper and handyman to keep down your overhead and repair costs.

What You Will Need: The major consideration is the location of your home, whether it is easily accessible and visible to tourists travelling along major roads and highways, or proximate to cities. If your home is attractive and unique in its appearance, this will be a drawing factor. It should have ample bathrooms, preferably a separate bathroom for your guests. The bedrooms should be well insulated and private, with sufficient closet and drawer space. You should check out any zoning restrictions and your insurance coverage.

The Plan: A comfortable and decorative home will create a cozy atmosphere to enhance your visitors' stay. Perhaps your first step is to visit some B & B inns, or to work at one to do your research and clarify your commitment to this type of business. Check the area hotel and motel occupancy rates to see if the demand exists. Once you have clarified any zoning and insurance considerations, and completed any home improvements to enhance its attractiveness, it is time to hang out your shingle. If your home is on a well-travelled route, an attractive sign mounted on your porch, window ledge, or gate post could announce your B & B services. Choose contrasting colours for easy visibility during the day and evening hours. Perhaps a small light will be necessary. An inexpensive brochure, preferably with a photograph of the outside of your home or an interior room, could be prepared. Personally deliver these to local tourist offices and chambers of commerce. Find out from these bureaus where most tourists come from. Then contact the tourist offices in those communities and send them your information and brochures, and encourage them to contact you for more when their supply is depleted.

You may prefer to list your B & B inn solely with an agency which handles all the booking arrangements for a fee of 20% to 30% or a fixed annual fee. These agencies sometimes also pre-screen the guests to minimize the risk involved. A small ad in a travel guide may produce leads.

You may wish to prepare a list of suggested things to see and do in your community, as an added service to your guests. Remember the importance of creating an atmosphere, which is the reason why people choose a B & B inn over a hotel room. With creativity you can make the most of national holidays by holding your own celebrations for your guests; you can perhaps get some free publicity at the same time.

Your days will start early as you put on a large pot of coffee and start to prepare an interesting, but not necessarily elaborate, breakfast. Your guests will arrive for breakfast at varying intervals between your preset times of 8:00 to 10:00 a.m., for example. After your guests have left their rooms, you will have the dishwasher set in motion and commence to strip and wash the bed linens and towels. Besides any shopping you may have to do, the rest of your day is relatively free of major tasks. If you employ a part-time housekeeper and an answering machine, you may be able to free yourself for additional periods. The trick is to arrange your free time to blend with the flow of your business.

Associations

Canadian Country Vacations Association, P.O. Box 2580, Winnipeg, Man. R3C 4B3.

National Bed and Breakfast Association, P.O. Box 332, Norwalk, CT 06852.

Tourism Industry Association of Canada, #1016-130 Albert Street, Ottawa, Ont. KIP 5G4.

Publications

Agent Canada: Canada's National Weekly Travel and Tourism Trade Magazine. Bizletter Publishing Ltd., 1425 W. Pender Street, 2nd Floor, Vancouver, B.C. V6G 2S3 (weekly).

Bed & Breakfast Guest. American Bed & Breakfast Association, #203-16 Village Green, Crofton, MD 21114 (bimonthly).

Bed & Breakfast Guide for the United States, Canada, Bermuda, Puerto Rico & the U.S. Virgin Islands. Norwalk, CT: National Bed & Breakfast Association, 1987.

Bed & Breakfast Inn (Start-up Business Guide XI 2 78). Irvine, CA: Entrepreneur Magazine.

Bed & Breakfast Shoptalk. American Bed & Breakfast Association, #203-16 Village Green, Crofton, MD 21114 (monthly).

Bed & Breakfast Update. Rocky Point Press, Box 4814, N. Hollywood, CA 91607 (bimonthly).

Innkeeping Newsletter. Mary E. Davies, P.O. Box 267, Inverness, CA 94937.

Notarius, Barbara and Gail Brewer. *Open Your Own Bed and Breakfast.* New York, NY: John Wiley & Sons, 1987.

Nykiel, Ronald. *Marketing in the Hospitality Industry.* New York, NY: Van Nostrand Reinhold, 1988.

Pantel, Gerda. *The Canadian Bed & Breakfast Guide.* Chelsea, VT: Fitzhenry & Whiteside, 1989.

Stankus, Jan. *How to Open and Operate a Bed and Breakfast Home.* Chester, CT: Globe Pequot, 1987.

Taylor, Monica, and Richard Taylor. *Start and Run a Profitable Bed and Breakfast Business.* Vancouver, B.C.: International Self-Counsel Press, 1982.

Zander, Mary. *How to Start Your Own Bed and Breakfast.* Spencertown, NY: Golden Hill Press, 1985.

(b) CARPET CLEANING

The Concept: Most houses, apartments, and offices have wall-to-wall carpeting which should be cleaned a couple of times a year. Although supermarkets and other stores rent shampoo equipment and sell cleaning fluids, the whole procedure can be expensive and tiresome for the office/homeowner. And while there may be numerous cleaning services listed in the Yellow Pages, a few phone calls to homeowners who have used a carpet cleaning service will indicate that there's a great opportunity for a quality service. Offices, retail shops, and restaurants are an additional customer source that can provide bigger jobs with greater efficiency. You can start the business on a part-time basis while still maintaining another job until you build the volume and customer base. As a sideline, many carpet cleaning machines also clean upholstery which offers better profit margins.

Money Matters: The major expenditure is a quality rug shampooer, which could range between $2,000 and $4,000. Advertising is the other major cost item at about 20% of your gross sales; this will lower your net profit, but it will be compensated for by a tremendous growth rate. Supplies will consist mainly of cleaning fluids, which should be purchased in bulk at wholesale prices. Usually the family car or van is sufficient to transport your supplies and equipment.

The going rate for carpet cleaning is about 20 cents per square foot. Properly cleaning 300 square feet of carpet takes one person about an hour and costs the customer $60. If you allow two hours' travel and setup time between jobs, and pay your worker $10 per hour, and the cost of the materials is $5, your net profit is $25. Your rate per square foot may increase to 30 cents if you are required to move furniture. Successful operators can handle 10 to 15 jobs per week per worker. Profits can accrue by hiring additional workers and carefully scheduling jobs.

Your Background: A customer-conscious and service-oriented attitude will be the determining factor for your business to grow through repeat and referral business. A strong promotional sense will help you to build and maintain a volume business. Equipment manufacturers may offer instruction on how to properly use their shampooing equipment and techniques to produce the best results. You may wish to practise in your own home and the homes of friends and relatives to test the drying times for various types of carpets. Perfect your technique so you can offer first-class work.

What You Will Need: Physical strength is required to carry shampoo equipment and move furniture. You will need an industrial-type vacuum cleaner, and large quantities of soap may be purchased at wholesale prices. At the outset you may choose to rent or lease a rug shampooer, or purchase a used heavy-duty unit at an auction or second-hand store. Be certain, though, the equipment is capable of producing professional results.

The Plan: Once you have researched the market and decided upon the rates you will charge, you will need to start advertising your services. Yellow Page listings, classified ads in local newspapers, inexpensive flyers delivered to neighbourhoods and businesses, are a few of the methods you should use. A direct telephone marketing campaign in November and March will trigger a response from those getting ready for Christmas entertaining and spring cleaning. Suggest starting with one room, and if the customer is satisfied, do the entire house. Keep in mind that one job well done equals three other jobs because of word-of-mouth referrals.

Provide an estimate over the telephone, if possible, to save travel time. Multiply the approximate square footage of the area to be cleaned by your rate per square foot to calculate the job cost. The job itself involves (a) moving the furniture, (b) vacuuming thoroughly, (c) shampooing with special liquid shampoo, and (d) vacuuming while the carpet is wet to draw out the excess moisture into a tank. Follow up with the customer to ensure satisfaction. Keep a diary for a business call in six months' time.

Associations

Association of Specialists in Cleaning and Restoration, #1408-One Skyline Place, 5205 Leesburg Pike, Falls Church, VA 22041 (also includes National Institute of Rug Cleaning).

Ontario Professional Carpet Cleaners Association, #2-2300 Finch Avenue W., Downsview, Ont. M9M 2Y3.

Publications

Carpet Cleaning Service (Start-up Business Guide X1053). Irvine, CA: Entrepreneur Magazine.

Cleaning and Restoration. Association of Specialists in Cleaning and Restoration, #1408-One Skyline Place, 5205 Leesburg Pike, Falls Church, VA 22041 (monthly).

Installation and Cleaning Specialist. Specialist Publications Inc., 17835 Venture Boulevard, Encino, CA 91316 (monthly).

Griffin, William R. *Rug and Carpet Cleaning: A Comprehensive Technical Guide for Training and Professional Certification*. Seattle, WA: Cleaning Consultant Services, 1988.

Kepka, Brian. *Taking the Mystique out of Carpet Cleaning*. BRK Enterprises, 1988.

Von Schrader Company (manufacturer of equipment and supplies), 2291 Place, Racine, VA 53403. Free booklet.

(c) CHILD CARE CENTRE

The Concept: There is an increasing trend toward double-income households, as well as toward women who want both a career and family. Therefore, there is a critical need for good day care facilities, and many parents prefer the homelike atmosphere rather than a cold, institutional setting. Babysitting in itself is not a lucrative business, but minding from six to 10 youngsters can earn you a comfortable income. However, your heart needs to be in it to enjoy this type of business.

As an extension of the child care services, you may decide to form an association of mature women who will go into homes to care for children who for some reason cannot attend the centre. You may offer "hostelling" services for children whose parents need to go out of town overnight or for up to a week or two at a time. Becoming a foster parent for one or two youngsters could bring in a stable income to cover your expenses for the day care centre. By expanding to a number of day care centres, with staff that you hire and train, you could accrue additional financial benefits.

Money Matters: Minimal investment is required to get started if you presently rent or own a suitable home. If you have raised your family, you may already have suitable toys and furniture. Weekly rates can run from $50 to $100 per child. If you multiply this by the number of children you feel you could manage, the income could be attractive. Your tax-deductible expenses will include a portion of your household rent or mortgage interest and related house expenses, the children's food costs, toys, advertising, and part-time help.

Your Background: The principal ingredient for success is the proper attitude toward children: patience, a sense of humour, a genuine love and respect for children, a good character, and reliability. You should also be healthy, with abundant energy — you can count on being tired at the end of each day.

Licensing: You should first check to see whether there are any municipal or provincial regulations governing in-home day care centres. If you care for a limited number of children, there may be no particular regulations that pertain to you. Apply for a licence, as required, as well as the proper insurance coverage. Remember, any regulations that apply are minimum standards and guidelines designed to safeguard children and to ensure that your premises are suitable. Typical items covered in regulations for day care centres are amount of floor space, number of exits, number of bathrooms, extent of your first aid training, size of staff, and maximum number of children.

What You Will Need: You need to provide the children with proper supervision, fresh air and exercise, sturdy toys, wholesome food, and conscientious leaders. As a day care centre operator, you care for, feed, and entertain your charges; you are not required to teach them. The degree of versatility you are ready to offer will depend on how much energy you wish to put into the centre. You should maintain file cards on each child's attendance, medical history, home telephone numbers and addresses, emergency telephone numbers for parents, etc. When selecting part-time or full-time staff to assist you, select individuals with special qualifications such as former teachers or nurses.

You should have sufficient space indoors and outdoors with a fenced yard. Sufficient toilet facilities should be provided, and a first-aid kit should be handy. Small furniture such as tables, chairs, cots will be more convenient for the children and you. Outdoor play equipment may include swings, slides, and a sandbox. Indoor activities may require toys, books, and materials such as colouring books, crayons, paints, plastic scissors, catalogues. Select sturdy toys so children will not injure themselves on them or wear them out quickly.

The Plan: Visit a day care centre to see how it is equipped and operated. Decide on the number of children, their preferred ages, and the days and times you will be offering services. While you could charge more for babies, you will need a greater staff-to-child ratio for the non-toilet-trained. Make arrangements at the outset about holidays, sickness, or unexpected changes in routine.

Calculate your actual disbursements costs such as meals, supplies, transportation for outings. Buying in bulk or from restaurant suppliers will help you cut costs. You will need to decide on how to set your fees. It may be based on a per-child, a per-family, or a per-hour rate, or some combination of these. You may also set a minimum rate for occasional drop-ins while parents attend to appointments or shopping. The type of facilities you offer, the demand for your services, the degree of certification and licensing, the location, and any special services you offer will largely determine the hourly rate you can charge.

Advertise your service in the Yellow Pages, local newspapers, community centres and schools, hotels/motels in the area, and local businesses. You may also choose to distribute flyers in your neighbourhood. A neat, brightly coloured sign could be prominently positioned on your lawn or fencepost advertising your service. You might choose a unique, descriptive name for your centre, such as "Wee Care Day Care" or "The Smiling Brook Nursery."

Associations

Association of Day Care Operators of Ontario, #705-5468 Dundas Street W., Etobicoke, Ont. M9B 6E3.

Canadian Child Care Management Association, #705-5468 Dundas Street W., Etobicoke, Ont. M9B 6E3.

Publications

Child Care Center. Lake Publishing Corp., 17730 W. Peterson Road, Box 159, Libertyville, IL 60048-0159 (bimonthly).

Child Care Quarterly. Human Science Press, 72 Fifth Avenue, New York, NY 10011 (quarterly).

Child Care Service (Start-up Business Guide XI 058). Irvine, CA: Entrepreneur Magazine.
Day Care and Early Education. Human Sciences Press Inc., 72 Fifth Avenue, New York, NY 10011 (quarterly).
Martin, Elaine. *Baby Games.* Philadelphia, PA: Running Press, 1987.
Pruissen, Catherine. *Start and Run a Profitable Day Care.* Vancouver, B.C.: International Self-Counsel Press, 1993.

(d) DRESSMAKING AND ALTERATIONS

The Concept: Many fashion-conscious and quality-conscious individuals insist on one-of-a-kind garments that are truly customized in style, size, colour, and/or texture of fabric. The personalized nature of dressmaking allows you to cater as well to atypical figures, the handicapped, and seniors. While urban centres will have many client sources, rural areas may also provide opportunities, as shopping facilities may be limited.

Annual changes in fashion, and the fact that people gain and lose weight, lead to a constant need for clothing alterations. Fashion retail stores can be a good source of alteration work when a slight adjustment will enhance the fit of a new outfit. Doing repair work on garments, such as replacing broken zippers and patching small tears, can provide additional revenue.

Money Matters: There is considerable profit potential if you are a skilled seamstress and cater to the special desires of professional businesspeople and the fashion conscious. They will keep you busy with regular orders and good referrals. The startup costs for your basic equipment could be as low as $1,000. Sewing work is based on hourly rates, and the total amount of income you make is dependent upon the amount of time you wish to devote and how efficient you are. You must be certain to keep careful records of all materials used and time spent so that you can determine the profit on each item. You may choose to expand your business by hiring assistants and actively soliciting more alteration and custom design work.

Your Background: An essential skill is the ability to enhance a good figure and flatter a difficult one. Final-touch craftsmanship and professionalism is the key to success. Creativity, a flair for fashion, and attention to detail in selecting and fastening the right buttons, zippers, and linings is important. Perhaps some evening courses will acquaint you with modern machines and new sewing techniques. Reasonable business acumen is required in the arranging of appointments, keeping simple records of costs, and acquiring the judgement to charge rates which are competitive yet profitable.

What You Will Need: An ideal setting is a room in your home set aside solely for the purpose of dressmaking and that has ample space and is equipped with good lighting and adequate heating. You will need a good sewing machine, a cutting table, an ironing board, a rack for hanging garments, a full-length mirror, and a tailor's dummy. A tidy storage area would be handy for storing materials such as scissors, thread, needles, pins, etc. Also, a book of patterns may be helpful in generating ideas or explaining garment features.

The Plan: Decide on whether you will specialize in certain types of clothing, or whether you will handle a wide range of work within your abilities. Familiarize yourself with the retail prices of garments that are similar in quality. Determine your hourly rate. As your reputation grows and demand for your creations increases, you will be able to increase your prices and profits. Advertise your dressmaking service in the classified section of local newspapers. Make personal contact with dry-cleaning shops and fashion boutiques. If they do not have an established arrangement with an alterationist, they may be pleased to direct referral work to you.

Space your appointments to allow sufficient time for initial discussion and subsequent fittings. Take customer measurements accurately and take the additional time and care necessary to add those extra touches that display quality and craftsmanship. Buy your materials and supplies from manufacturers or wholesalers. You will be able to make a small profit on these items when you resell them to your customers at retail prices. To give your creations an identity and enhance your image, choose an appropriate name for a label to be sewn into each item. Ensure the garments are completed on time. Keep a careful record of all costs and the time spent on each item and bill out accordingly.

Taking on alteration and mending work will increase your customer base and source of referrals. You may hire someone on a part-time basis to perform the straightforward hemming and the replacement of zippers and worn elastics, and keep the more intricate work for yourself. However, you should conscientiously supervise the work of your assistants to ensure it meets your standards of workmanship.

As a method of expanding your volume, you may choose to contact two or three dressmakers with whom you could work together on projects. If you pool your expertise, garments which lend themselves to semi-mass-production could be made at competitive prices while retaining a degree of individuality. While you may decide to offer your garments to retail shops for sale, keep in mind that you can expect the retailer to offer you approximately half of the selling price. You should deal with the more exclusive shops, as it would be difficult to profitably design and hand-sew low-priced items.

Associations

Canadian Home Sewing & Needlecraft Association, #204-224 Merton Street, Toronto, Ont. M4S 1A1.

National Association of Milliners, Dressmakers and Tailors, c/o Harlem Institute of Fashion, 157 W. 126th Street, New York, NY 10027.

Publications

Canadian Home Sewing and Needlecraft News. Canadian Home Sewing & Needlecraft Association, #204-224 Merton Street, Toronto, Ont. M4S 1A1 (monthly).

Making It in the Exciting World of Fashion, Sewing and Crafts. Home-sewing Trade News, 330 Sunrise Highway, Box 286, Rockville Center, NY 11571 (quarterly).

Sew News: The Newspaper for People Who Sew. P.J.S. Publications Inc., One Fashion Center, Box 3136, Harlan, IA 51537 (monthly).

Vogue. Condé Nast Publications Inc., 350 Madison Ave., New York, NY 10017 (monthly).

Carrol, Frieda. *Sewing as a Home or Small Business — Possibilities.* Houston, TX: Prosperity and Profits Unlimited, 1984.

Roehr, Mary A. *Sewing as a Home Business.* Memphis, TN: Mary Roehr, Custom Tailoring, 1987.

Smith, Judith and Allan Smith. *Sewing for Profits.* Palm Beach Gardens, FL: Success Publications, 1984.

(e) PAINTING CONTRACTOR

The Concept: While almost everyone has the ability to paint or hang wallpaper, few relish doing the work themselves. After homes have suffered the elements of winter weather, many homeowners are receptive to having a spruce-up indoors as well as outdoors. Apartment managers may be interested in contracting out the painting of suites as tenants move out. After learning the ins and outs of the business by working for an experienced painter, you can then hire junior labour at the minimum wage to do the work. As a contractor you will spend your time making client contacts, writing careful estimates, purchasing supplies, overseeing the job, and following up with clients.

Money Matters: Approximately $500 is all that is required for you to be set up in a business as a painting contractor, as minimal equipment is necessary. Advertising will be your major ongoing expense. Taking care to complete jobs on budget and on time will ensure profitability and repeat or referral business.

Your Background: The skill required to paint a house, inside or out, is mainly a combination of neatness and speed. If you have an artistic flair and a knack for understanding your client's needs, this will help to build client confidence in your expertise, suggestions, and quotation.

What You Will Need: You will need ladders, a power paint sprayer, brushes, rollers and pans, paint thinner, sandpaper, and drop sheets. Energetic college students may be a good source of part-time or seasonal painters who may work for minimum wage.

The Plan: Crucial to the success of your business is being able to provide a good estimate on the job. You will need to know how much paint will be required and how long a job will take. If you underestimate either of these, it will cost you time and money to finish the job. If you overestimate, you may lose out to a more competitive bid. Paint wholesalers may be able to provide some guidance on the quality of different kinds of paint and how to estimate the amount of paint to cover a given area. A typical contractor's calculation includes purchasing the paint at wholesale price and then adding 30% to 40% markup to reach the retail cost to your customer. Once you have estimated the length of time to complete the job, add 50% to that labour cost as your profit margin. You must train your staff to do quality work and be cost-efficient.

Advertising is a must to bring in a steady flow of work to keep your staff busy and your profits high. Advertising in the Yellow Pages is a good source of leads. A small classified ad in the local newspapers will also generate business. Your ads may contain phrases such as "quality service," "free estimate," "fast service," "every job guaranteed for two full years." You may also choose to distribute neighbourhood flyers, conduct a postal mail drop, or leave a supply of your business cards at local paint stores. Also look for possible business leads from other contractors (e.g., subcontracting work) or from independent tradesmen (e.g., carpet layers, carpenters).

A natural sideline or expansion of a painting contractor's business is to supply and hang wallpaper and special fixtures.

Associations

Canadian Paint and Coatings Association, 9900 Cavendish Blvd., Ville St. Laurent, Que. H4M 2V2.

Independent Professional Painting Contractors Association of America, P.O. Box 1759, Huntington, NY 11743.

Master Painters and Decorators Association of British Columbia, 4090 Graveley Street, Burnaby, B.C. V5C 3T6.

Ontario Painting Contractors' Association, #508-150 Consumers Road, Toronto, Ont. M2J 1P9.

Publications

House Painting (Start-up Business Guide XI 249). Irvine, CA: Entrepreneur Magazine.

Independent Professional Painting Contractors Association of America Newsletter. P.O. Box 1759, Huntington, NY 11743 (quarterly).

Painting and Wallcovering Contractor. Painting and Decorating Contractors of America, 7223 Lee Highway, Falls Church, VA 22046 (bimonthly).

Matis, Dave and Jobe H. Toole. *Paint Contractor's Manual.* Carlsbad, CA: Craftsman Book Co., 1985.

Percival, Bob. *How-To-Do-It Encyclopedia of Painting and Wall Covering.* Blue Ridge Summit, PA: TAB Books, 1982.

Thornung, William J. *Roofing, Siding and Painting Contractor's Vest Pocket Reference Book.* Englewood Cliffs, NJ: Prentice Hall, 1984.

(f) TUTORING OR SPECIAL INSTRUCTION

The Concept: Many people who dislike the traditional school environment enjoy the comfortable learning atmosphere and non-competitive nature of one-on-one or small-group lessons in the home. Instructional classes are offered in a wide range of areas including academics (languages, mathematics, bookkeeping); artistic (music, sketching, calligraphy, photography); crafts (pottery, quilting, macramé, knitting); culinary (ethnic cooking, wine and beer making); consumer awareness; fitness and health; hi-tech; etc. Outside of academics and the professions, there are few subjects that require an educational degree or special credentials. All that is required is knowledge and expertise in a skill or hobby, and the ability to present your thoughts in an orderly and easily understood manner.

Once you have developed your training program, you may be able to see areas to customize it or alter it slightly to offer it to a different audience. For instance, you may decide to offer different levels, from beginners to intermediate and advanced, thereby encouraging students to enroll in subsequent levels. You may offer classes for different age groups (children, adults, seniors), keeping in mind their varying special needs, attention span, dexterity, and capabilities. You can establish your own time schedule and dictate your own income by accepting as many or as few students as you like. As you expand, you may need to hire additional teachers to assist you.

Money Matters: Startup costs are almost nonexistent, except for what you will need for advertising your classes. Once you have established a good reputation and make the public aware of your classes, you could earn upwards of $50 an hour and have a wailing list for your next classes. This figure is based on, for example, accepting 10 students into a three-week quilting class which includes a total of six hours of instruction at an enrollment cost of $50. If you are tutoring on a one-to-one basis, you may charge $20 to $25 per lesson, but you would need to spend some time preparing the lesson and correcting homework.

Your Background: Formal credentials or an exceptional ability in a skill that people are eager to learn, the talent to teach it, and marketing know-how are what you require. A patient and friendly disposition will build your reputation as much as your teaching ability. You may decide to start by teaching a night school course on your specialty for your local school board or community centre. This will provide you with an opportunity to practise your teaching ability.

What You Will Need: You will need to have a marketable skill and a place to offer classes. It is best if your home is in a central location, or at least has good accessibility by bus and car. The room in your home where you will offer the lessons should be suitably lit, heated, and equipped for the purpose, with minimal distractions. A telephone answering machine will free you from telephone interruptions while you are teaching.

The Plan: You will first want to check out the demand for your classes. Find out if local night school classes are offered in your subject area, and if they are well attended. Ask what are other instructors are charging for courses of a similar nature.

There are many things you can do to build a reputation for being a credible authority. You could write short articles on your area of specialty and submit them to the local newspapers, which are constantly in search of human-interest stories to use as fillers. Include a photograph of you interacting with your students. Radio and local TV programs may also offer opportunity for such free publicity, if you take the initiative to spark an interest. Such publicity commands more acknowledgement and respect than paid advertising which is quite costly.

Some newspapers publish a "what's happening" column free of charge which lists courses, seminars, and workshops scheduled throughout the upcoming week. You may consider placing a small classified ad in the local newspaper. Neatly prepared flyers which outline the course content and registration information may be left in community centres and libraries, delivered to the neighbourhood, posted on bulletin boards, etc. If what you are teaching will help people to make or save money, or be more marketable in their jobs, stress these points. If you are offering music instruction, perhaps the local music store will display your business cards and course pamphlets in return for your referring students who need instruments. If you are giving instruction in beer and wine making, perhaps you could also sell beer- and wine-making kits to your students, and earn an additional profit through product sales.

Develop an application or registration form that gives the course outline, dates and times of classes, and the fee. Include a tear-off portion at the bottom to be completed with the student's name, address, and phone number and returned with payment in advance of the course. Make every lesson interesting and exciting. Avoid unrealistic assignments that may discourage your students' ambition and make your efforts unpopular.

In the case of music instruction, place particular emphasis on teaching proper techniques and instill in your students the desire to learn and practise. You may decide to start with a free exploratory lesson to get an idea of the student's goals and current level of musicianship.

Observe and chart each student's progress. Demonstrate a genuine interest in your students. Consider presenting in the community a demonstration of their work. This will give you increased publicity and increase the demand.

Associations

Canadian Association for Adult Education, 29 Prince Arthur Avenue, Toronto, Ont. M5R 1B2.

Publications

How to Tutor. Boise, ID: Paradigm Co., 1987.

Learning: The Magazine for Creative Teaching, P.O. Box 2580, Boulder, CO 80322 (9 issues per year).

Teaching Today. Teaching Today Magazine Inc., #6112-102 Avenue, Edmonton, Alta. T6A 0N4 (5 issues per year).

Tutoring Service (Start-up Business Guide XI 239). Irvine, CA: Entrepreneur Magazine.

Arkin, Marian and Barbara Shollar. *The Tutor Book*. White Plains, NY: Longman, 1982.

Moore, David P. and Mary A. Poppino. *Successful Tutoring: A Practical Guide to Adult Learning Processes*. Springfield, IL: C. C. Thomas, 1983.

Myer, Emily and Louise Z. Smith. *The Practical Tutor*. New York, NY: Oxford University Press, 1987.

Shaw, Sylvia. *How to Make Money Teaching Reading at Home*. Los Angeles, CA: Mark of Excellence Publishing Co., 1984.

CHAPTER

14

Product Businesses

Most people find it more difficult to market a service than a product, because a service is intangible. A product, on the other hand, can be inspected before it is purchased. It can be photographed, demonstrated, displayed, and illustrated. It can be seen, felt, tasted, smelled, or touched before it is bought. You can therefore appeal to your customers' sensory impulse buying habits.

Another advantage of a product-type business is that there is no limit to the amount you can sell. Products can be mass-produced and inventoried for volume sales during peak seasons. Conversely, there is a finite number of sales that can be made in a service business, because it usually relates to your personal time spent. There are only a certain number of chargeable hours in a day, and therefore only a certain number of jobs that can be handled during that time. A service business sometimes needs to "close temporarily" while the owner takes a vacation, which is not necessarily the case in a product-type business.

There are certain factors that will enhance the success of your product business. You must have a unique product that is superior to and/or different from those of the competition. Literally every product in existence can be changed, improved, presented, or sold in a new way, or simply offered to a different audience. You must be creative to find a uniqueness to offer. Set high standards for the product quality and the related services you provide. Have technical competence in the production of your product. Gain hands-on experience and knowledge of what is happening in your industry. Use of an effective marketing approach is crucial to your success. Studies show that 75% of product failures can be attributed to poor marketing. The chapter on marketing will assist you with the major considerations.

The type of product you choose will depend upon your financial resources, your special interests and talents, and the market demand in your area. It will be either one that you produce (you are the manufacturer), or one that you purchase from a manufacturer for resale (you are the distributor).

1. PRODUCTS MADE BY YOU

A lot of home-based businesses have been started by turning a hobby into a profitable enterprise. Arts and crafts-type businesses, for example, account for a growing percentage of product-type businesses operated from home. Many are operated on a part-time basis to suit the owner's lifestyle needs. Others, through astute marketing, have found a high demand for their products and have expanded their operations into manufacturing plants in order to mass-produce large quantities to fill major supplier orders on a national and international basis. Some of these outgrow their home-based status at this point and have to face factors such as leasing larger premises, hiring staff, accessing bank financing for equipment, supplies, etc. At the outset of your business planning you should address such issues as expansion, market demand, and staffing, and decide on the direction you wish to take. Ensure that your profitability increases substantially with the expansion process. Otherwise, it may not be worth the additional risk, overhead, and managerial problems that you will face. Product liability insurance may be an important consideration and should not be overlooked.

The following pages include an overview of five types of made-at-home product businesses and an overview of the startup considerations. They are: (a) booklet and directory publishing, (b) craft manufacturing, (c) growing plants and herbs, (d) specialty food products, and (e) woodworking. Some additional product businesses that you may wish to consider are:

Art or photographic greeting card designs	Clothing design and manufacture	Macramé plant hangers
Bakery	Customized candles	Millinery
Beekeeping products (honey, wax, polish)	Dried-flower arrangements	Quilt making
Christmas ornaments	Hand-knitted sweaters, etc.	Rug making
	Jewelry making	Stained-glass window manufacturing
		Toy/stuffed animal manufacturing

(a) BOOKLET AND DIRECTORY PUBLISHING

The Concept: There is a growing demand for sources of specialized information and easy-access directories. If you can come up with ideas for specialty books, directories, how-to manuals, cookbooks, etc., and identify those who would be interested in buying your publications, you have the potential for starting a small publishing house. Directories rarely remain current longer than it takes to get them printed, so you could provide annual updates for an additional fee. A how-to manual may develop into a series on similar but different topics. Cookbooks provide a good example of how you can diversify; each book might specialize in certain types of recipes such as soups, breads, cakes, etc. In many instances your audience for each book will be the same, which makes your marketing easier. By selecting a publication that may require subsequent updates, or develop into a series of publications, you can count on repeat sales. The subsequent booklets will require less time and effort in terms of writing, compiling, and distributing than for the initial edition. If you are selective and sell only booklets in high public demand, your efforts of one year could be rewarded with continued sales for years to come.

Instead of preparing the original work yourself, you may become a "vanity publisher" — that is, you do not assume any risk and the writer pays you all the publishing costs in advance. As major publishing houses reject hundreds of thousands of manuscripts each year, many would-be writers are happy to pay the full cost of having their work of art finally put in print. Your responsibility is limited to and ends with your providing the required number of books. The author then has to do the marketing and selling. Often the book is not a huge financial success, but this risk is accepted by the author in exchange for the pure pleasure of seeing his or her manuscript in print.

Money Matters: To keep your predictable costs down, you should consider doing the inputting and layout on your own computer with desktop publishing software. Such a system could run you $5,000 to $10,000. As you will rarely receive advance payment (unless you are a vanity publisher), you should budget for your living expenses and overhead costs until your publication is available for sale. Your major expense will be to a printer to produce the required copies. Printing a larger quantity will lower your per-copy cost. However, this may be false economy if there is little demand for the publication.

Your Background: You should be computer-literate and have some research, writing, and organizational ability. Some marketing and business sense will help you to recognize and seize opportunities to meet a high demand. You will then have to establish a fair price for your product, and aggressively market and sell it.

Requirements: A personal computer with desktop publishing software, your telephone, desk and chair, and numerous reference manuals will be your essential tools. You will need to identify a printer who can produce quality work and deliver on time.

The Plan: In the research and planning stage you will spend a considerable amount of time reading and talking to people. What frustrations do people have in finding information or learning a particular skill? The local libraries may give some clues as to the most frequently asked questions. Find out which night school courses have a continued high enrollment and check to see if there are up-to-date manuals that might be required to supplement the classroom instruction. Often instructors of these courses do not have the patience or the organizational skills to pull together their notes into a manual format. Directories need to be updated annually or possibly semiannually.

Once you have identified a need, it's a matter of doing your research and gathering data. You should try to keep this aspect to a short time frame, as information becomes out-of-date so quickly. As you are researching, don't lose sight of the marketing aspect. Who will buy your publication and what price will they pay? Collect contact names and marketing ideas. If you're not afraid that someone will take your idea and get it published before you do, talk about the end product to test out the need and create an interest. This will provide you with a ready list of customers, and give you an idea of the quantity you will need to print. Give some thought to a catchy title and attractive cover design.

Prepare the booklet in an easy-to-read format. Point-form lists or steps and numerous side-headings make it easy for the reader to speed-read or search out certain parts for reference purposes. A detailed table of contents, reference section, and index are useful features. If your booklet or directory will be used in an office environment, you may consider providing it in a three-hole-punched format so it can be easily inserted into binders. Remember to provide ordering information at the back to encourage further orders. If it's feasible to include a tear-out page to encourage readers to write you for more information, feedback, workshops, etc., this is a means of building a mailing list for your other publications. You may decide to hire a part-time typist or freelance editor, depending upon the size and complexity of your project.

Make contact with printers who do quality work in printing and binding books. Investigate the various production options and the costs of each. Since you will probably be able to supply a large volume of work, you should be able to negotiate a reasonable price and satisfactory terms of payment. Confirm quotations in writing along with estimated delivery time. Establish your costs for printing, binding, freight, and advertising and add your markup.

Be creative when selecting the vehicles you will use to sell your publications. If you sell to local bookstores, specialty gift stores, or supermarkets, be prepared to provide a 40% to 50% discount. Libraries, book clubs, mail order, community and professional associations, and craft fairs may provide you with substantial orders. Of course, when presenting yourself as a publisher, use high-quality paper, colours, and printing for your brochures and business cards.

Associations

Association for the Promotion of Independent Printing and Publishing, #702-27 Queen Street E., Toronto, Ont. M5C 2M6.

Association of Canadian Publishers, 260 King Street E., Toronto, Ont. M5A 1K3.

National Association of Independent Publishers, 2299 Riverside Drive, Box 850, Moore Haven, FL 33471.

Small Magazine Publishers Group, One Main Street, Freedom, ME 04941.

Publications

Booknotes: Resource Information for the Small and Self-Publisher. Interpub, Box 555, W. Linn, OR 97068 (quarterly).

Brilliant Ideas for Publishers. Creative Brilliance Associates, 4709 Sherwood Avenue, Box 4237, Madison, WT 53711 (bimonthly).

Canadian Printer and Publisher. Maclean Hunter Ltd., 777 Bay Street, Toronto, Ont. M5W 1A7 (monthly).

Small Press: The Magazine of Independent Book Publishing. Meckler Corporation, 11 Ferry Lane W., Westport, CT 06880-5808 (bimonthly).

Crook, Marion and Nancy Wise. *How to Self-Publish and Make Money.* Leonia, NJ: Sandhill Publications, 1987.

Holt, Robert L. *How to Publish, Promote, and Sell Your Own Book.* New York, NY: St. Martin's, 1986.

Mathieu, Aaron M. *The Book Market: How to Write, Publish and Market Your Book.* New York, NY: Andover Press.

Poynter, Dan. *The Self-Publishing Manual: How to Write, Print and Sell Your Own Book.* Santa Barbara, CA: Para Publishing.

(b) CRAFT MANUFACTURING

The Concept: One of the reasons why crafts are becoming big business is that people are tired of the factory-produced look, and instead want to decorate their homes with one-of-a-kind items that reflect their individual tastes. Another reason is that nostalgia makes people yearn for the "good old days" of natural products, ingenuity, and craftsmanship. The possibilities are endless: patchwork, weaving, crocheting, ceramics, sculpting, pottery, découpage, painting, woodworking, glass staining, wall hangings, glass etching, and toys. The manufacturing process, once learned, can be easy to operate.

Money Matters: Startup costs will vary depending upon the materials you need and the type of workspace required. It will also depend on the volume of work you wish to handle. If kept on a small scale, an initial investment of $200 could produce revenues of $350. By reinvesting your profits to buy more supplies, you can increase the volume gradually to coincide with your gradually increasing customer base. On the other hand, if you have a product that is quite unique and has a high demand, you may prefer to corner the market and substantially increase your initial investment to $10,000 or $15,000. This amount of working capital will be required to buy professional expertise on creating a unique design and packaging, marketing tactics, booth and entrance fees to wholesalers' gift trade shows, travel and accommodation expenses, and production of sufficient volume to handle potential trade show orders. Of course, if your product is successful, your return could be five to seven times your original investment.

Your Background: Most people are drawn to craft works as an outlet for their creativity. The degree of talent, knowledge, and artistic ability that is required may be minimal, although this will vary depending on the craft. You will no doubt have to have patience and an eye for quality and precision in your work. Many training courses and books are available. Some business sense and marketing abilities will help you to choose a craft that has market appeal and profit potential. These skills will also help you to discover new avenues of selling your products.

What You Will Need: Your material and space requirements will vary widely depending on the type of craft you choose. A quilting business will need a clean, dust-free room, with a cutting and ironing board and a large open area to accommodate an 8-foot by 12-foot quilting frame. Alternatively, woodworking would best be done in a heated garage or unfinished basement area where lumber and cutting saws could be easily loaded and safely stored. If working on your craft causes loud noises, excess heat, or fumes to be generated, or any other type of disturbance, be certain to check into any municipal regulations or by-law restrictions. Also, it would be a good idea to discuss your plans with your neighbours to avoid problems or confrontations.

The Plan: As with any business, you should do your market research first. Become familiar with the variety of crafts, where and how they are sold and in what quantities, and which ones do well only during certain seasons as opposed to year-round. Find out the costs involved to get started and the cost to make each item. After the costs of startup, production time, packaging, transportation, and materials are factored in, what price can the item be sold at to earn a reasonable profit? Be astute, and business-minded enough to recognize that some crafts are much more profitable than others. A careful analysis will narrow your choices. Materials and time costs will be the major factors. Buying in bulk direct from a raw materials plant is one way to reduce supplies cost. However, it may be more time and cost-efficient to buy partially prepared material. For example, if you buy precut glass to your specifications, you will pay a higher price than if you purchased full sheets, but you would have saved a lot of time, spoilage, and other frustrations of cutting the glass yourself. Practise your craft until you have developed it to the point where your work is saleable. Make it outstanding in quality, design, value, and attractiveness.

Through your careful research and study of the craft industry and subsequent selection of a craft to manufacture, you probably have formed a few ideas on how to market and sell your product. There are almost as many vehicles as there are types of crafts. Swap meets, flea markets, and craft fairs draw large crowds of people who enjoy crafts and novelty items. This may be a way to test your product's appeal. By talking to customers and other craftspeople you may get tips on how to modify and improve its appeal, colour, and size and on variations of the product that you could try. Negotiate for a prime location at the fair. Be creative in your display, and create an interest and enthusiasm in your product.

Craft stores, boutiques, or department stores may buy your products to display and resell. You will need to convince them, though, that you can meet their quantity and delivery requirements. They will expect you to sell to them at a lower price so that they can add up to 50% markup or more (relative to selling price). If you meet some resistance from shop owners, suggest you leave a few products "on consignment." If they sell, the shopkeeper usually retains 10% to 40% (of the selling price) and remits the rest to you. If they don't sell after a period of time, you take them back.

Mail order is another popular approach for products that are unique and will not become damaged in shipment. Advertise in publications that appeal to those with interests related to your product line. The price you charge should include the cost of advertising and delivery. If you specify "Allow four to six weeks for delivery," you can keep your stock low and wait until orders are received before producing more inventory.

By far the most costly means of selling your product is through trade shows. You will need to pay an exhibitor's fee of $500 to $1,500 and arrange to have an attractive booth display. Your time will be required to man the booth for the duration of the show, which may be three to four days. Be prepared with a quantity of brochures and business cards. Be selective about the shows you enter to ensure the people attending are truly prospective buyers. If you have a high-priced product and display at a show which appeals to the medium- to low-income bracket, you may find your audience admiring, but not buying, your products. Instead, enter trade shows that attract wholesale and retail buyers where orders placed are in bulk.

As your sales increase, you will need additional help to manufacture your products. If you pay your help on a piecework basis, you can tightly control your labour cost, but ensure the quality is maintained.

Associations

Canadian Craft & Hobby Association, #3640-26 Street N.E., Calgary, Alta. TIY 4T7.

Canadian Crafts Council, #16-46 Elgin Street, Ottawa, Ont. K1P 5K6.

Canadian Guild of Crafts (Quebec), 2025 Peel Street, Montreal, Que. H3A 1T6.

Metal Arts Guild (Ontario), 38 Kippendavie Avenue, Toronto, Ont. M4L 3R4.

Publications

Craft International. World Crafts Foundation, 247 Center Street, New York, NY 10013 (quarterly).

Craft News. Ontario Crafts Council, 346 Dundas Street W., Toronto, Ont. M5T 1G5 (8 issues per year).

Crafts Plus. Camar Publications, 130 Spy Court, Markham, Ont. L3R 5H6 (6 issues per year).

Craft Businesses (Start-up Business Guide No. X1304). Irvine, CA: Entrepreneur Magazine.

Fusion Magazine. Ontario Clay and Glass Association, 140 Yorkville Ave., Toronto, Ont. M5R 1C2 (6 issues per year).

The Quality Crafts Magazine: The Business Magazine for Craftspeople. National Information Center for Crafts Management and Marketing, 15 West 44th Street, New York, NY 10036 (quarterly).

Starting a Business to Sell Your Craft Items. Nashville, TN: Business of Your Own Publishers, 1988.

Brabec, Barbara. *Creative Cash: Making Money with Your Crafts, Needlework Designs and Know-how*. Huntington Beach, CA: Aames-Allen Publishing Company, 1986.

Hynes, William G. *Start and Run a Profitable Craft Business*. Vancouver, B.C.: International Self-Counsel Press, 1986.

Jefferson, Brian. *Profitable Crafts Marketing: A Complete Guide to Successful Selling*. Portland, OR: Timber Press, 1985.

Schultz, Kathleen D. and Robert L. Schultz. *How to Sell at an Arts and Crafts Show*. Mosca, CO: Sandune Press, 1987.

Scott, Michael. *The Crafts Business Encyclopedia*. San Diego, CA: Harcourt Brace Jovanovich, 1979.

Note: See also the section "Arts and Crafts Consignment Shop" beginning on page 199.

(c) GROWING PLANTS AND HERBS

The Concept: There is an increasing demand for green plants in homes, offices, and businesses for the warmth and beauty they add to the environment. And experts expect this "back to nature" trend to continue indefinitely. It is a confirmed notion that having plants in your home is a sign of good taste and good decorating. Business owners recognize that appearance is vital to attracting customers. Office managers agree that a pleasant and comfortable work environment improves productivity. However, few people put enough time and interest into the proper care of their plants. They tend to view plants as a decoration, and quite often pick poor locations for their plants. As every plant has different light, watering, and food requirements, plants that are poorly cared for will droop and eventually die. This creates an ongoing need for new, healthy plants, and a plant specialist to advise on the proper care of plants. So, if you have a "green thumb" and an appreciation for beautiful and healthy plants, this could be a profitable home business as well as a labour of love.

Money Matters: Minimal investment is required to purchase your basic supplies of shelves, pots, plant foods and additives, a lighting system, and an initial supply of plants and seeds. Since your actual cost per plant will be low, each sale will provide a high profit margin. Your overall financial success will depend upon the quality, type, and volume of plants that you produce.

Your Background: Naturally, a love of plants and a "green thumb" is the right combination to be happy and successful in this type of business, although growing plants is not as difficult as many people might think. Most public libraries have books and magazines that can supplement your knowledge of plant diseases, breeding, and the ideal environment for plants of different species.

What You Will Need: The amount of space you need will depend on the size of plants you carry and how much volume you wish to produce. The area in your home where you set up your "greenhouse" should have adequate heating, lighting, and shelving. You will need a workspace for repotting plants and storing soil, pots, etc. Expendable supplies include pots, seeds, soils, plant foods, and additives, and may be purchased from a wholesaler.

The Plan: Your initial research will include checking out the market to identify those plants in high demand and those that are not readily available from other sources in your area. Consider offering your plants to individuals, offices, and retail businesses. If you plan to do a large-scale business, you should look into making volume sales to retail outlets such as supermarkets, corner grocery stores, and hospital and nursing home gift shops. However, you will have to offer a discount price to allow them to resell your plants for a profit. Offer your selection of herbs to health food and produce stores. Sales could be made directly to the public by renting a table or booth space at a flea market, craft sale, or farmers' market.

You can start off with a small selection of plants that are in high demand. These can be grown under fluorescent lamps and on windowsills. As your business grows you can expand your variety of plants and move them to a separate area of your home such as a sun room or heated and windowed garage or basement. You may be able to build suitable shelving or buy warehouse racks to house your plants. A moveable type will ensure the plants get optimum levels of heat and light.

You can keep your costs low by buying supplies in bulk at wholesale prices. Ensure you get a quality grade of soil, free from fungus and insects. Then experiment with mixing your own soils and additives. You will be able to take cuttings from one plant to grow many others, which will further reduce your actual cost per plant. When you sell your plants, be certain to include instructions regarding their care, lighting, and watering.

You can easily regulate your income and the amount of time you devote to your business by the volume of plants you choose to produce. A supplementary income source could be through the sale of decorative flowerpots, plant hangers, terrariums, and other specialty items. For an additional fee, you may offer to nurse a sick plant back to good health. You may also want to provide a plant-sitting and/or maintenance service for businesses or individuals.

To increase your reputation as a plant specialist, you may offer to write a column for your local newspaper or be a guest on a radio phone-in program. You could offer a seminar or adult education night school program on the proper care of indoor plants. Charge a small enrollment fee and bring samples of your plants. Provide a fact sheet printed on your letterhead stationery with your name and phone number for further reference. Sell your samples at the end of the class.

Publications

Harrowsmith Magazine. A Maclean-Hunter publication.

Herb Farming (Start-up Business Guide No. X1282). Irvine, CA: Entrepreneur Magazine.

Black, David and Anthony Huxley. *Plants*. New York, NY: Facts on File, Inc., 1986.

(d) SPECIALTY FOOD PRODUCTS

The Concept: Specialty home-baked goods and products are always in demand. If you can make a quality product and sell it in a large quantity, you have the makings for a profitable business. You may choose to specialize in home-made pies, fruitcakes, preserves, candies, or party appetizers, and expand your offering later. Or you may identify a market for baked goods for special diets such as diabetics, heart patients, or those with certain food allergies. By providing a quality specialty product to bulk purchasers such as restaurants, gourmet food stores, delicatessens, and convenience stores, you can build a stable and profitable home business.

Money Matters: Assuming you already have the necessary cooking appliances and utensils, your startup costs will be minimal. The cost of your ingredients, packaging, equipment, utilities expense, and labour will form the base for your charges. You should charge about double this figure when you sell your products. Advertising costs can be limited to the cost of business cards and transportation to deliver samples or orders and to make "cold calls" (unscheduled phone calls or visits to prospects or customers, which can often result in impulse orders for your goods). To promote specialty products at gift trade shows, the cost of a booth, setup, and promotional material may be from $1,000 to $1,500.

Your Background: You must enjoy baking and be good at it. Although this type of business is labour-intensive, it can be scheduled to allow you free time after your orders have been filled. You may know of others who are willing to assist when you have a high volume of orders, or when you need to spend time away from your kitchen.

What You Will Need: Ensure that you can comply with provincial and federal health codes and regulations that pertain to the preparation and sale of food. If you sell you products through mail order, there may be federal shipment regulations that apply. For the most part you probably already have the necessary equipment and utensils to get started. Major considerations may include ample food storage (cool and dry), shelving and counter space, a large oven, and a refrigerator/freezer.

The Plan: Your friends and family will reap the rewards of your research and planning stage as you experiment with different recipes. Find a product that is unique. Identify trends and adapt your products to capture the market interest. Chart the total costs of each product you make. In addition to your ingredients, factor in an amount to cover your time, the packaging, and the use of utilities and equipment. Recognize that these costs will be reduced when you buy in bulk at wholesale prices and when you prepare your products in large quantities. After doubling this amount, compare your prices with those of commercial manufacturers to ensure it is neither too high nor too low. You can charge more if your product is specialized and has a high demand.

The importance of packaging should not be overlooked in your marketing decisions. When checking out your options, consider maximizing the freshness and protecting the quality of your products. Transparent wrap and containers will enable the product to be seen, a crucial factor when enticing impulse buyers. A creative design, distinctive motif, appealing colour combinations, and clear labelling will enhance your product's marketability. By using only healthy ingredients and listing these on the label, cautious, health-conscious shoppers can be swayed into buying your product. If you add a recipe or a list of serving suggestions on a card tied around the neck of a jar of marinade, this could increase its use and boost sales.

Find clients who will buy in bulk. If your products are diet- or health-oriented, nursing homes, hospitals, and health food stores are strong markets for you. Dessert-type goods and candies may be sold to gourmet shops, catering wagons, grocery stores, restaurants, delicatessens. Products that preserve well such as fruitcakes, salad dressings, condiments, pickles, jams, and jellies may sell well at all these locations as well as gift boutiques, offices, and factories and even by mail order. Seasonally you may rent a booth at a farmers' market or Christmas craft fair.

Perhaps the best ways to establish contacts are by personal visit and, of course, by offering samples. Spending a few minutes on the telephone before you start making your round of "cold calls" will ensure that you speak with the decision-makers and buyers. You may suggest starting with a small order on a trial basis or on consignment. As your business grows through regular orders and the recognition and demand for your product increases, you may need to hire assistants. Be certain, however, to maintain quality control to protect your reputation.

Catering is a natural sideline you may consider. If your sights are on large-scale production, you may consider displaying your specialty product at a trade fair. A creative booth and lots of samples will attract attention. Should wholesale buyers for department and specialty stores like your product, you may need to consider virtually overnight growth to a small manufacturing plant.

Associations

Canadian Health Food Association, #102A-1093 W. Broadway, Vancouver, B.C. V6H 1E2.

Canadian Specialty Food Association, P.O. Box 305, Station Q, Toronto, Ont. M4T 2N5.

Publications

Bakery Production and Marketing. Gorman Publishing Co., 8750 W. Bryn Mawr Avenue, Chicago, IL 60631 (14 issues per year).

Harrowsmith Magazine.

Gurvich, Philip B. et al. *Canadian Food Trade Directory and Buyers Guide.* Pro-Trade, 1987.

Harris, Catherine. *Cash from Your Kitchen: A Complete Guide to Catering from Your Home.* New York, NY: Macmillan, 1984.

Lawrence, Elizabeth. *The Complete Caterer. A Practical Guide to the Craft and Business of Catering.* New York, NY: Doubleday, 1988.

(e) WOODWORKING

The Concept: Beautiful woodwork will always be in demand. This appreciation for fine wood products creates opportunities for those who have a skill and interest in carpentry. The variety of applications stretches from artistic ornaments and sculptures to clocks, bookends, wine racks, planters, birdhouses, and furniture items such as cedar chests, bookcases, cabinets, tables, and chairs. The higher the quality and craftsmanship, the higher the price you will be able to demand.

Money Matters: To set up a workshop in your basement or garage will cost you between $1,000 and $2,000. This will cover the cost of a suitable work table (which you could build, of course), a band saw, a table saw, an electric drill, a planer, and an assortment of smaller tools and materials. Your profitability will depend on your product line, time efficiency, how cheaply you can buy materials, and of course how high you can price your products. Simple items that require little labour can be marked up two or three times the cost of materials. For more complex items, you will build in an hourly rate along with the cost of materials.

Your Background: You should have some experience and expertise in carpentry, and an appreciation for quality craftsmanship. To assist you when selecting materials, you should have a knowledge of different types of wood, and their texture, colour, and grains. There are books and courses available on woodworking techniques; proper care and use of saws, planers, and routers; and articles that can be built for sale.

What You Will Need: You will want to have easy access to your workshop for delivery of wood, and use of a van or truck to transport materials and finished products. Check into any bylaw restrictions regarding the operation of small machinery. Your workshop should be set up in an orderly fashion with sufficient space for working, safe storage of equipment, and materials when not in use.

The Plan: Spend some time studying wood products that are sold in department stores and specialty shops to make note of their quality and approximate cost of materials. Roughly calculate the steps and costs involved and the profit margin, keeping in mind that a retail store will add about 20% to 30% markup. Identify a product line that is in demand and that you can readily produce in quantity at a profit. Be aware of what similar products sell for, and price your own within a competitive range. Your aim should be to produce and sell in volume in order to keep costs low and revenues high. Continue to experiment and further develop your techniques and products. When taking on helpers, though, remember to insist on quality workmanship to maintain your reputation.

Construct a few samples giving a variety of sizes and colour of stain or paint. Find out who does the buying for the gift and specialty stores in your area. Take samples of your products to their shops when they're not busy to show your wares and negotiate an arrangement. (It's a good idea to have photographs of your products mounted in a binder for display purposes because, depending upon their size and weight, it may not be feasible to carry them with you.) Merchants will want to get your products at a low enough price to provide room for their markup. Of course, you want to protect your own profit margin, so beware and don't lose sight of your bottom line.

Preparing kits of do-it-yourself furniture may be an idea you wish to pursue and offer through mail order or retail. Easy-to-assemble furniture items — such as outdoor and children's furniture, or antique furniture reproductions — are examples of high-demand products.

Associations

Canadian Woodwork Manufacturers Association, 33 Atomic Avenue, Toronto, Ont. M8Z 5K8.

Woodworking Association of North America, P.O. Box 706, Plymouth, NH 03264.

Publications

Canada's Furniture Magazine. Victor Publishing Co., #8-7777 Keele Street, Concord, Ont. L4K 1Y7 (6 issues per year).

Canadian Workshop. Canmar Publications (1984) Ltd., 130 Spy Court, Markham, Ont. L3R 5S6 (monthly).

Fine Woodworking. Taunton Press, 63 S. Main Street, P.O. Box 355, Newtown, CT 06470 (bimonthly).

2 x 4. Éditions C.R. Inc., Box 1010, Victoriaville, Que. G6P 8Y1 (bimonthly).

Feirer, John L. *Furniture and Cabinet-Making.* New York, NY: Charles Scribner's Sons, 1983.

Harris, Edward. *Introduction to Woodworking and Construction.* Toronto, Ont: McGraw-Hill Ryerson, 1984.

Lyons, Richard A. *Making Country Furniture.* Englewood Cliffs, NJ: Prentice Hall, 1987.

Rowan, Bob and Melvin Fenn. *Tradesmen in Business: A Comprehensive Guide and Handbook for the Skilled Tradesman.* Betterway Publications, 1988.

2. PRODUCTS DISTRIBUTED BY YOU

There are actually a host of products that could be marketed through a distributorship. Any product that does not have a local supplier or distributor is a potential opportunity for you. You should research the market demand for that product, and then contact the manufacturer to make a proposal to distribute in your area.

With a distributorship, your main business function is selling. You will need to use effective communication and people skills to establish a bond with and trust among your prospective customers. You need to exude confidence in your product and in yourself as a salesperson. Of course, having an ability to handle objections and close the sale (get the order) is all part of good salesmanship. As well, you will need to keep proper business records and handle a variety of arrangements to ensure proper follow-through of orders from the order-taking to final delivery and installation.

Before signing a distributorship agreement with the manufacturer, you should have the contract reviewed carefully by a lawyer. Details that could be clearly specified include:

• Terms of the agreement.
• Sales territory.
• Exclusive or non-exclusive territory.
• Amount of commission paid on sales and when it is due.

- Who is responsible for arrangements such as advertising, delivery, installation, repairs, and returns, and paying the cost for all these arrangements.

You may wish to negotiate a sliding-scale commission wherein you receive a different commission dependent upon volume of sales. For instance, if sales exceed a base level, a higher commission rate is applied. You may wish to negotiate three or four different rates depending on the volume of sales.

In the following pages, three businesses have been profiled: (a) antiques and collectibles dealer, (b) arts and crafts consignment shop, and (c) home product sales through multi-level marketing. Examples of other opportunities in products for resale include:

Art broker/gallery	Costume rentals	Household appliances
Balloon decorator	Food products	and gadgets
and delivery	(with long shelf	Limited-edition sales
Books	life)	Office equipment
Car broker	Garage sales	Pet breeding
Children's toys,	Gift basket design	Picture framing
furniture	and delivery	Used books

(a) ANTIQUES AND COLLECTIBLES DEALER

The Concept: There are many people who treasure the charm, beauty, and rarity of antique furniture and ornaments, and who will pay dearly for them. Some people identify with the historical periods which antiques represent, while others appreciate their high investment value. Some antiques may provide a remembrance of special times in a person's life or family heritage. Whatever the reason, there is a high demand for a variety of antiques. Your items may include furniture, clocks, dolls, rare books, household tools, etc. All it takes is a trained eye to spot a genuine bargain at a flea market or auction and then to resell it in an area where there is a high demand. This may mean taking certain items to a different part of your city or province, or even across the country. If demand for certain articles is rising, you may decide to purchase as many as you can and hold onto them until the price and demand has peaked, and therefore be able to command a much higher price. Being an antique dealer is a great way to combine a love of rare and beautiful objects with a money-making venture.

Money Matters: In the antique business, it takes money to make money. To establish an initial inventory of collectibles, you will need to invest from $3,000 to $5,000. Your profit on each item will vary according to how low a price you paid for it and how high you can sell it for. It all depends on the supply and demand. An average markup is 50% to 70%.

Your Background: The essential factor in being successful as an antique dealer is your knowledge of and appreciation for valuable objects. You will need to have the ability to identify a genuine antique when you see one. You may increase your knowledge by studying world history and culture. By talking to antique dealers and attending auctions and flea markets, you can learn much about the business. Subscribe to publications and develop a reference library on antique articles.

What You Will Need: You will, of course, need to have a sufficient amount of space in your home in which to store your collectibles. You will need shelving and display cases, and a small work table where you could do some small repairs, polishing, and refinishing work. A vehicle to haul large items may also be necessary.

The Plan: If you plan to specialize in a particular type of antique or certain era, you may be able to acquire the necessary knowledge to get started fairly quickly. Your study, observation, and knowledge of other types of antiques could develop with more time and experience. By attending antique shops and auctions and searching through guidebooks, you will learn how to value your items. Although the governing principle is supply and demand, the reality is whatever a person is willing to pay for it.

Once you have the ability to identify the features of genuine antiques, you are ready to start collecting. You should attend flea markets, garage sales, second-hand shops, pawn shops, and auctions where you may pick up items at a very low price if the owner is unaware of its true value. Estate and bankruptcy sales can also produce bargains. While there may be some treasured objects for which you will pay a higher price, you should aim to have a minimum markup of 50% to 60%. Also, you should try to turn over your inventory quickly so that your cash investment is not tied up for long periods of time.

The means of selling your antiques may vary. If the zoning in your area permits it, you may have a small retail shop in your home. You may rent a table at an antique show to display and sell your products. Be certain you are skilled at bargaining so you can tread the fine line of maintaining the highest price for an item while not losing the customer. If you have a sufficient inventory, you may decide to hold an auction sale. Be certain those names on your mailing list are qualified buyers of antiques and collectibles. You may have to hire a professional auctioneer and rent suitable space. Or you could offer your products to an auction house where they will advertise and conduct the auction for a percentage of the total sales made.

Associations

Canadian Antique and Fine Arts Society, #406-27 Carlton Street, Toronto, Ont. M4B 1L2.

Canadian Antique Dealers Association, P.O. Box 517, Station K, Toronto, Ont. M4P 2E0.

National Association of Dealers in Antiques, 7080 Old River Road, R.R. 6, Rockford, IL 61103.

Publications

Antiques Magazine. Old Mill Road, P.O. Box 1975, Marion, OH 43306.

The Antique Trader. P.O. Box 1050, Dubuque, IA 52001.

Barlow, Ronald. *How to Be Successful in the Antique Business*. Charles Scribner's Sons, 1983.

Johnson, Bruce. *How to Make up to Twenty Thousand Dollars a Year in Antiques and Collectibles without Leaving Your Job: An Expert Shows How*. New York, NY: Rawson Associates, 1986.

(b) ARTS AND CRAFTS CONSIGNMENT SHOP

The Concept: The fascination with arts and crafts products is a growing trend as they provide uniqueness and personality to a home or office decor. And there are many more people producing such items than there are selling. Many consider their crafts as a hobby rather than a business venture, and therefore are satisfied with receiving a reasonable payment, which in turn buys more supplies for their particular craft. You will earn a percentage of the selling price for displaying and selling the goods. If the goods do not sell, they are returned at no cost to you. You may find it particularly rewarding to run a business where you are meeting the public and providing work for interesting craftspeople.

Money Matters: If you only offer goods on a consignment basis, your investment is minimal. A budget of $500 to $1,000 will cover the cost of some shelving, display tables, an attractive sign, and printed brochures. Since you will receive a percentage of the selling price, you can estimate a 20% to 40% markup.

Your Background: A creative flair for displaying products and some retail experience will help you to maximize your potential sales. You will need to keep careful records of the products, suppliers, sales, and consignment fees paid.

What You Will Need: You will need to ensure that the zoning regulations permit you to have a small retail shop in your home. Ensure that your home insurance coverage is upgraded. Equal in importance is that the location be on a well-travelled route, preferably with walk-by traffic. If your house has an enclosed sun porch that is visible from the street, this may be an ideal location for the shop.

Your window displays will be eyecatching. Your shelving and display tables may be furniture items such as dressers with drawers open and laden with linen products for sale. Check into provincial sales tax requirements to see if you are required to collect and remit tax on the type of products you carry.

The Plan: As with any retail-type business, the three most important considerations are location, location, and location! If your home doesn't meet the zoning regulations, you may search out a rental home that does comply and is in a high-traffic area. Your research may include finding out from craft sale organizers which items are the best sellers on a year-round basis. You can always supplement and decorate with seasonal items, but these have short-term interest. Find out the profile of the typical buyer. For example, you may find that middle-income working women between the ages of 30 and 50 are the customers you are appealing to. This type of information is crucial when choosing your location, marketing tactics, and ancillary products you will carry.

To find craftspeople to make products for you, contact local crafts stores and craft associations, place small ads in local newspapers, or distribute flyers to residential neighbourhoods. You may decide to be specific about the type of products you wish to carry. Meet with each of the artisans to view the quality and attractiveness of their products. Do not accept products which you feel are substandard.

The craftspeople will deliver their products to you during certain hours that you stipulate. Together you decide on a reasonable selling price. Each item will then be tagged with the price and coded to identify the craftsperson and the date the products are delivered. You may set a maximum time limit (three to six months, for example) for displaying items, after which time the craftsperson agrees to pick up unsold items. When an item is sold, you receive a percentage of the sales price and remit the remainder to the craftsperson. Establish the percentage you will receive and set a schedule for paying him or her. You may stipulate that you will not be responsible for stolen items. It's a good idea to have these matters outlined clearly in writing beforehand and given to each craftsperson so that he or she knows and understands your procedures. Have them sign a copy confirming receipt.

Creatively display the products in and on top of dressers, chairs, and tables, taking advantage of every nook and cranny. Ensure that you have some particularly eyecatching items to the right of your entrance-way, as most people are right-eye-dominant and will instinctively work their way around your shop in a counterclockwise fashion. Carry a variety of products in sufficient quantity to fill your shop. Avoid overcrowding, though. A combination of low-, medium-, and high-priced items will ensure that they fit everyone's budget. If you display products unwrapped, your customers will be inclined to touch the fabrics, which may be all that is required to close the sale. Also, a soft perfume scent helps to create a pleasant ambiance.

Associations

Canadian Craft & Hobby Association, #3640-26 Street N.E., Calgary, Alta. TIY 4T7.

Canadian Crafts Council, #16-46 Elgin Street, Ottawa, Ont. KIP 5K6.

Canadian Guild of Crafts, 2025 Peel Street, Montreal, Que. H3A 1T6.

Publications

Craft International. World Crafts Foundation, 247 Center Street, New York, NY 10013 (quarterly).

Craft News. Ontario Crafts Council, 346 Dundas Street W., Toronto, Ont. M5T 1G5 (8 issues per year).

Crafts Plus. Canmar Publications, 130 Spy Court, Markham, Ont. L3R 5H6 (6 issues per year).

Handcrafts Co-op Gallery (Start-up Business Guide No. X1118). Irvine, CA: *Entrepreneur* Magazine.

Hands. Hands Publishing, Box 340, Station L, Toronto, Ont. M6E 4Z2 (6 issues per year).

The Quality Crafts Magazine: The Business Magazine for Craftspeople. National Information Center for Crafts Management and Marketing, 15 W. 44th Street, New York, NY 10036 (quarterly).

Hynes, William G. *Start and Run a Profitable Craft Business.* Vancouver, B.C.: International Self-Counsel Press, 1993.

Jefferson, Brian. *Profitable Crafts Marketing: A Complete Guide to Successful Selling.* Portland, OR: Timber Press, 1985.

Scott, Michael. *The Crafts Business Encyclopedia.* San Diego, CA: Harcourt Brace Jovanovich, 1979.

(c) HOME PRODUCT SALES THROUGH MULTI-LEVEL MARKETING

The Concept: The most well known home product sales companies which have been in the business for several decades are Amway, Fuller Brush, Avon, and Tupperware. Their products range from house cleaners, vitamins and food supplements, and hand and body lotions to airtight food storage containers. You can become a distributor and make money by selling the products to your friends and neighbours. You will earn a percentage of your total sales. In addition, you receive a discount on your own purchases.

A further and even greater source of revenue, though, can be earned by recruiting additional salespeople. In this *multi-level marketing* concept, the salespeople that you recruit report to you in the sales structure. They in turn can recruit salespeople to report to them.

You would receive a commission on the sales made by those you have recruited, and receive a (lesser) commission on the sales made by their people. If there are a sufficient number of enthusiastic people within your sales structure, you can earn a substantial amount from the commission on total sales. Therefore, you would spend less time selling products and more time motivating your sales force. The most successful salespeople advance in the firm, and supervise large territories of sales representatives. Handsome commissions and benefits are earned at this level. A word of caution: Make sure that the multi-level marketing business concept and operation conform with provincial and federal legislation.

Money Matters: A modest amount of approximately $100 may be required for your starter kit of products and/or the training program. (Beware of any firm that demands a substantial investment at the outset.) Your earning potential is unlimited if you approach your selling vigorously. You can double and triple your earnings by recruiting other salespeople who will earn commissions for you based on their sales volumes.

Your Background: The ability to sell will come easily if you have a pleasant, outgoing personality and enthusiasm for and belief in the product. You must be willing to constantly approach people with a sales pitch. Don't be afraid to develop your own selling style. It is likely to be far more effective than trying to mimic your sales instructor's antics.

What You Will Need: You will need an automobile to pick up and deliver products to customers' homes. A fold-up luggage cart will be useful when transporting large amounts of products to people's homes for demonstrations.

The Plan: Through your local telephone book or library you will find the phone numbers for a local representative of the major home product sales companies. Talk to the district manager to find out how to get started, what commissions you can expect, and the sales potential. While each company will vary, you will want to know what sales training is provided, the cost (if any) of a starter kit of sample products, ordering procedures, and their sales incentive programs. Before making any investment, compare these features with those of other companies. Especially if it is your plan to participate in the multi-level marketing concept by recruiting salespeople, compare the incentive programs and commission structures to identify the most lucrative arrangement.

Once you have made your decision and you have been given the introductory course, the rest is up to you. You have to go out and drum up sales. Your options will include telephone and door-to-door sales (often called "cold calls") and home parties. Many salespeople find home parries more relaxing with better results. To hold a home party, you would ask a potential customer to host a product demonstration. That person would invite eight to ten friends and neighbours to his or her home and provide refreshments to the invited guests. In return, you would present the host with a gift from your product selection. After your presentation of the products, during which you have given examples for their multiple uses, you distribute order sheets to each of the guests. The host usually earns an extra gift if the sales exceed a certain amount.

If you keep good records of all your customers and their preferred products, you can make repeat sales by staying in contact with them. Put their names on your mailing list to regularly receive a catalogue or announcement of new products. You can do much of the work at home, although you will have to make some deliveries. In this type of business you can put in as many or as few hours as you wish.

Associations
Direct Sellers Association, 4950 Yonge Street, 14th Floor, North York, Ont. M2N 6K1.

Publications

How to Develop Multilevel Marketing Sales (Start-up Business Guide No. X1222). Irvine, CA: Entrepreneur Magazine.

Bohigian, Valerie. *How to Make Your Home-Based Business-Grow: Turning Products into Profits*. New York, NY: New American Library, 1984.

Hutton, Shirley and Constance Deswaan. *Pay Yourself What You're Worth: How to Make Terrific Money in Direct Sales*. New York, NY: Bantam, 1983.

Hyatt, Carole. *The Woman's Selling Game: How to Sell Yourself and Anything Else*. New York, NY: Warner Books, 1988.

Scott, Gini Graham. *Get Rich through Multi-Level Selling*. Vancouver, B.C.: International Self-Counsel Press, 1989.

SECTION THREE

PROFILES OF SUCCESSFUL HOME-BASED BUSINESS OWNERS

It has been said, "A prudent person learns from personal experience, a wise one from the experience of others." In this section we profile 27 successful home-based business owners from across Canada to bring you their insights, experiences, challenges, and advice. They are listed below alphabetically by type of business.

Some of those profiled eventually intend to move their businesses out of their homes, many do not, and some already have. Those who have moved out were already operating a viable business out of their homes before doing so. Their comments are included to show their retrospective thoughts on their home-based experience and their reasons for relocating their operations.

At this point you may already know what type of business you wish to start. Nevertheless, we suggest that you read all the profiles, because many of the suggestions are transferable to any type of business operation. The energy, enthusiasm, and commitment expressed by these entrepreneurs toward their businesses are a source of encouragement and inspiration. The profiles also show the innovative attitudes and diversity of enterprises by Canadians, regardless of the size or geographic location of the community.

PROFILES PRESENTED IN THIS SECTION

Nature of Business	Owner(s)	Location
Bakery and Bed and Breakfast Inn	Peter & Candice Sotropa	Pangman, Sask.
Broker — Printing and Stationery	Debbie Nider	Yellowknife, N.W.T.
Business Services	Barbara Moyle	Whitehorse, Y.T.

Nature of Business	Owner(s)	Location
Business Training and Management Consulting	Gordon Cameron	Amherst, N.S.
Candy-Making	Priscilla Pollock	Summerside, P.E.I.
Catering	Cindy Boffey	Olds, Alta.
Christmas Craft Business	Karen Booy	Matsqui, B.C.
Delivery Service	Les & Frances Warren Quentin & Shirley Warren	Prince Albert, Sask.
Editing/Publishing	Lesley Wyle	Toronto, Ont.
Fashion Design	Michèle Houle	Laval, Que.
Film Production	Alan Booth	Yellowknife, N.W.T.
Health Care	Bev & George McMaster	Brandon, Man.
Home Inspection	Ralph Braun	Sidney, B.C.
Importing	Michele de Gendt	Toronto, Ont.
Landscaping	Randy & Rachael Lewis	Whitehorse, Y.T.
Manufacturing Airfield Signs	Charlene Davis	Edmonton, Alta.
Manufacturing Children's Clothing	Cindy & Ralph Eeson	Calgary, Alta.
Manufacturing Glass Products	E. Jane Midgley	Maple Ridge, B.C.
Pottery	Marlene Penner Poole	Corner Brook, Nfld.
Pre-Kindergarten Instruction	Thérèse Naggar	Chateauguay, Que.
Processing Ocean Sediments	Ron Sampson	Winslow, P.E.I.
Sewing	Karen Wiebe	Manitou, Man.
Tent Rentals	David H. Nelson	Dugald, Man.
Tours and Convention Services	Regina McCarthy	Conception Bay, Nfld.
Translating and Consulting	Brigitte Bryant	Waterloo, Ont./ Hudson, Que.
Woodworking	Ross Phinney	St. John, N.B.
Writing	Jane Widerman	Toronto, Ont.

BAKERY AND BED AND BREAKFAST INN

Owners:　　　　　Peter and Candice Sotropa
Company Name:　Harvest Pie Co. Ltd.
Location:　　　　Pangman, Saskatchewan
In Business:　　8 Years

After moving to a large, new 4,600-square-foot home on 17 acres of forested land, Candice was looking for something new to do at home in her pleasant surroundings. She and her husband had previously owned several businesses, including a restaurant. When presented with an offer to purchase 800 pounds of Saskatoon berries, Candice quickly recognized a business opportunity that she could operate from her home. "My pies were enjoyed when I had owned a restaurant, so that was the natural thing to do." The Harvest Pie Co. Ltd. was launched.

The company markets frozen wild berry pies and wild Saskatoon jams, marmalades, and sauces made from blueberries and cranberries. These products are sold to restaurants, service clubs, conventions, and the general public throughout the province. The business soon will be too large to operate from Candice's kitchen, so a 20-foot by 36-foot garage is being remodelled into a processing kitchen.

When her daughter left home to attend university, another business opportunity arose. Candice converted the extra room into a guest room and started providing bed and breakfast services to tourists wanting a farm vacation. In addition, her guests like to buy her food products as souvenirs of their stay. The marketing techniques she uses includes brochures, packaging, signage, direct mail, media interviews, and word of mouth.

Candice admits that she had the necessary background to prepare her for this business. She had had previous experience in the food service industry, had been in various businesses since 1968, and possessed teaching experience that helped her in dealing with people. Her husband set up her first accounts, and the provincial government offices (the Department of Small Business and Tourism, the Buy Saskatchewan Agency, and the Department of Agriculture) assisted with marketing and sourcing raw materials.

What factors are critical to your success? I enjoy working at home. The business I chose involves work I know well and have always enjoyed. The whole family enjoys the work and participates.

What would you do differently if staring over? I would approach government agencies sooner. There is much helpful research available. Also, I would abandon the "cottage industry" idea sooner. If you think small, you stay small!

What words of advice would you offer to someone starting a home-based business? Have interests outside of the home. Everyone has to get away from the business from time to time. Pick work you enjoy, as you can't go home at night to get away from it. Have the backing of the entire family, since everyone will be immersed in the work. You have to exude confidence in yourself and your product when marketing. You need to be able to understand and communicate with all kinds of people. Understanding the ups and downs of business is also necessary.

BROKER – PRINTING AND STATIONERY

Owner: Debbie Nider
Company Name: The Invitation House
Location: Yellowknife, N.W.T.
In Business: 13 Years

When the Nider family moved to Yellowknife, Debbie started looking for something she could do on a part-time basis at home while minding her two young children, and would help her get to know the people in her new community. She soon realized there was a need in the area for someone to sell wedding invitations and related products. She and her husband had previously operated a similar business in Vancouver, so she knew what was required. The Invitation House commenced operations as a retail printing and stationery broker for the Territories. Wedding stationery and accessories (matches, napkins, plume pens) are sold by catalogue, although some items are stocked. Other products include advertising specialties (pens, balloons, pins, decals), stationery, bulk paper and envelope supplies, letterheads, and business cards. They also handle custom printing orders. While she advertises her products by direct mail, mail order, media ads, and signage, Debbie finds that word of mouth is the most effective marketing strategy, followed by mail order for out-of-town business.

Debbie speaks highly of the support and understanding she receives from her husband and children. In addition they help her in the business during busy times, at trade shows, and with the pricing of products.

What factors do you feel are critical to your business success? I gained the necessary background experience with our Vancouver home-based business. I knew the products and suppliers and what they would and would not do on special orders. I had attended trade shows and talked to people in the industry. My research was current. Most importantly, there was a need for my service and my first customers were pleased with my work. They helped to spread the word. I have good communication and social skills, and am confident talking with people. My prices are reasonable, and I keep evening hours, which is more convenient for some of my customers.

What would you do differently if starting over again? In hindsight I wish that I had organized my accounting on a computer system right from the start. If/when we move, I would try to have a separate business entrance and storage area, which would be more convenient when receiving deliveries from suppliers.

What words of advice would you offer to someone starting out in business? Develop slowly and expand only as fast as you can comfortably. Have the support of your family. If they aren't willing to experience some inconveniences, it'll be an uphill battle! Have a business plan. Know where you want your business to go. Should it stay a home-based business, or do you want to expand to commercial space? Don't be afraid to ask questions of your customers; check out information with them.

BUSINESS SERVICES

Owner:	Barbara Moyle
Company Name:	Barbara Moyle Business Services
Location:	Whitehorse, Yukon
In Business:	2 Years

Barbara's background experience provided everything she needed to start up her business which offers conference and event organizing, training, bookkeeping, and word-processing services to local businesses in Whitehorse. It was primarily through her one and one-half years as Manager of the Yukon Chamber of Commerce that she identified the market need for her business. Her experience provided an overall awareness of what services were not being offered, what the local business community needed and, most importantly, a wide network of important contacts. She had previously held training and management positions, and handled the bookkeeping aspects for a business she and her husband owned. She says that she likes and relates well to people, has a sense of humour, and pushes herself to do new things.

As her children were getting older (ages 8 and 10), Barbara found that she had more time and flexibility. Operating a service from her home still allowed her to be available to her children and kept her start-up and overhead costs low. Her children occasionally assist her with small tasks which save her time. She found it easy to obtain a business licence for her type of home-based business. Barbara doesn't need to use conventional means of advertising her business because her networking and word-of-mouth referrals are so effective.

After two years of operating from the "kitchen table," she is planning to renovate her home to better suit her business. She is looking forward to improving her workspace, which will enhance her time management and organization. She enjoys having the house to herself during the daytime, and sometimes uses the answering machine to screen calls in order to protect her from interruptions.

What challenges have you encountered in your business growth? Separating work and family at times is difficult. I need to set clear boundaries around my workday, both for myself and for my clients. Setting priorities and keeping to a schedule is always a challenge. I now also need to be more selective on the type of work I accept, instead of being so diversified.

What factors are critical to your business success? Having made many business contacts while in my highly visible position as manager of the Chamber was instrumental. I have continued to expand my network as a member of the Chamber of Commerce and the Women's Business Network. Conference organizing exposes me to many different people who see first-hand the quality of my work. I have received a lot of positive feedback from my business associates. I receive encouragement and support from my family, especially my husband who is my "sounding board."

What words of advice would you offer to someone starting out in business?   Focus your business; don't be all over the map! Set clear boundaries for your home and work life, and set up a proper workspace with the equipment and materials you need to operate efficiently.

BUSINESS TRAINING AND MANAGEMENT CONSULTING

Owner: Gordon Cameron
Company Name: Gordon Cameron & Associates Inc.
Location: Amherst, Nova Scotia
In Business: 6 Years

While he has operated two other businesses, Gordon says this one was not planned, but "happened by accident." For years he had been offering sound, profitable advice to his customers for free. After giving a client an idea that could have increased his profits by $25,000 a year, Gordon decided to start charging for his "consulting" services. Three years later he started teaching a small business management course in Amherst which opened up a new source of client contacts. Gordon says his lucky break came when he was asked by the Cumberland Development Authority to serve as a consultant to a committee to help businesses in crisis. Within a year he had become very busy and saw the potential need and opportunity in the marketplace. The company employs two full-time consultants who work as a team in meeting a variety of client needs under the umbrella of business training and management consulting. The company's mission is "to develop successful people and businesses." It also services local and provincial government departments, entrepreneurs, managers, and employees.

Gordon says, "I love this work; every day is a challenge and something new! All my life I have gained experiences and skills which I am utilizing to their fullest. My past activities which have been beneficial to me in business include my involvement as a youth group leader, toastmaster, volunteer teacher, coordinator of conferences, director of conferences, member of groups, clubs and their executives. My love for case-study problems in business courses at university, and for the businesses I have operated, have all led me to this point."

Gordon says the office occupies virtually all of his basement, which is becoming cramped with a large library of resource books, files, and office equipment. He says working from home keeps the overhead costs low and allows for ease of access when working evenings and weekends. A training room in an office complex is rented as required. When Gordon's wife is not working in her own retail business, she assists as a proofreader, sounding board, and counsellor. "She is level-headed, exudes common sense and is a big asset to the firm." His 12- and 13-year old children assist with some of the clerical work. His son enjoys having easy access to the computers for games and desktop publishing technology for preparing "awesome" school projects! Being able to balance home and business life is a challenge Gordon says he needs to work on.

What challenges did you encounter in your business growth? Initially we found that the "local" flavour of our business was an obstacle to our growth. It was a Catch 22. When competing for business outside the local area, potential clients wanted references of work done locally. However, in the local market the attitude prevailed, "If it's local, it cannot be any good." Until we had done work outside the area, it was difficult to be recognized locally. It was the credibility we earned through teaching and working for the Cumberland Development Authority and associated agencies that helped us to establish our reputation for top-quality work. This has resulted in business, both locally and regionally.

What factors are critical to your business success? The desire and commitment to provide "phenomenal" customer service and market our firm every opportunity we have. Continuous improvement is fundamental to our long-term success. We provide a written money-back guarantee to our clients if they are not completely satisfied. (No one has ever wanted to collect on it.) We also invest heavily in our own professional development, plus having the fastest and latest technology to assist our work. When all you have to sell is time, time is money. Perhaps most of all, working with my father for 12 years provided me with the understanding of people and the ability to work through any and all situations. I watched and learned from a real "pro."

What advice would you offer to someone starting out in business? Buy the best technology they can afford. This means computers, faxes, laser printers, and copiers. Our business is value-added. Initial presentation and impact is vital. Regardless of the insightful content, poor first impressions are difficult to overcome.

CANDY-MAKING

Owner:	Priscilla Pollock
Company Name:	Cilla's Homemade Chocolates
Location:	Summerside, Prince Edward Island
In Business:	12 Years

With five young children, Priscilla wanted to find something to do at home to supplement the family income. She liked the challenge that operating a small business offered. It was a natural decision for her, since both she and her husband came from family business backgrounds. Priscilla's previous work selling Avon products gave her the sales and customer service experience that she needed. Doing the bookkeeping for her husband's business provided her an inside awareness of the financial bottom-line. Since she enjoyed working with her hands, she decided to start a candy-making shop. She took a course on making chocolates and set out to turn her family kitchen into a chocolate factory. "In this line of work you have to be creative, artistic, and fast with your hands because the work is all hand-done." The chocolates are made with the finest of pure milk — white and dark chocolate. Other products include peanut brittle, fudge, and cakes for birthdays and special occasions, and are sold locally to over 80 retail and wholesale outlets. Telemarketing, media advertising and interviews, signage, packaging, and word-of-mouth advertising are techniques she uses to market her business.

After having the business in her home for five years, limited space became a problem. She moved Cilla's Homemade Chocolates to a store outlet in the lane of their property. In this way she was still within close proximity of her children. This move has increased the number of her customers. They enjoy coming into the shop and watching them make the chocolates. Priscilla does recognize, though, that her overhead has increased substantially and wishes that she had assessed this more closely beforehand. "When I was working from my house I made chocolates whenever I needed to. If something came up and I had to leave, I would just leave. Now that I have a store open seven days a week, though, it is a lot different. I have to have someone there all the time."

What factors do you feel are critical to your business success? I believe my perseverance has really paid off. I have great children and a husband who is a big help and supports me 100%. By having my business in the home, I was able to involve the whole family. I've shared with them the good as well as the bad news about the business. My children help with labelling bags, and my daughter makes chocolates along with me after school and on weekends. The community support and government assistance that I received when I was starting out was an important factor for me.

What challenges did you encounter in your business growth? It is hard to fit everything into a day — being a mother of five children, a wife, and a bookkeeper for my husband's business, besides making and selling the chocolates to stores. But I really enjoy all the things that I do. I find it very hard to find, screen, train, and keep staff. It seems that they only want to work for 10 weeks and then they leave. But I have one person who has been with me for almost two years, and she is doing really well.

What words of advice would you offer to someone starting out in business? Don't start unless you have the support of your family. Make sure you can deal with the ups and downs, because there are a lot of them. Be certain what you are doing is something that you intend to stick with.

CATERING

Owner:	Cindy Boffey
Company Name:	Catering by Granny Jacks
Location:	Olds, Alberta
In Business:	10 Years

Cindy says it was her mother's and her sister's wish as well as her own to operate a family gourmet catering business. That and a "sheer pleasure for cooking" motivated her to start. Cindy had taken professional cooking training in vocational school and apprenticed after leaving her studies. She enjoys testing new recipes and recreating original recipes. Cindy takes pride in her ability to present food in an artistic manner. She uses fancy serving dishes and tries to maintain a touch of class while keeping the food homemade. She says that eye appeal is as important as the quality of the food.

The decision to operate from home was a deliberate one in order to keep the business small and personal. And it was convenient. Within three years the business had grown so much, though, that it was no longer practical to do the cooking in her home. A separate building was built on their property which housed a commercial kitchen. This also satisfied local regulations which required the cooking to be done in commercial facilities. Cindy says that "the business keeps growing and people keep stretching our capabilities." Word of mouth is her best method of advertising. She leaves business cards on the buffet tables she sets to help spread the word. At present she employs two full-time and 10 part-time workers in the business to provide services throughout the region.

What factors are critical to your business success?   I believe it is the homemade flavour of our food and the manner of presentation which has helped us to grow quickly. Our personal touch and willingness to adapt to our customers' needs is also important.

What assistance did you receive in your business startup?   We received a lot of family assistance which was invaluable when starting out and funds were low. My husband and children often help me in the business. When we expanded we got assistance from a bank, and then things became much easier in the larger facility.

What words of advice would you offer to someone starting out in business?   Do your research. Check your area and see what type of catering might be in demand. Check with health officials regarding any regulations that have to be followed. Probably one of the biggest problems we faced when in our homes was cleaning up all the china dishes, cutlery, etc. There was always an immense amount of dishes and nowhere to do them!

CHRISTMAS CRAFT BUSINESS

Owner: Karen Booy
Company Name: Country Keepsakes
Location: Matsqui, B.C.
In Business: 8 Years

Karen's business was born out of a love of Christmas, her enjoyment in making handcrafted Christmas ornaments, and the encouragement of her friends and family to sell her crafts. Since she was approaching "burnout" as a dental hygienist, Karen decided to invest her full-time efforts into making crafts. She found this to be both therapeutic and profitable. Although the crafts were labour-intensive, she found that they could be sold at a reasonable price and still generate a profit.

Working from home allowed her to pick the hours she wished to work, involve her family in the business and save on unnecessary overhead costs. She mass-produced her crafts and sold them to 30 giftware stores within the region. When she could no longer keep up with demand, Karen started sub-contracting work to six other people. However, Karen says, "this turned into a nightmare — costs went through the roof, supply waste increased and, worst of all, the product quality suffered." She now subcontracts to only one other person who does the work of six people with incredible attention to detail. Karen does all the finishing which provides the quality control, and concentrates on selling her products at the prestigious Circle Craft Christmas Market in Vancouver and at her annual Open House in Matsqui.

Country Keepsakes actually was a springboard for a number of other related businesses which Karen now operates. She publishes West Coast *Craftlink*, a quarterly newsletter for professional crafters mailed to over 3,000 subscribers. In addition, she is an author, speaker, teacher, and pattern designer and publisher. Fortunately Karen says she has a very supportive and understanding husband who runs his own business, a 20-acre dairy farm. She says she's learned to set time aside for personal as well as business goals.

What would you do differently if starting over? I would have concentrated my efforts on the 20% of the stores which were my best customers and let go of the rest.

What words of advice would you offer to someone starting out in a craft business? Use the best quality supplies and equipment you can possibly afford. Realize that to get the optimum price you may have to travel to a different market outside your community. Strive to improve your skills, read, take classes and keep learning.

DELIVERY SERVICE

Owners:	Les and Frances Warren, Quentin and Shirley Warren
Company Name:	Warren's Parcel Express Inc.
Location:	Prince Albert, Saskatchewan
In Business:	14 Years

Faced with the news that his employer was going out of business, Les decided to turn his job as a taxi-cab driver into one of self-employment as a courier driver. He realized that no one offered local deliveries as well as provincial and national deliveries, and decided to seize the opportunity to offer a complete courier/delivery service for businesses in the area. Les enlisted his wife, son and daughter-in-law. Since all had a very hard-working family background, and most of their previous years of work were spent dealing with the public, they were confident in their approach to the new venture. Their decision to set up the business office in the basement of their home was initially for budgetary reasons. However, after 14 years, they still have no plans to relocate the business. Les says, "The space is adequate and serves our purpose. As we do not offer storage of goods, and deal only in pickup and delivery of goods, we don't feel a need to have a store-front business."

The four family members now have three full-time employees and an accountant who does the year-end bookkeeping and financial statements. The locally-owned courier business is an agent for Motopak, Tiger Courier and Star Phoenix. Local deliveries accounts for 70% of the business, while provincial and national deliveries makes up 25% and 5%, respectively. They say that being well-known in the community and accepting advice/criticism from other local business people were factors that made a considerable difference in the growth and development of their business. "Our business strives upon courteous and dependable service." Having a good credit rating at the financial and banking institutions helped us in securing a business line of credit.

What challenges did you encounter in your business growth? The competition would frequently under-bid in pricing of deliveries. We overcame this by making the customer aware that the quality of service would considerably outweigh the cost. Our children are young and require a great deal more of our time. There seems to be not enough hours in the day to squeeze everything in. Occasionally we have a day to ourselves and do what we want, and those days make it all worthwhile.

What would you do differently if starting over again? We would have a better liaison between employer-employee-customer. It is important to get feedback from the customers about our employees before they quit or we let them go. Improved communication with our customers about our overall service would help us to ensure our quality standards are being met.

What factors do you feel are critical to your business success? We always find time to deal with customers, whether it is for a compliment or a complaint. Having solid business ethics such as that your word and honour are equal to your signature on a contract is critical. Treating everyone fairly, and keeping in mind that a small account today could prosper into a larger account in the future, or generate more business through his network of business contacts. Having four people in the business giving their own opinions on business matters assists with effective decision-making which has seldom failed us. Each of us has separate duties, and we meet to discuss all major decisions. We keep our minds open to new techniques to help improve the business.

What advice would you offer to someone starting out in business? You must enjoy your line of business. Never follow a trend or enter a trade just because you think it might be a money-maker. And don't overlook the importance of good customer relations.

EDITING / PUBLISHING

Owner: Lesley Wyle
Company Name: Lifestories
Location: Toronto, Ontario
In Business: 6½ Years

The desire to be in business for herself and a love of books were Lesley's motivating factors to start Lifestories, a company that provides a comprehensive service for individuals who wish to write and publish their memoirs.

Having sensed a growing trend among her senior friends to talk nostalgically about the past, usually comparing today's attitudes and lifestyle with those that prevailed when they were young, Lesley realized that there was a demand for this type of service. Although a few have succeeded to get their stories down on paper, many more abandoned the task at the halfway mark because they found it too overwhelming.

After doing some in-depth research and a market analysis, Lesley was able to identify the basic reasons why people want to write their autobiographies: strong family and personal pride, a keen sense of history, and a desire to respond to the requests of adult children, in search of their roots, to have chronicles of their parents' lives, including meaningful anecdotes about other family members.

Lifestories has developed and tested a unique method that makes writing an autobiography and/or a family history an enjoyable experience. After the manuscript has been professionally edited, printed, and attractively bound, the finished book is privately published as a limited edition for distribution to family members and friends.

Lesley is a professional book editor who has worked for a number of prominent Canadian publishers, and has authored four non-fiction works. Apart from hiring competent freelancers to interview her prospective "authors," she handles all the editorial work and supervises the production of each book from start to finish. To promote Lifestories, she does some media advertising, as well as extensive P.R. work that includes speaking engagements and the distribution of brochures and flyers to special-interest groups. However, she has found that word-of-mouth referrals are still the most effective means of obtaining new contracts.

To work from home was an easy decision for Lesley, as she had an extra room in her house that could be converted into an office. Customers are met there or in their own homes.

What provided you with the confidence to start your own business? A thorough knowledge of book publishing, editorial work, and production procedures. The ability to establish and maintain good rapport with clients and to gauge their special needs, enables me to turn an often "raw" manuscript into a very readable piece of writing, all the while preserving my author's unique personality as the central character of his/her personal story.

What challenges did you encounter in your business growth? Since Lifestories' print runs usually are much smaller than those for commercial books, it was not easy to find typesetters, printers, and bookbinders who were willing to handle small quantities, often as low as 15 books. I now work with a group of very competent people who, having recognized the uniqueness of my enterprise, gladly assist me in turning out a first-class product.

What words of advice would you offer to someone starting out in business? Thoroughly research your market beforehand, and make sure you are really familiar with the techniques required to do a good job. Have sufficient capital available to pay for startup costs, including funds for printing stationery, advertising matter, etc. Make sure that those who share your home wholeheartedly support your endeavour. Establish a routine that does not interfere with their inherent rights. Since considerable discipline is required to work at home, politely discourage friends and family members from telephoning or visiting during office hours.

FASHION DESIGN

Owner:	Michèle Houle
Company Name:	Créations Michèle Houle Enr.
Location:	Montreal, Quebec
In Business:	6 Years

Encouraged by the praise she received for her designs, Michèle decided to turn her hobby into a fashion design business. Like many others, she was motivated by the desire to own and manage her own business. Créations Michèle Houle Enr. designs and manufactures exclusive prestige knits. All designs are hand-knitted and blended with an array of different fibres and textures such as feathers, leather, rhinestones, etc. Exclusivity is assured through originality and limited quantifies of each design and colour. She promotes her products throughout Quebec through the use of media advertising and interviews. She provides a sample photo album of her line of clothing to those who purchase from her collection. This is much appreciated and has helped to generate tremendous interest in her collection. Michèle makes a point of personally visiting potential customers to discuss their needs. She employs pieceworkers to assist with her products, and gets help from family members on a part-time basis.

Michèle started her business at home because of limited cash flow, but hopes to expand into larger facilities. This will allow her to regroup all aspects of the operation under the same roof. She says that her husband has been most supportive, and has made the transition between the working and the home environment easier. She says, "Space management is critical. We've had to make adjustments to be able to live in our intimate corners! My daughter, who is nine years old, has been very helpful and understanding. In retrospect, I feel fortunate to have taken my time in getting started. I feel that I needed that time to mature and understand the business before expanding."

What provided you with the confidence to start your business? It takes a tremendous amount of imagination to be able to meet the fashion needs of today's men and women without focussing on any one particular tendency. One of my major attributes is the ability to compose a look and create my own fashion statement. For the last 10 years I've been involved in fashion. I've managed clothing boutiques and have established many business contacts within the industry! It has given me the drive and perseverance to become a success story in this industry! I feel my success is owed to the originality of my product, its quality, and the service rendered.

What challenges did you encounter in your business growth? Limited cash was a major obstacle. This was alleviated when a bank finally approved a credit line for me, which was more practical than a loan. In addition, a friend provided me a personal loan. Also, I was able to obtain government subsidies through "Le Centre entreprise jeunesse," whose mandate it is to help young entrepreneurs.

What words of advice would you offer to someone starting out in business?   Be disciplined. Avoid the temptation to be lazy when you are at home working by yourself. Be professional. Demonstrate that although your business is home-based, your product and/or service is of high quality. Have the desire to succeed.

FILM PRODUCTION

Owner: Alan Booth
Company Name: Yellowknife Films Ltd.
Location: Yellowknife, N.W.T.
In Business: 12 Years

Alan says that he has had a lifelong interest in filmmaking and photography. He was inspired by the vast and rugged landscape of Great
Slave Lake, where he once spent three summers in commercial
fishing. From his experience, he developed a desire to communicate
to others through film the frontier-style way of life in the North. At
age 30, with a diploma in filmmaking and an independent entrepreneurial spirit, he launched Yellowknife Films in 1981. He admits
that at times he wished he had started earlier.

The company's primary business activity is motion picture and
video production which includes documentaries for broadcast, com-
mercials, public relations films, career and information videos, and
slide shows. His main interests are documentary and dramatic films.
Alan's company has received many national and international
awards. Many of the film programs he has produced have been seen
on television throughout the world. Because of the high cost of office
space in Yellowknife, he decided to start the business at home. In so
doing, he was also able to take care of his young child at the same
time. He was able to do the consulting and editing aspects in his
home, and most of the filming was done on location. He kept his
overhead low, bought only what he needed to achieve his goals, and
did most of the work himself where possible. He saved money by
paying cash for quality used equipment. He says that flexibility and
versatility allowed him to change with the market. After four years
and a move to a smaller house, the workload had increased suffi-
ciently to warrant a move to larger, rented premises. Also, more
space was needed to accommodate client visits and some freelance
workers.

Eight years later, he is now moving back to a home occupancy in a
commercially zoned five-level building. The top two levels will be his
home and the bottom three will be for office and editing purposes, as
well as warehousing. The move is intended to keep all costs down as
much as possible.

What challenges did you encounter in your business growth?
The N.W.T. did not have a large market for film production. The
government did not and still does not have a film production fund like
most provinces. I had to do a lot of work to develop the market by
educating prospective clients and by producing a high-quality prod-

uct. Being far from the centre of the filmmaking industry, I had to be self-sufficient until I could train freelancers to assist me. It was difficult to maintain liaisons with southern lab and video post-production houses. At times I would fly thousands of miles to meet my clients in person so that I could establish a solid working relationship. Southern sources of funding such as the National Film Board, Supply and Services Canada, and Broadcasters had not been aware of my skills and services due to my remote location. I had to increase my presence by keeping these parties informed of my activities. In addition, I have completed many projects internationally for clients, as well as doing co-productions to provide a larger resource base, and to compete for larger projects.

What assistance did you receive in your business startup? I owe my start to CBC North which had the funding to enter into co-productions with private-sector producers. The government of the N.W.T. contracted with me to produce the high-profile feature film presentation in the N.W.T. Pavilion at Expo '86 in Vancouver. The film and pavilion were very well received. Employment and Immigration has helped me train people, the Canada Council has helped me to develop my craft, and the government of the N.W.T. has helped me through their Northern Preference Policy.

What advice would you offer to someone starting out in business? Make quality the first priority. A product that is poorly made doesn't help business and says very little for Canadians' ability to compete in a world market. Listen to your banker. Bankers will give you free advice and because they are on the conservative side, they can keep you out of trouble. Try to enjoy your work and your clients. A good attitude goes a long way on the road to success.

HEALTH CARE

Owners: Bev and George McMaster
Company Name: We Care HomeHealth Services
Location: Brandon, Manitoba
In Business: 10 Years

We Care HomeHealth Services was founded in Brandon, Manitoba, in 1984 by Bev and George McMaster. At the time, Bev was a nurse at Brandon General Hospital, and George was a Doctor of Computer Science in systems analysis at Brandon University. Their four boys were doing well in school, were actively involved in the community and high school sports, and were supportive of the new venture.

While visiting the dying father of a close friend, Bev was disturbed that excellent health care was not available to the man on his own terms: a person to clean his home once a week; a nurse to come in several times a day to administer medications; someone he could call at any time when he needed help or advice. The motivation to create We Care was born.

We Care would become the extended family to those in need. Bev made the operations side of the business fly, with business and health-care contacts, hiring staff and operating the business. George created the computer, management, marketing and training systems to make it run. Soon a complete system was created so that people anywhere could obtain care and support that was of the highest quality every time.

From their home, the McMasters managed the nurses, caregivers, and home-cleaning staff that were We Care's employees. The major hurdle at this point in time was to educate people on a new concept and attitude in health care. After eight months, it became more and more difficult to work at home due to the coming and going of numerous employees, so they moved into a rented office and hired office staff.

Since that time, the company has expanded throughout Canada utilizing franchising as a vehicle, and now has 28 franchise offices in cities in Ontario, Manitoba, Saskatchewan, Alberta, and British Columbia. We Care is now expanding into the Maritimes and the United States. We Care now employs 3,000 people — both full and part-time across Canada.

We Care uses brochures, direct mail, telemarketing, radio, word-of-mouth, media advertising, a national newspaper that they publish, and corporate marketing firms to market the business.

What factors are critical to business success? To be successful, we had to be totally focused and committed to the business and to work long hard hours and to never give up. Being determined and persistent is the bottom-line. You have to be enthusiastic and have a positive attitude and be convinced that in every difficulty lies the seed of an equal or a greater opportunity. We are committed to innovation and to providing the highest quality service. We have had an excellent board of directors that provided timely advice, and consulting firms such as Management 2000, and Diversa Group that offered sound advice at critical stages. We were fortunate to have available, both business and academic advisors of the highest quality at all times. The book *Beneath the Golden Arches* provides an excellent blueprint for any new business that wishes to do well.

What assistance did you receive in your business startup? We did not receive any financial assistance. We attended FDBD courses, attended seminars offered by consulting companies, and worked on a network of supportive advisors.

What words of advice would you offer to someone starting in business? Have a vision that you passionately believe in, keep a low overhead, seek advice and the support of others, have a lot of personal energy, take care of your health, and constantly learn by reading, listening to tapes, attending seminars, and from your network of advisors. Surround yourself with people who have complementary strengths.

HOME INSPECTION

Owner: Ralph Braun
Company Name: AmeriSpec Home Inspection Services
Location: Sidney, British Columbia
In Business: 2 Years

After being in the construction industry for 20 years, Ralph was ready for a change and a new challenge. He had been monitoring the home inspection business over the previous eight years and, with the changes happening in the real estate industry, he knew the timing was ideal. His background as a carpenter, carpenter foreman and superintendent provided him with a solid foundation and perspective on which to base his new business. Ralph researched the industry and decided to buy an AmeriSpec franchise, with over 160 offices throughout North America. He says an average inspection takes two hours which involves a thorough visual inspection of the property including the heating, plumbing, and electrical systems. The findings of the inspection are then conveyed to the prospective purchaser in verbal and written form. He feels that such disclosure of the true condition of the property is an essential part of the real estate transaction and protects the prospective purchaser, the vendor, and the realtor.

Ralph and his wife work full-time in the business. Operating it out of their home has not presented any complications as it requires minimal space, and all clients are met on the inspection site. Because of the low overhead, money is instead directed into marketing to generate additional business. While they actively network and use signs, brochures and direct mail to promote the business, word-of-mouth referrals are their most effective vehicle. Ralph admits that, "At first I was not used to marketing and public speaking, so my initial meetings and presentations to realtors and office managers were rough. But with time and additional product knowledge, the marketing has become easier."

What type of assistance did you receive in your business start-up? We have received a multitude of assistance from the franchise organization, from initial set up through to the day-to-day operation. They assist with inherent problems and questions which arise as part of the business. The extensive resources available through the organization far exceed that which would be available to an individual.

What factors do you feel are critical to your business success? My knowledge of the industry and ability to communicate well with clients, as well as my drive to continuously expand the business and refine the product. Having become involved with a franchise operation has probably been the most critical key to our growing success. In addition to the initial set up and outline of business operation, the support marketing programs and technical up-dating have helped us to double our sales over this same time last year. Being associated with the largest home inspection company in North America has enhanced our corporate image.

What advice would you offer to someone starting out in business? Do your homework first. Know your market and its growth potential. Research your competition. Most of all, research the opportunities available through franchise organizations.

IMPORTING

Owner:	Michèle de Gendt
Company Name:	EURIMPEX
Location:	Toronto, Ontario
In Business:	1 Year

On several trips to Canada to visit family, Michèle became aware of opportunities for importing high-quality European products. She recognized that there was a lack of knowledge and initiative on the part of European manufacturers, who are often intimidated by the North American market. The personal challenge and desire for independence in business motivated her to move to Canada from Brussels and establish an import business. She had had 18 years' experience as an entrepreneur and manager, and experience dealing with professional and government agencies.

EURIMPEX does business in four areas. It is an import agent on commission for European consumer goods manufacturers, which includes client contact, marketing to potential clients, market analysis for European companies, and trade show representation and research. It provides consultancy services for North American and European companies that wish to export overseas. This involves research on agents, distributors, and joint ventures, market and procedural research, and collecting business information. The company also handles direct import of consumer goods and provides language translations. It markets its products through direct mail, word of mouth, and media interviews. Also, networking has been beneficial. Many contacts have been made through official channels such as trade commissions, chambers of commerce, and professional associations.

Michèle chose to operate her business from home because the startup cost savings allowed her to conserve her capital for marketing and servicing client needs. Also, it provided freedom and flexibility in scheduling trips, meetings, etc. The flexible office hours enabled her to serve clients in Europe and North America across all time zones. She says that the style and decor of her home has had a positive impact on her clients. Certain decoration items she brought from Europe when she moved to Canada caught clients' attention and created new additions to her import lines.

What factors are critical to your business success? I had previous experience both as an entrepreneur and as a company manager. I am fluent in several languages and have a master's degree in international trade, which provided the necessary theoretical basis in business. I did my research and was aware of the market conditions.

I am independent, self-motivated, ambitious, and persistent. Seeing the opportunities, I wish I had started earlier!

What assistance did you receive in your business startup?   As no outside capital was required, most assistance came from professional organizations such as the Canadian Importers Association, foreign trade commissions and, last but not least, friends who provided experience, background, and contacts.

What words of advice would you offer to someone starting out in business?   Make sure that you have both the necessary education and the necessary experience. Be prepared to work nonstop, especially being home-based, as most clients will expect your services at all times. Have the self-discipline and motivation required to run a business from your home — without the encouragement from colleagues, or the organization of an office — and to separate business and private life.

As an import agency, it has proven vital to be aware of legal considerations when making a contract with foreign manufacturers. Agencies are very vulnerable and should therefore be protected in the best way possible. Careful attention should be given as to the nationality of applicable law, and the ease of enforcement of that law. Furthermore, one should keep informed about these matters, considering the risks.

LANDSCAPING

Owners:	Randy and Rachael Lewis
Company Name:	Decora Landscaping (1980) Ltd.
Location:	Whitehorse, Yukon Territory
In Business:	13 Years

In 1991, Decora Landscaping became owned and operated by two of its original four partners. Taking a new direction, Randy and Rachael Lewis moved back to the residence located on the property and renovated the home during the winter months in preparation for the next season. Randy and Rachael, with their two children, are really enjoying the convenience of being right where it all happens. Keeping the greenhouse and nursery in top shape are two of the benefits of being back, and with intense schedules during the summer months they have time to spend with their children in the off-season.

Decora Landscaping (1980) Ltd. acts as a landscape contractor. It handles design consulting, regular property maintenance, construction of decks, installation of lawn and irrigation systems, and supplies garden plants, trees and shrubs, seed and fertilizers.

Even though management costs are down, Decora has been maintaining its annual revenues and still hires up to 10 seasonal employees. Decora has also expanded into native seed production under the trade name Arctic Alpine Seed, and will harvest its second crop of indigenous grasses in 1994.

What factors are critical to your business success? Maintaining high standards and consistent service are critical when a company undergoes a management change. Everyone watches you and wants to be sure you are the same company or better. Maintaining customer loyalty is everything and we feel we've managed to be the leading edge in our industry. We were thrilled this year to receive a Gold Georgie Award for "Best Expression of Environmental Awareness" from the Canadian Homebuilders' Association, especially since we were competing against 300 other landscapers in British Columbia.

What challenges did you encounter in your business growth? You are usually so busy just running the company it is often difficult to find the time to sit down and differentiate between what works well and what doesn't. A period of reflection while the summer is still fresh in your mind makes all the difference to the next season.

What words of advice would you offer to someone starting out in business? Be prepared for a considerable change in lifestyle and to being one hundred percent committed to making it a success. Your reputation and personal presentation will make or break your business.

MANUFACTURING AIRFIELD SIGNS

Owner: Charlene Davis
Company Name: Davis Airfield Fiberoptek Ltd.
Location: Edmonton, Alberta
In Business: 6 Years

Motivated by a good idea passed on by her father who was working at airports at the time, Charlene seized the opportunity to start a business in manufacturing and selling fiberoptic airfield lighting products. They saw that fiberoptically illuminated signage would improve the safety of air travel, especially during low visibility weather conditions. During the past six years, Charlene has supplied her signs to over 15 international, commercial, military, local, and private airports. Charlene now works in the business about 30 hours per week and employs up to 15 part-time employees and independent contractors. Word-of-mouth referrals from her customers have been the most effective means of acquiring new business, although she has used direct mail and trade shows to distribute her brochures and show her short video. Undoubtedly, Charlene believes in her product and is proud of the contribution she has made to the air-travel industry throughout Canada and internationally.

The timing to set up the business was right for Charlene. As a single mother, she was just starting to look at re-entering the job market after having her two children. With regard to her background and suitability for her new venture, Charlene says, "being an ex-police officer, backhoe operator, disc jockey and TV talk-show host indicates my willingness to try unusual and challenging things!" As she did not have large amounts of cash for startup costs, the decision to operate the business from her home enabled her to keep the capital investment reasonable amount. A separate office was constructed in the basement of her home. Being home-based also meant that she could spend more time with her young children. Charlene finds that she is able to control interruptions and stay on schedule by diligent use of her day-timer and using an answering machine for her home telephone while she is "at work." Whenever possible, though, her children come first. Charlene's family has provided financial and moral support and her new husband now actively participates in the decision-making process.

What challenges did you encounter in your business growth?
Getting the product accepted by the national approval body took a lot of time and persistence in weaving through the bureaucracy. I had to work harder to prove my credibility, being a female entering a male-dominated area. I have had to deal with unscrupulous competitors,

purchasers who renege on work-in-progress, and reverse engineering of my product by the federal government in order to provide competition.

What assistance did you receive that made a difference in your business? I received federal government funding under the IRAP [Industrial Research Assistance Program]. This financing enabled me to advance four separate projects to the manufacturing stage. Throughout the various stages of the business I have received technical advice from my husband and moral support from my family.

What advice would you offer to someone starting out in business? Set rules and schedules for yourself and stick to them. Properly set up and maintain your bookkeeping procedures, and remember to accurately keep track of your product costs.

MANUFACTURING CHILDREN'S CLOTHING

Owners:	Cindy and Ralph Eeson
Company Name:	Kids Only Clothing Club Inc.
Location:	Calgary, Alberta
In Business:	5 Years

After being at home with her young children, Cindy had made the decision not to go back to the practice of law. She enjoyed being at home and wanted to remain close to them. Therefore, if she was going to go back to work, it would have to be something that offered flexible hours. The idea for her business actually came from her own frustrations in shopping for her children. She had difficulty finding reasonably priced and well-designed children's wear on the Canadian market. She also found that the conventional retail setting was not conducive for busy mothers with young children.

Cindy decided to design, manufacture and distribute high quality, innovative children's clothing. She uses easy-care fabrics that are comfortable, yet durable. Instead of the conventional retail distribution, she found that using the home-party sales method was the better way for mothers to shop for clothing for their children. It offered them convenience and flexibility, and saved them a lot of time.

Although Cindy had no previous retail business experience on which to base her business plans, she felt that as a mother she knew what consumers were shopping for and what children would want to wear. She did have a previous, unsuccessful business venture, so was aware of what the basics were, and pitfalls to avoid. Cindy says, "You must be a risk-taker and enjoy making decisions and working with people. You can't be a quitter when the going gets tough." When it came to specialty areas, she hired experts to provide the necessary advice and expertise. To supplement her own financing for the start-up business, Cindy took on a partner for the first year.

For the first six months, the business was operated from the attic of the Eeson's three-storey house. They found it was imperative to separate the business area from the living space in the home. "We set definite rules so that all family members knew certain work times were *sacred* while other work times were flexible. Customers also needed to know definite times when we could be reached. Other times we left our answering machine on to record messages."

The rapid growth of the business soon meant a home-based business was no longer viable. The Kids Only Clothing Club Inc. now has 125 full-time employees working in the factory including both Cindy and her husband Ralph (also a former lawyer), and employs 700 part-time independent contractors and commissioned salespeople.

What type of assistance did you receive in your business start-up? When moving the business to the factory, I hired a consulting engineer who was extremely helpful in setting it up so that all operations ran smoothly. My husband was a big support in the financial planning for the business. He was also a lawyer who left his practice to join me in the fourth year of business.

What factors are critical to your business success? We were fortunate that the timing for the new marketing concept was good. As well, women were looking for ways to work from their homes, which provided us a ready and willing base of sales agents. I feel it was my creativity and ability to look at new situations in an unconventional way, that gave me the competitive edge to capitalize on a unique opportunity.

What words of advice would you offer to someone starting out in business? Study as many similar businesses as possible. Don't be afraid to try something completely different. Look for unconventional solutions. If you don't have experience, you can always rely on the common-sense approach. You must be seen as professional when running a business from home, or people won't take you seriously. But don't *live* your work; remember to *turn it off* when it's time for other responsibilities and R & R.

MANUFACTURING GLASS PRODUCTS

Owner: E. Jane Midgley
Company Name: Elite Art Glass
Location: Maple Ridge, B.C.
In Business: 15 Years

Jane had been a crafts instructor for four years and taught a wide variety of crafts. She then chose the craft that she enjoyed the most and started a business. "I've always wanted to be my own boss," says Jane. "I wanted to be home with my children while they were young, and operating a business from home with the craft I enjoy gives me the best of both worlds." It also gave her the flexibility to set her own schedule. Most often she worked at night while the children slept. She admits that balancing time for her children and work is a challenge for her. She has had to learn to be organized.

Jane designs, handcrafts, and distributes "Italian green" art glass place-settings and decorative serving trays. Through trial and error she has developed a product that is truly unique and attractive. She purchases glass of different sizes and shapes, and then takes it through various steps of cutting, grinding, firing in the kiln, and washing before it is packaged and ready for sale. Besides building her kilns, her husband works with her through the various stages of the manufacturing and packaging processes. She sells her finished product on a wholesale basis to retail gift store buyers throughout Canada. Since having her products featured on the front cover of a recent issue of *Food and Wine* magazine, Jane has started selling her products internationally. Trade shows and word-of-mouth advertising have proven to be her best marketing techniques, besides the gift store displays. Because the business outgrew the basement workshop of their Vancouver home, Jane and her husband purchased a home on a large property out of the city. The two full-sized workshops on the property have given them ample work and storage space and room to expand further.

What factors do you feel are critical to your business success? My creativity and ingenuity has enabled me to develop a unique product. I started out making stained-glass products, but when that became really popular and my ideas were being copied by hobbyists, I knew I had to create something new and different to maintain my market position. I have drive and perseverance and am committed to the business. My husband has been very supportive from the outset, and is now joining me in the business on a full-time basis.

What assistance did you receive in your business startup? I participated in the New Enterprise Program at Simon Fraser University, which helped me to get a business plan on paper. This intensive six-week program involved attending school one night a week for six hours. It changed my way of thinking. Instead of thinking of my craft as a hobby, I began considering it as a business. Instead of $2,000 in sales, I started projecting for $200,000. Besides teaching me about pricing, market research, and approaching banks and venture capitalists, it also provided me with a network of astute business associates. Also, I joined the Association of Women Business Owners, a networking and support group to women in business. I was able to get feedback and advice from my colleagues who had successful businesses of their own. I am constantly taking business courses which help me broaden my ideas, knowledge, and skills.

What words of advice would you offer to someone starting out in business? You should create a product that is different and new. Be prepared to work hard and persevere. Don't underprice your product. Especially in a craft business, if you underprice, people will feel that they can make the products more inexpensively themselves. Know what your time is worth, and be certain to add to that figure all your costs before arriving at a price. Start out with a good bookkeeping system and know how to keep it up to date. Know how to read a balance sheet and income statement — that's your bottom-line! In the five years since the move and expansion of the business, we have learned you have to keep on top of the collections. A bookkeeper/accountant and a "friendly" collection agency are helpful in this area. We know that size orders are normal for our customers and danger signals flash when that extra large order comes in quickly without some explanation attached. To sell your products successfully, you need to find agents that are in love with your line and don't look upon it as a little something extra to sell.

POTTERY

Owner:	Marlene Penner Poole
Company Name:	Marlene Penner Poole's Pottery Studio
Location:	Corner Brook, Newfoundland
In Business:	16 Years

Marlene says that she considered doing pottery as a hobby, but because the supplies were so inaccessible and expensive, this was not feasible. She had to go into business to justify the expense. She recognized that a need existed. There were few potters in Newfoundland, so her work was in great demand, and selling it was easy. She took a one-year business-oriented pottery course at a local vocational school, which prepared her for selling her work.

Marlene decided to operate her business on a part-time basis to accommodate her lifestyle needs. She works four to five hours per day during the months of April, May, June, September, October, and November. "My lifestyle includes a lot of volunteer work, hobbies, and a very active family and social life. For six months of the year I work very little or not at all." She considers her pottery business a very satisfying occupation which is high in "job satisfaction," though low in financial return. She sells her stoneware and functional pottery wholesale in craft shops within the province. She sends a wholesale catalogue to her customers which generates most orders by phone and mail. People hear about her products through word-of-mouth advertising and media interviews. A craft booklet published by the provincial government has proven to be an effective marketing tool.

Working at home offered numerous conveniences for Marlene. She was able to be at home with her children, and was able to work odd hours for short periods spread throughout the day. Space was not a problem, because she had a large home with ample space for her studio.

What factors are critical to your business success? I work quickly, which is very valuable in any work which is sold "piecemeal." And I exert lots of energy. This is important because this type of work is physically demanding. My husband assisted me financially to get started. Although he does not help in a concrete way, he is very encouraging and supportive. My children, too, are very understanding of my work priorities. Local and provincial craft associations have provided me with encouragement and support. My business is vital to my sense of well-being. My life has become integrated with my work in a very satisfying way.

What would you do differently if starting over again? I would start at a younger age and seek further training in my field. I have supplemented my knowledge by taking summer courses for three years. At first I lacked confidence in my abilities in designing work and formulating glazes; however, time and experience has overcome this. I would be more disciplined and strict about my working hours and those spent with family and friends. I allow interruptions, because I have difficulty saying no to people. So a lot of time is wasted.

What words of advice would you offer to someone start out in business? Especially in the first few years, your business should have priority in your life. Persistence is very important to achieve what you want. Set a definite work schedule, and have others (including yourself) respect your working hours.

PRE-KINDERGARTEN INSTRUCTION

Owner:	Thérèse Naggar
Company Name:	Pré-maternelle "Le Brin d'éveil"
Location:	Chateauguay, Quebec
In Business:	9 Years

One of Thérèse's personal goals was to create her own enterprise. She recognized it would have to generate a respectable financial return, and be one that she could operate from home so that she could supervise her young children through her working hours. Working at home also had the advantage of requiring minimal financial investment and avoiding transportation problems. With an Educational Science degree and a background of seven years' teaching of kindergarten students, Thérèse decided to open a or "pré-maternelle" pre-kindergarten school. She converted the basement of her home into a suitable facility, and hired a full-time person to assist with supervising the children, cooking, and cleaning. Thérèse takes in small groups of eight to twelve children from three to five years of age, and offers a very personalized service of preparing them for attending regular kindergarten classes. Activities include drawing, plasticine art, music, singing, and group entertainment and presentations. Her school gets a lot of good publicity by staging an annual show with songs, dances, and sketches performed by her pupils in front of a large audience. She distributes brochures to local schools and churches, places announcements in newspapers, and advertises on local radio stations to market her business. Also, word-of-mouth advertising has been effective.

What challenges did you encounter in your business growth? My only obstacle has been the zoning of my home, which was designated as "residential." This allows me the right to operate by business with groups of limited size, but it does not permit me to display an attractive sign outside my residence to promote the business. I do have a small sign inside my front window, which is somewhat visible. If I had to do it over again, I would do everything the same, except that I would have checked into zoning earlier, and chosen a home that was in a mixed zoning area (residential and commercial). This would have been more advantageous to me.

What assistance did you receive in your business startup? My mother and father helped me with the accounting and clerical aspects of the business. Also, when it is busy, my husband helps me. Friends and relatives have also assisted with various tasks. I have received valuable help from SAGE in Chateauguay. This group specializes in helping young promoters to obtain subsidies for their projects.

What factors are critical to the success of your business? I have good business sense and am not afraid of investing hours and energy for the success of my enterprise. I am patient with the children and have a lot of imagination. Also, I am open-minded and understanding with the children and their parents.

What words of advice would you offer to someone starting out in business? Don't be afraid to make decisions. Solve one problem at a time, but solve it to the best of your abilities. Conform with all municipal laws in order to avoid problems.

PROCESSING OCEAN SEDIMENTS

Owner: Ron Sampson
Company Name: PEI Mussel Mud Inc.
Location: Winslow, Prince Edward Island
In Business: 5 Years

Ron, who was a graduate of Agricultural College, had worked along-side farmers for 15 years. He had often heard stories from elderly farmers about how "mussel mud" from the riverbeds was used to fer-tilize the farmland. Once applied, the soil remained enriched which aided the growing of crops for periods of 35 to 50 years. In the 1920s, new products became available that were much more convenient, although they had a far less lasting effect, requiring re-application every two to three years.

At the tender age of 40, Ron decided to go to work on re-discover-ing the "mussel mud" product for sale in a convenient fashion. This was done after considerable research. He explains that, "It's not mud at all — it's the naturally occurring sea compost of oysters, mussels, quahogs, clams and other shellfish and minute sea creatures. The mussel mud is rich in lime which neutralizes soil acidity and provides other valuable nutrients to enrich the soil. Since it is a naturally occurring product, it represents a renewable resource. It's found in the clean estuarial waters abundant on PEI, then dried, crushed and packaged."

Ron spent three years on research and development of accessing the "wasted" resource and turning it into a useful, environmentally friendly product. The business was started from the basement of his family home, where his employees worked shifts from 7:00 a.m. to 7:00 p.m. It was a low cost, easily accessible and convenient process. He admits separating work and family time was very difficult. Just recently he has purchased a plant on 29 acres where he employs six full-time employees, eight to 10 months of the year. During his busiest season he employs an additional six part-timers. His products are now sold in 160 stores throughout the Maritime provinces and Que-bec and Ontario. Media advertising and interviews (ATV, CBC and CTV) have helped to promote his products as well as brochures, packaging, signage and product give-aways. Ron is now trying to bring more balance to his life by spending more time with his wife and three children.

What assistance did you receive in your business startup? I applied for and received federal funding from the National Research Council which was necessary to get the project to the development stage. I later received assistance from the Atlantic Canada Opportunities Agency.

What factors do you feel are critical to your success? I started with a good credit rating, but very little money. I took chances with personal guarantees, but my determination, hard work, and personal credibility has paid off.

What words of advice would you offer to someone starting out in business? You must believe totally in your product. You must do your research thoroughly, so that you know your business concept has the strong potential for success. Hold on through the tough times, like with a marriage. Expand slowly and concentrate on the profitable parts.

SEWING

Owner:	Karen Wiebe
Company Name:	Karen's Sewing Centre
Location:	Manitou, Manitoba
In Business:	17 Years

Karen's Sewing Centre was created out of a need to fill a role other than wife and mother. The idea of being her own boss, setting her own schedule, and earning an income without leaving the home environment appealed to her. Staying at home on their farm was a priority for her because of her young children and the farm work that she did during peak seasons. Besides, she felt that a home-based business could be more profitable than outside employment. The idea for her business stemmed from a similar one that her parents operated from their home when she was going through high school. She took training courses and seminars to give her a background in teaching.

Retail sewing machine sales and service is the mainstay of Karen's Sewing Centre. In addition, sewing lessons are offered to children and adults. Children ages six to twelve attend weekly classes to learn to sew garments they can wear. The adult classes centre around "serger" sewing machine instruction techniques. Dressmaking classes offer colour and wardrobe consulting, personalized fabric shopping service, dressmaking, and design. The business is operated from a 12-foot by 22-foot room on the third level of their home, which has a private entrance. Karen's husband does the service and warranty work on the sewing machines, with cleaning and tidying help from her children. Her oldest son did the bookkeeping, including invoicing, mailing lists, newsletters, etc., on their computer. She says that she has plans to move the business out of the family home into a separate building on their property. The move would create a more efficient business and working atmosphere, with fewer distractions, and would allow the business to continue to grow. Signage, direct mail, word of mouth, media ads and interviews, and networking are the techniques Karen uses to market her business throughout the region. As a separate business operation, Karen's family also operates a farm vacation home which specializes in historic tours of the area, and group holidays and country campouts.

What challenges did you encounter in your business growth? Strong local competition in the sales end of the business led me to expand on the teaching area. My local competitor retails large numbers of serger sewing machines. To compete, as well as fill a void in the market area, I developed a sewing workshop specializing in serging techniques. If starting over again, I would spend less time procrastinating. I would have a greater belief in myself as a business person, and would view my business as a business rather than a hobby. Interruptions are one of my greatest challenges, although I have tried to train my family, friends, and customers.

What factors are critical to your business success? I have energy, determination, vision, and belief in the future viability of my home-based business. I feel I relate well to people and to their interests and needs in the sewing field. I enjoy teaching and learning from my class participants. I work well under pressure, and work quickly and competently. Respect and credibility from fellow business associates was certainly an encouragement in the beginning. Last but not least, my family's support and cooperation, especially from my husband, has been a major factor.

What words of advice would you offer to someone starting out in business? Set up a strong business image from the start, and make sure your customers know that you operate in a businesslike manner. Make sure you are in control of your time.

TENT RENTALS

Owner:	David H. Nelson
Company Name:	Nelson Industries Ltd.
Location:	Dugald, Manitoba
In Business:	14 Years

With past experience in theatrical lighting and design, David foresaw a market demand for a party tent rental business. He brought with him technical abilities, experience in construction methods and materials and theatre design, and aesthetic appreciation. His company, Nelson Industries Ltd., designs and manufactures rental equipment and accessories such as tents, dance floors, lighting, etc. He says that he got his education in design and manufacture through trade magazines, seminars, and trial and error. Approximately 75% of his business is party-oriented (i.e., weddings, anniversaries, graduations), while the remaining 25% comprises commercial venues, grand openings, and fund-raising events. In addition to his own full-time efforts, and those of his wife, he has the assistance of six part-time employees for the installation and maintenance of equipment. The condition of the equipment must be clean and well maintained, and often clients request a site inspection prior to installation. "We accommodate our customers' needs in every way possible, including assisting them with colour coordination, decorations, and choice of a theme. Customer satisfaction is our trademark." To market the business throughout the province, David uses direct mail to send brochures and actual photographs of the equipment installed. "The Yellow Pages ad is necessary, but word of mouth is the most effective. Our satisfied customers are our best advertising."

Since David lived out of town, commuting to an urban location would have been inconvenient and expensive. Therefore, running the business from his 14-acre property afforded him the luxury of ample storage and expansion space, and low overhead expenses. His office is part of the dining room, which he admits gets cluttered occasionally. "Scheduling was chaos in the beginning, but we're better at it now. Customers came to our home at random hours. Our son was then at preschool and needed more attention. He is now 11 years old and has a full day at school. Of course, our busiest time is during his summer holidays. That has been hard on all of us, but especially on our son."

What challenges did you encounter in your business growth?
Finding suitable employees for our busy summer season is an ongoing problem. During our busy period the phone was ringing day and night, until we hired a telephone answering service to take calls after

hours. If starting over again, I would spend more time researching manufacturing methods and all other related aspects of the business.

What factors are critical to your business success? We have quality products and ensure customer service and satisfaction. We are able to meet difficult demands, and view these as challenges, which in turn brings the reward. A government "Career Start Program" has provided financial assistance by subsidizing employee wages.

What words of advice would you offer to someone starting out in business? Be prepared for difficulty in keeping business and family life separate. Scheduling your time is important. Everyone seems to think that because you are at home, you aren't working. They expect you to drop everything and socialize.

TOURS AND CONVENTION SERVICES

Owner: Regina McCarthy
Company Name: McCarthy's Party Ltd.
Location: Topsail, Conception Bay, Newfoundland
In Business: 11 Years

Regina had been at home raising her four sons for 20 years. The boys were all "university material," and since summer jobs were hard to come by in Newfoundland, she decided to start a business in which they could work in the summer to earn their tuition for the fall. After researching the market, she found that there was no one locally offering tour bus services. She had been a tour guide as a teenager and enjoyed the work, and felt that she could offer a better service.

McCarthy's Party Ltd. — Tours and Convention Services provides tours of Newfoundland and Labrador on an hourly, daily, or weekly basis, or by special itinerary. They also offer pre- and post-convention package tour services for groups as large as five or six hundred delegates. They arrange spousal programs, local tours, entertainment, "screech-in" ceremonies, transportation, meal arrangements, and everything else to do with the social side of a convention. Regina uses brochures, direct mail, media advertising, and interviews to market her business. She displays her brochures at trade shows and networks at business association meetings. Word-of-mouth advertising, though, has been the most effective for her. As her customers are mainly tourists from Ontario, the United States, and Europe, Regina has contracted with well-known operators in those areas to sell her tours for her. During her busy season she employs seven part-time staff (including her four sons) to operate the tours.

Operating her business from home was the most practical thing to do. The work was seasonal, and most of the office work was done by phone and mail. When Regina met with clients, she would go to their offices. Her office is in the lower floor of her house. "We remodelled the basement and created a separate entrance for staff to give more family privacy. It helps define the work area from the living area, and was worth the price. Working from home is never easy — it's a juggling act. Balancing social, family, and work time becomes a real challenge. Because the office is in the home, you are never away from it. Self-motivation becomes a true challenge. I get up, shower, and dress as if I was going to work for someone else (including high heels and makeup). Then I go to my office. I make a 'to do today' list and itemize it from most to least important. I enjoy working at home for many reasons: I don't have to travel each day; I'm at home if my children need me; I'm my own boss and can set my own schedule; and I can 'run home' for lunch!"

What type of assistance did you receive in your business startup? My family encouraged me tremendously. Then they all gradually became involved in the business. They all feel very much a part of the business. I received financial assistance with marketing from government agencies, and dealt with very helpful government officers at both the provincial and the federal level.

What factors are critical to your business success? Hard work. I gave personal attention to detail and was willing to do everything and anything myself that needed doing. My personality and organizational skills, and being a doer, helped me along the way. I actively participated in business-related associations. From time to time I gave away my time and effort for free in order to demonstrate our services.

What words of advice would you offer to someone starting out in business? Make sure there is really a need for such a service. Research your idea well. Find a way to make your product "the best." Don't be afraid of hard work and long hours. Try to separate work from home life. Keep specific hours whenever possible, and take time out for lunch. Instead of feeling guilty about the "state of the house," solicit family members or hire someone to do it for you.

TRANSLATING AND CONSULTING

Owner:	Brigitte Bryant
Company Name:	French With Flair (a division of Econotrends Ltd.)
Location:	Waterloo, Ontario
In Business:	7 Years

Company Name:	Stratec Communications Inc.
Location:	Hudson, Quebec
In Business:	3 Years

Brigitte says her frustration of working for other people and her need for more independence and flexibility led her to the decision to start her first business, "French With Flair." She was fluently bilingual and had had experience in freelance translation for several years. Business advice was provided by her accountant and husband, and she had established a set of contacts that provided an initial customer base. French With Flair, that later became a division of Econotrends Ltd., specializes in French/English, English/French translation. The company's activities were maintained after a personal move to Quebec, and a separate company, Stratec Communications Inc., was incorporated to deal with Quebec clients. Documents are provided in camera-ready form through desk-top publishing equipment or on floppy disks. Business had developed largely through a personal contact network. In association with her husband, both companies also provide consulting and training services in the economic development field. For the first year of French With Flair, Brigitte worked from a home office to keep overhead low, but then moved to a downtown office in order to get more social contacts. Since moving home, she runs her new business again from a home office.

What factors do you feel are critical to your business success? I enjoy dealing with people, and make the effort to ensure customer satisfaction and I had some good contacts. I had the right kind of experience and was trained on a number of computer systems.

What challenges did you encounter in your business growth? I often find that customers do not understand or appreciate the amount of time involved in translations. Over time, I have had to educate my regular customers, and this has helped.

What words of advice would you offer to someone starting out in business? In my type of business you need excellent language skills. There is an absolute need to do your work onto a computer system, and to communicate by fax or modem. A set of good contacts is essential for both the translation and the consulting businesses.

WOODWORKING

Owner: Ross Phinney
Company Name: Seaside Woodworks
Location: Saint John, New Brunswick
In Business: 11 Years

Ross was building scenery and props for a professional theatre company when he decided he needed a change. He had always enjoyed woodworking and liked the idea of being his own boss and setting his own work schedule. He studied commerce at Mount Allison University, and had a natural interest in design. "I have a strong interest in running a business, from the bookkeeping to the shop work. I believe in moving with technology, and have recently purchased an XT-compatible computer for word processing, accounting, estimating, and data keeping."

The primary objective of Seaside Woodworks is to design and build furniture. Designing may range from receiving a set of drawings or a photograph of a piece, to a client describing a piece of furniture. He finds the designing aspects most challenging. He must interpret the style, type of wood, etc. He builds a variety of furnishings such as office desks, display cabinets, household items, yacht furnishings, and doors, with styles ranging from period reproductions to contemporary pieces. He markets his products within his region of the province through the use of brochures, media interviews and word-of-mouth advertising. He also participates in craft and home shows, and recently started advertising in entertainment programs and association newsletters. In hindsight, though, he says that he should have spent more money on advertising in the early years of his business.

For the first four years he operated the business from his parents' garage, as it was free of charge and the space was available. When he built his own home he designed a 500-square-foot attached wing for his workshop, and a further 350-square-foot area of workspace. His home overlooks the Bay of Fundy, which provides a pleasant and relaxing setting. "Initially I dedicated a lot of time to my business and not so much to my personal life. That has changed in the past few years, though, especially since the birth of my son six years ago."

What assistance did you receive in your business startup? The best assistance I received was the moral, financial, and business management support from my wife and parents. Their advice, along with that of my friends, has been extremely helpful and readily available.

What challenges did you encounter in your business growth? My first challenge was getting my name known. I started participating in craft shows, and my profile grew through friends, family, and clients. Another challenge is dealing with the isolation I feel when working alone. I make a conscious effort to get away from the shop and meet new people. This benefits both me and the business.

What factors are critical to your business success?   The quality of my work and the good relationships I maintain with my clients has been most important. I have always maintained a positive outlook toward the success of my business.

What words of advice would you offer to someone starting out in business?   Start small and do not fall heavily into debt. Purchase equipment as you need it. Let time dictate your needs for a certain item. For example, I allow one and one-half years to decide whether I should purchase a major expense item. Ask friends and colleagues for advice on business or techniques in manufacturing.

WRITING

Owner: Jane Widerman
Company Name: Jane Widerman Communications Inc.
Location: Toronto, Ontario
In Business: 12 years

Soon after receiving her master's degree, Jane decided she wanted to write professionally. She wanted to work on her own because she felt that working for a company or a publication would limit her interests. She acknowledges the help of her parents in providing her with the confidence to be an independent thinker. She came from a long line of seer-employed professionals who acted as role models. "They showed me that with a little time management and an ounce of assertiveness, you can make it as your own boss." Jane provides a variety of writing, editing, and media relations services. Her clients include magazines, public relations firms, government offices, corporations, and nonprofit organizations. An area of related expertise is script writing for a video production company and government clients. She services clients locally as well as provincially and nationally. They hear of her services largely through word-of-mouth advertising and networking. "I have the gift of the gab, which I use *everywhere*! I always carry my business cards, which I hand out shamelessly. Also, I belong to the YMCA Health Club, where I've made many profitable connections."

Jane decided to operate her business from home because she didn't need much workspace and she could minimize her costs. Most importantly, though, she enjoyed the overall sense of comfort and calm in being able to work at home.

What assistance did you receive in your business startup? I have a number of computer-literate friends, who have given me invaluable advice on computer setup. Also, I am an active member of the Periodical Writers Association of Canada, which gives seminars on practical topics such as office management and freelancing as a business.

What challenges did you encounter in your business growth? Initially, I had to make a small space ergonomically viable! I overcame this with an economic use of my living/dining room, where I had a small computer table, filing cabinet with printer on top, and dining table which doubles as a desk. A challenge for me was enforcing self-discipline. Aggressive time management has helped me to organize my day as I would if I were in an office.

What factors are critical to your business success? My independence, aggressiveness, and optimism have enabled me to hustle to keep the work flowing. There are lots of peaks and valleys in my line of work. I have had to learn to accept the rollercoaster nature of life. My flexibility has given me the ability to do a wide variety of writing and editing jobs — in double time!

What words of advice would you offer to someone starting out in business? Be sure that you have what it takes to work on your own as your own boss, without someone else to impose on you a sense of order and direction. Be extremely organized. Pare down your office needs to the essentials. You don't need bells and whistles to be successful.

SUMMARY

Now that you have read the profiles, you will no doubt recognize that there are similar entrepreneurial traits and attitudes: endless energy and stamina, a positive attitude, optimism, enthusiasm, commitment, pride, self-confidence, goal orientation, knowledge of the business, initiative, and flexibility.

There are also some common themes in the advice that was given. Do your research thoroughly beforehand, and have a business plan. Start a business that you enjoy. Enlist the support of your spouse and family. Have personal activities outside of the home to provide balance. Keep regular "office" hours to minimize outside distractions or disruptions. Have a designated area in the home for your business activities. And most importantly, maintain high quality control of your product or service.

SECTION FOUR

CHECKLISTS, SAMPLES, APPENDIXES

CHECKLISTS

CHECKLIST 1
(See Chapter 2)

Action Plan Checklist

Step	Estimated Date of Completion	Actual Date of Completion	Comments
1. Preliminary research on business idea completed	_____	_____	_____
2. Feedback on business idea from family and friends obtained	_____	_____	_____
3. Feedback from partners (if any) obtained	_____	_____	_____
4. Adequate work/storage space in your home determined	_____	_____	_____
5. Licensing and zoning regulations checked	_____	_____	_____
6. Advice from provincial small business counsellors obtained	_____	_____	_____
7. Advice from FBDB CASE counsellor obtained (if applicable)	_____	_____	_____
8. Advice from lawyer and accountant obtained	_____	_____	_____
9. Legal form of business structure determined (e.g., proprietorship, partnership, corporation)	_____	_____	_____
10. Market survey completed	_____	_____	_____
11. Personal commitment to business venture finalized	_____	_____	_____
12. Market segment goal determined	_____	_____	_____
13. Market share goal determined	_____	_____	_____
14. Cash flow projection completed	_____	_____	_____

15. Operating forecast completed for Year One   _____ _____ _____

16. Personal financial statement prepared   _____ _____ _____

17. Detailed business plan completed   _____ _____ _____

18. Feasibility study completed   _____ _____ _____

19. Sources of financing identified   _____ _____ _____

20. Sources of financing explored   _____ _____ _____

21. Adequate financing arranged   _____ _____ _____

22. Equipment and machinery ordered   _____ _____ _____

23. Fixtures, furnishings, supplies, and printing ordered   _____ _____ _____

24. Permits and licences obtained   _____ _____ _____

25. Company logo, business cards, and stationery designed and printed   _____ _____ _____

26. Insurance protection arranged   _____ _____ _____

27. Telephone answering service arranged   _____ _____ _____

28. Bookkeeping and accounting systems set up   _____ _____ _____

29. Business bank account established   _____ _____ _____

30. Employees selected, hired, and trained   _____ _____ _____

31. Signs and advertising completed   _____ _____ _____

32. Equipment and machinery received   _____ _____ _____

33. Fixtures, furnishings, supplies, and printing received   _____ _____ _____

34. Inventory priced, marked, and placed   _____ _____ _____

35. Review of business
    plan to ensure all
    steps on schedule   _____ _____ _____
36. Work schedule
    established   _____ _____ _____
37. Candid assessment
    of administrative
    effectiveness on a
    daily basis   _____ _____ _____
38. Actual and projected
    sales measured after:
    - 1 week   _____ _____ _____
    - 1 month   _____ _____ _____
    - 3 months   _____ _____ _____
    - 6 months   _____ _____ _____
39. Actual and projected
    cash flow measured:
    - Weekly   _____ _____ _____
    - Monthly   _____ _____ _____
40. Operating forecast
    tested after:
    - 1 month   _____ _____ _____
    - 3 months   _____ _____ _____
    - 6 months   _____ _____ _____
41. Customer survey to
    measure satisfaction
    and feedback
    completed at end of
    first month of business   _____ _____ _____
42. Candid assessment of
    overall business plan
    accuracy completed   _____ _____ _____
43. Modifications made to
    business plan, if
    required   _____ _____ _____
44. Changes to
    management
    decisions, if required   _____ _____ _____

CHECKLIST 2
(See Chapter 4)

Business Regulations

Business Regulations/ Legislation	Applies to Me	Does Not Apply to Me	Need Further Info	Further Info Obtained
A. Municipal				
• City Business License				
• Zoning Bylaws (opening hours and location)				
• Zoning Bylaws (home-based business)				
• Zoning Bylaws (noise, fumes, etc.)				
• Land Use Regulations				
• Business Taxes				
• Property Taxes				
• School Taxes				
• Water Taxes				
• Building Permits (applicable to alteration also)				
• Building Codes (plumbing, electrical, fire, and health hazards				
• Health Regulations (preparation of food, removal of waste products, training of staff, etc.)				
• Other: _____				
B. Provincial				
• Business Registration (proprietorship, partnership, and/or trade style name)				
• Bulk Sales				
• Incorporation (provincial charter)				
• Land Use Regulations (certain provinces)				
• Environmental Protection Regulations				

Business Regulations/ Legislation	Applies to Me	Does Not Apply to Me	Need Further Info	Further Info Obtained
B. Provincial (continued)				
• Director's Liability to statutory creditors (that is, to provincial government departments with such legislation and claim rights as employment standards, Workers' Compensation Board, sales tax, environmental protection, human rights, etc.)	_____	_____	_____	_____
• Provincial Business License	_____	_____	_____	_____
• Provincial Income Tax (corporate or personal)	_____	_____	_____	_____
• Quebec Place of Business Tax (Quebec only)	_____	_____	_____	_____
• Provincial Sales Tax	_____	_____	_____	_____
• Provincial Building Codes (electrical apparatus and equipment, fire and health hazards)	_____	_____	_____	_____
• Minimum Age for Employment	_____	_____	_____	_____
• Minimum Wage for Employment	_____	_____	_____	_____
• Trade Practices	_____	_____	_____	_____
• Consumer Protection	_____	_____	_____	_____
• Sale of Goods	_____	_____	_____	_____
• Hours of Employment	_____	_____	_____	_____
• Annual Vacations and Public Holidays	_____	_____	_____	_____
• Workers' Compensation	_____	_____	_____	_____
• Quebec Pension Plan (Quebec only)	_____	_____	_____	_____
• Safety and Health Standards	_____	_____	_____	_____
• Liquor License	_____	_____	_____	_____
• Provincial Health Insurance	_____	_____	_____	_____
• Maternity Leave	_____	_____	_____	_____
• Termination of Employment	_____	_____	_____	_____
• Other _____	_____	_____	_____	_____

Business Regulations/ Legislation	Applies to Me	Does Not Apply to Me	Need Further Info	Further Info Obtained
C. Federal				
• Incorporation (federal charter)	_____	_____	_____	_____
• Federal Income Tax (corporate or personal)	_____	_____	_____	_____
• Director's Liability to statutory creditors (that is, to federal government departments with such legislation and claim rights as employment standards, GST, income tax, environmental protection, human rights, etc.)	_____	_____	_____	_____
• Goods and Services Tax	_____	_____	_____	_____
• Export/Import Permit	_____	_____	_____	_____
• Customs Duties	_____	_____	_____	_____
• Building Codes	_____	_____	_____	_____
• Health and Safety Standards	_____	_____	_____	_____
• Environmental Protection Legislation	_____	_____	_____	_____
• Unemployment Insurance	_____	_____	_____	_____
• Canada Pension Plan (except Quebec)	_____	_____	_____	_____
• Payroll Tax Deductions (monthly remittances to government)	_____	_____	_____	_____
• Hazardous Waste	_____	_____	_____	_____
• Trademarks	_____	_____	_____	_____
• Copyrights	_____	_____	_____	_____
• Industrial Designs	_____	_____	_____	_____
• Patents	_____	_____	_____	_____
• Product Safety	_____	_____	_____	_____
• Competition Act (includes false or misleading advertising)	_____	_____	_____	_____
• Other _____	_____	_____	_____	_____

CHECKLIST 3
(See Chapter 4)

Partnership Agreement Checklist

1. Date of agreement: _____
2. Description of partners:
   (a) individuals have attained the age of majority
   (b) each partner is acquiring interest for own benefit
3. Firm name:
   (a) name search to ensure no conflict with existing trade, corporation, or partnership name
   (b) registration of name as required by law
   (c) continued use of name after death or withdrawal of any partner or after reorganization
   (d) restriction on use of name in any other activity
4. Term of partnership:
   (a) commencement
   (b) termination at specified time or on specified events
5. Place of business:
   (a) specify geographic limits if desired
6. Business purpose of partnership:
   (a) description of authorized business activities
   (b) limitations on business activities
   (c) provisions for future changes in business activities
7. Capital contributions:
   (a) percentage contribution of each partner
   (b) form of contribution (cash, assets, etc.)
   (c) when contribution to be made
   (d) valuation of non-cash contributions
   (e) interest on contributions
   (f) adjustments to contributions
   (g) loans to partnership
   (h) future capital contributions:
       i) circumstances when required
       ii) amount and form
       iii) apportionment of contribution among partners
       iv) redistribution of partnership interest for nonproportional contributions
8. Division of profits and losses:
   (a) proportion of division among partners
   (b) salaries and benefits as elements in profits for distribution
   (c) guarantee of minimum profits to certain partners
   (d) reserve fund for partnership expenses paid into prior to distribution
   (e) limitation on partner's share in profits or losses
   (f) distribution to partnership

9. Records of business:
   (a) nature of records
   (b) partners' access
   (c) statements to be given to partners
10. Appointment of accountant/auditor
11. Fiscal Year: _____
12. Accounting and valuation principles:
    (a) generally accepted accounting principles (specify if desired)
    (b) valuation principles (book value, multiple of earnings, etc.)
13. Banking arrangements:
    (a) bank and branch
    (b) kinds of accounts
    (c) signing authority
    (d) maximum loan amount without approval of all partners
14. Financial restrictions on partners:
    (a) prohibition against partner giving bonds or guarantees, charging his partnership interest for his separate debts or otherwise impairing his financial position to the detriment of partnership
    (b) prohibition against any one partner borrowing for partnership or releasing debt of partnership
    (c) indemnity by partner breaching these provisions
15. Attention to business:
    (a) partners to devote full time and attention to business
    (b) partners not to engage in competing business, or any other business
    (c) liability of partners to account for outside income (e.g., director's fees)
    (d) salary for full-time partners
    (e) specify responsibilities
16. Control of policy:
    (a) majority rule or unanimity
    (b) voting:
        i) one partner — one vote
        ii) votes proportional to interest
17. Management:
    (a) designation of responsible partners
    (b) division of functions (e.g., administration, sales)
    (c) provision for business meetings
    (d) records of decisions
    (e) establishment of policies
    (f) simple or special majority or unanimous approval
    (g) authority to enter contracts, negotiate loans, pledge credit, hire and fire employees
    (h) provision for review of decisions by all partners
18. Drawing arrangements and benefits:
    (a) frequency
    (b) maximum amount or percentage
    (c) vacations
    (d) other benefits

19. Powers of partners and limitations:
    (a) engaging in nonpartnership business
    (b) defining scope of partners' authority, collectively and individually
    (c) delegation of powers to management committee
    (d) acting outside scope of partnership committee
    (e) patents and trade secrets
20. Restrictive covenants (to prevent competition in the event of departure):
    (a) reasonable time, scope, and geographic area
21. Retirement or death:
    (a) provide for continuance notwithstanding retirement or death
    (b) purchase of retiring partner's interest — valuation criteria and method of payment
    (c) purchase of deceased partner's interest or provision for estate to act as partner
22. Sale of partnership interest:
    (a) prohibit
    (b) allow, with right of first refusal to remaining partners, compulsory buy-sell, etc.
    (c) restriction on who may purchase
    (d) terms of sale
    (e) right to sell or to compel purchase by partnership on reorganization, or on being outvoted on major decision
23. Expulsion of partner:
    (a) majority vote or unanimity of remaining partners
    (b) specify grounds:
        i)   insolvency
        ii) fraud
24. Dissolution:
    (a) specify grounds
    (b) specify events that are not to result in dissolution (e.g., death, insolvency)
    (c) dissolution on vote in case of major split among partners
    (d) tax effects
25. Admission of new partners:
    (a) special majority or unanimity on vote of partners
    (b) acceptance qualifications
    (c) new partner's capital contribution
    (d) allocation of new partner's interest from others
    (e) method of payment
26. Purchase of partner's interest:
    (a) obligation to purchase on death, retirement, expulsion, insolvency
    (b) option-to-purchase terms
    (c) right of first refusal
    (d) compulsory buy-sell

27. Partnership property:
    (a) identification of assets
    (b) valuation of assets including goodwill
    (c) title to assets
    (d) control of assets
    (e) maintenance, repair, and replacement
    (f) restrictions on personal use
    (g) distribution on termination
28. Insurance:
    (a) kinds, limits, and deductibles
    (b) fire, boiler, theft, automobile, tenant's liability, personal injury, products liability, errors and omissions
    (c) life insurance on other partners sufficient to fund purchase of other partner's share, and agreement of partners to facilitate obtaining such insurance (provision if a partner is uninsurable)
29. Partners' liability:
    (a) to one another
    (b) to third parties
    (c) partnership liability
30. Arbitration:
    (a) named individual (auditor for financial matters)
    (b) Arbitration Act
31. Registrations:
    (a) grant irrevocable power of attorney to other partners for purpose of effecting all necessary registrations
32. Amendment:
    (a) written
    (b) majority rule or unanimity
33. Applicable law (province)
34. No assignment of agreement
35. Addresses of partners
36. Partners' signatures on agreement

CHECKLIST 4
(See Chapter 5)

Business Deductions

Note: The tax laws are constantly changing, so be sure to verify annually the following deductible items with a professionally qualified accountant or other tax authority. Some exceptions to the following deductions may apply.

_____	Accounting or bookkeeping services
_____	Advertising expenses
_____	Automobile expenses
_____	Bad debts/bounced cheques
_____	Books related to business
_____	Briefcase or samples case
_____	Business development expenses
_____	Business gifts
_____	Business identity plan (I.D.)
_____	Christmas cards for business associates
_____	Cleaning services (supplies, equipment, service)
_____	Commissions (sales representatives, agents, others)
_____	Computer hardware and software (depreciated)
_____	Consulting fees
_____	Conventions and trade show expenses
_____	Delivery charges
_____	Donations (charitable or business-related)
_____	Dues to professional organizations
_____	Educational expense (business seminars, workshops, classes, handbooks, manuals)
_____	Entertainment, business-related (80% deductible; must be carefully documented)
_____	Equipment lease costs
_____	Equipment purchases (may be depreciated or expensed)
_____	Freight and shipping charges
_____	House-related expenses (mortgage interest, depreciation, utilities, services, repairs)
_____	Insurance premiums (product liability, special riders on homeowner's policy, computer insurance, etc.)
_____	Interest on business loans or charge cards, bank charges
_____	Labour costs (independent contractors or employees)
_____	Lease payments (equipment, etc.)
_____	Legal and professional fees
_____	Licences and permits
_____	Mail box rental
_____	Mailing list development and maintenance
_____	Maintenance contracts on office equipment and other repairs
_____	Membership fees in business-related organizations

_____ Office furnishings (depreciated)
_____ Office supplies
_____ Postage
_____ Product displays
_____ Professional services (designers, artists, copywriters, etc.)
_____ Refunds to customers
_____ Rent (apartment or house)
_____ Research and development expense
_____ Safety deposit box (if it holds documents related to business)
_____ Salaries (including those paid to spouse or children)
_____ Salary expense (employer's contributions to CPP, UIC, WCB, etc.)
_____ Stationery and printing
_____ Subscriptions to business magazines and periodicals
_____ Supplies and materials
_____ Tax preparer's fee
_____ Telephone (equipment, monthly service charges, long-distance calls, etc.)
_____ Telephone answering service/machine
_____ Tools of your trade
_____ Travel expenses connected with business (meals and lodging for overnight stays, plus airfare, train, bus, taxi, auto expense, tips, and tolls)
_____ Other (itemize.)

CHECKLIST 5
(See Chapter 7)

Creative Sources of Financing or Money Saving

Sources of Financing	Possible Source	Need Further Info	Further Info Obtained
1. Modifying Personal Lifestyle			
• Reducing personal long-distance telephone calls	_____	_____	_____
• Minimizing entertainment expenses	_____	_____	_____
• Minimizing transportation costs	_____	_____	_____
• Cutting down on tobacco and alcohol	_____	_____	_____
• Reducing number of meals out	_____	_____	_____
• Converting your holidays into part-business trips	_____	_____	_____
2. Using Personal Assets			
• Remortgaging your home	_____	_____	_____
• Selling personal assets to the business	_____	_____	_____

- Using credit cards to conserve cash   _____ _____ _____
- Using personal line of credit   _____ _____ _____
- Reducing premiums by reassessing insurance policy   _____ _____ _____
- Using funds in personal bank accounts   _____ _____ _____
- Renting out part of your home or garage   _____ _____ _____
- Selling stocks and bonds   _____ _____ _____
- Cashing in pension plans (e.g., RRSPs)   _____ _____ _____
- Selling unnecessary personal possessions (e.g., second car)   _____ _____ _____

3. Using Potential Private Investors Known to You
- Previous employers   _____ _____ _____
- Previous coworkers   _____ _____ _____
- Friends and neighbours   _____ _____ _____
- Lawyer, accountant, stockbroker   _____ _____ _____

4. Family Assistance
- Loans from relatives   _____ _____ _____
- Loans from immediate family members   _____ _____ _____
- Equity financing from relatives   _____ _____ _____
- Equity financing from immediate family members   _____ _____ _____
- Employing family members   _____ _____ _____

5. Using Customers' Funds
- Having a "cash only" policy   _____ _____ _____
- Invoicing on an interim basis   _____ _____ _____
- Asking for advance payments or deposits   _____ _____ _____
- Providing discounts for prompt payments   _____ _____ _____
- Charging purchases on customers' credit card accounts   _____ _____ _____
- Getting signed purchase orders or contracts (collateral for bank)   _____ _____ _____
- Third-party billing of long-distance phone calls to customer's account   _____ _____ _____

6. Using Suppliers' Funds
- Supplier loans   _____ _____ _____
- Establishing credit accounts with suppliers   _____ _____ _____
- Buying goods on consignment   _____ _____ _____
- Equipment loans from manufacturer   _____ _____ _____

- Installment financing   _____ _____ _____
- Conditional sales agreement   _____ _____ _____
- Co-op advertising   _____ _____ _____

7. Leasing
- Selling your assets and leasing
  them back through a commercial
  leasing company   _____ _____ _____
- Leasing assets rather than
  purchasing   _____ _____ _____

8. Volume Discounts
- Buying groups   _____ _____ _____
- Agency discounts   _____ _____ _____
- Co-op advertising   _____ _____ _____
- Group rates on insurance   _____ _____ _____

9. Other Creative Financing Techniques
- Advance royalty deals   _____ _____ _____
- Licensing your product or service   _____ _____ _____
- Franchisor financing   _____ _____ _____
- Franchising your business   _____ _____ _____
- Contra bartering (exchanging
  service/product for service/
  product)   _____ _____ _____
- RRSP (defer tax)   _____ _____ _____
- Assigning exclusive rights to
  copyright or patent, etc.   _____ _____ _____

CHECKLIST 6
(See Chapter 7)

Credit and Correction Procedures

Credit Approval	**Yes**	**No**	**N/A**
1. Have you thoroughly considered the advantages and disadvantages of extending credit?	_____	_____	_____
2. Is a written credit application required with every credit request?	_____	_____	_____
3. Do you have a standard form for credit applications prepared by your lawyer?	_____	_____	_____
4. Are you a member of your local credit bureau? Dun & Bradstreet?	_____	_____	_____

5. Are applicants checked out with their bank, the credit bureau, or the credit agency (e.g., Dun & Bradstreet) before credit is extended? _____ _____ _____

Terms of Sale

6. Do you offer a discount for cash payments? _____ _____ _____
7. Do you encourage COD sales? Or require an advance deposit for a large order? _____ _____ _____
8. Do you charge interest on overdue accounts? _____ _____ _____
9. Are the payment terms and time limit for payment clearly stated on invoices, statements, and credit contracts? _____ _____ _____

Invoices

10. Are invoices prepared and mailed promptly or on a regular basis? _____ _____ _____
11. Is the invoice preparation always accurate? _____ _____ _____
12. Are payment terms clearly stated? _____ _____ _____

Statements

13. Do you have an efficient, organized system for rendering statements? _____ _____ _____
14. Are monthly or bimonthly statements mailed to all open accounts? _____ _____ _____

Identification of Problems

15. Do you have a monthly aging of all outstanding accounts receivable? _____ _____ _____
16. Do you compare your average collection period:
    • With industry averages? _____ _____ _____
    • With your previous experience? _____ _____ _____
    • With your payment terms? _____ _____ _____
17. Do you calculate your monthly bad debt percentage and is this acceptable to you? _____ _____ _____

Collection

18. Do you have a systematic procedure to follow up slow accounts? _____ _____ _____

19. If you use the telephone to contact delinquent accounts, is it effective? _____ _____ _____

20. Do you write a letter of confirmation following all collection calls? _____ _____ _____

21. Do you accurately record on the client's account details of the collection conversations? _____ _____ _____

22. Do you have a late payment penalty or interest charge, and do you attempt to collect it? _____ _____ _____

23. Do you try to retain the goodwill of your customers in your collection procedures? _____ _____ _____

24. Do you sell to delinquent accounts on COD terms? _____ _____ _____

25. Do you send all overdue accounts over 45 or 60 days to a collection agency (credit bureau or Dun & Bradstreet) or to your lawyer, or both? _____ _____ _____

Credit Policy

26. Have you taken any seminars on credit and collection techniques from Dun & Bradstreet, FBDB, or others? _____ _____ _____

27. Are your credit terms comparable to those of your competitors? _____ _____ _____

28. Have you contracted with a cheque verification service for unknown clients? _____ _____ _____

29. Do you have a stamp you place on back of a cheque requesting details from an unknown customer? _____ _____ _____

30. Do you take credit cards for customer payment (VISA, MasterCard, American Express)? _____ _____ _____

CHECKLIST 7
(See Chapter 8)

Competition Checklist

Compare the characteristics of your competition with those of your own business. Who are your major competitors? What are their strengths and weaknesses? What does this tell you about your business and your marketing strategy?

	Competitor 1			Competitor 2			Competitor 3			Your Own Situation		
	Better	Equal	Worse	Better	Equal	Worse	Better	Equal	Worse	Good	Avg.	Poor
Prices												
Quality												
Product selection												
Customer attention												
Special service												
Reliability												
Expert advice												
Guarantees												
Credit cards												
Location												
Business hours												
Business image												
Advertising												
Product packaging												
Distribution method												

The time to analyze the competition is *all the time!* Be sure of your market position by knowing what your competitors are doing with their products, prices, and services.

SAMPLES

SAMPLE 1
(See Chapter 2)

Personal Net Worth Statement
(Format Commonly Requested by Lenders)

Name	Date of birth	Social insurance number

Street address	City	Province	Postal code

Home phone ( )	Residence ___ Own ___ Rent ___ Other	How long at address? ___ years ___ months

Occupation	Currently employed with:	How long with employer? ___ years ___ months

Employer's phone ___ Married ___ Unmarried ___ Separated
( ) ___ Number of dependants

Your principal financial institution and address

Personal Data on Your Spouse
Under the laws of Canada and of some provinces, your spouse may have legal interest or obligation arising from your business dealings and may also have an interest in your personal assets.

Spouse's name   Spouse's occupation

Spouse currently employed by:	How long with employer? ___ years ___ months	Spouse's work phone ( )

Financial Information
As at _____ _____, 19___ .
         Day   Month

Assets
(List and describe all assets.)   **Value**

Total of chequing accounts	$_____
Total of savings accounts	$_____
Life insurance cash surrender value	$_____
Automobile: Make _____ Year _____	$_____

Stocks and bonds (See Schedule A attached.) $ _____
Accounts/notes receivable (Please itemize):

_____ $ _____

_____ $ _____

_____ $ _____

Term deposits (cashable) $ _____
Real estate (See Schedule B attached.) $ _____
Retirement plans:

_____ RRSP $ _____

_____ Employment pension plan $ _____

_____ Other $ _____

Other assets (household goods, etc.):

_____ Art $ _____

_____ Jewelry $ _____

_____ Antiques $ _____

_____ Other $ _____

TOTAL ASSETS (A) $ _____ (A)

Liabilities
(List credit cards, open lines of
credit, and other liabilities including
alimony and child support.)

	Balance Owing	**Monthly Payment**
Bank loans	$ _____	$ _____
Mortgages on real estate owned (See Schedule B attached.)	$ _____	$ _____
	$ _____	$ _____
	$ _____	$ _____
Monthly rent payment	$ _____	$ _____
Credit cards (Please itemize):		
_____	$ _____	$ _____
_____	$ _____	$ _____
_____	$ _____	$ _____
_____	$ _____	$ _____
_____	$ _____	$ _____
Money borrowed from life insurance policy	$ _____	$ _____
Margin accounts	$ _____	$ _____
Current income tax owing	$ _____	$ _____
Other obligations (Please itemize):		
_____	$ _____	$ _____
_____	$ _____	$ _____
_____	$ _____	$ _____

Total monthly payments		$ _____
TOTAL LIABILITIES (B)	$ _____	(B)
NET WORTH (A – B)	$ _____	(A – B)

Income Sources

Income from alimony, child support, or separate maintenance does not have to be stated unless you want it considered.

Your gross monthly salary	$ _____
Your spouse's gross monthly salary	$ _____
Net monthly rental (from Schedule B attached)	$ _____
Other income (Please itemize):	
_____	$ _____
_____	$ _____
_____	$ _____
TOTAL	$ _____

Sundry Personal Obligations

Please provide details below if you answer yes to the following question.

_____

Are you providing your personal support for obligations not listed above (i.e., cosigner, endorser, guarantor)?
___ Yes ___ No
Details of any of the above:

_____

Schedule A: Stocks, Bonds, and Other Investments

Quantity	Description	Where Quoted	Market Value	Pledged as Collateral? Yes	No
_____	_____	_____	_____	_____	_____
_____	_____	_____	_____	_____	_____
_____	_____	_____	_____	_____	_____
_____	_____	_____	_____	_____	_____
_____	_____	_____	_____	_____	_____

TOTAL _____

Schedule B: Real Estate Owned

Please provide information on your share only of real estate owned.

_____

Property address (primary residence)   Legal description

_____

Street   City   Province

_____

| Type of property | Present market value
$ | Amount of mortgage liens
1st $ 2nd $ |

| Gross monthly income rental
$ | Monthly mortgage payments
1st $ 2nd $ |

| Monthly taxes insurance maintenance
and miscellaneous
$ | Net monthly rental income
$ |

| Name of mortgage
holder(s) | First mortgage | Second mortgage |

| Percentage ownership
       % | Month/year acquired | Purchase price
$ |

General Information

Please provide details if you answer yes to any of the following questions.

Have you ever had an asset repossessed?	___ Yes	___ No
Are you party to any claims or lawsuits?	___ Yes	___ No
Have you ever declared bankruptcy?	___ Yes	___ No
Do you owe any taxes prior to the current year?	___ Yes	___ No

Details:

The undersigned declare(s) that the statements made herein are for the purpose of obtaining business financing and are to the best of my/our knowledge true and correct. The applicant(s) consent(s) to the Bank making any enquiries it deems necessary to reach a decision on this application, and consent(s) to the disclosure at any time of any credit information about me/us to any credit reporting agency or to anyone with whom I/we have financial relations.

| Date | Signature of applicant(s) above |

SAMPLE 2
(See Chapter 2)

Business Plan Format

Note: Modify as appropriate for your needs. Not all sections will be necessarily applicable to you at this time or at all.

Introductory Page
- Company name
  (include address and phone number)
- Contact person
  (presenter's name and phone number)
- Paragraph about company
  (nature of business and market area)
- Securities offered to investors (if applicable)
  (preferred shares, common shares, debentures, etc.)
- Business loans sought (if applicable)
  (term loan, operating line of credit)

Summary
- Highlights of Business Plan
  (your project, competitive advantage, and "bottom line" in a nutshell —
  preferably one page maximum in length)

Table of Contents
- Section titles and page numbers
  (for easy reference)

PART 1: BUSINESS CONCEPT

Description of the Industry
- Industry outlook and growth potential
  (industry trends, new products and developments) (State your sources
  of information.)
- Markets and customers
  (size of total market, new requirements, and market trends)
- Competitive companies
  (market share, strengths and weaknesses, profitability)
- National and economic trends
  (population shifts, consumer trends, relevant economic indicators)

Description of Business Venture
- Product(s) or service
  (pictures, drawings, characteristics, quality)
- Product protection/exclusive rights
  (patents, copyrights, trademarks, industrial design, franchise rights)
- Target market
  (typical customers identified by group; present buying pattern and
  average purchase in dollars; wants and needs)
- Competitive advantage of your business concept
  (your market niche, uniqueness, estimated market share)

- Business location and size
  (location[s] relative to market, size of premises)
- Staff and equipment needed
  (overall requirement, capacity)
- Brief history
  (principals involved, development work done)

Business Goals

- One year
  (specific goals, such as gross sales, profit margins, share of market;
  moving out of home and opening new store, plant, or office;
  introducing new product; etc.)
- Over the longer term
  (return on investment, business net worth, sale of business)

Marketing Plan

- Sales strategy
  (commissioned sales staff, agents, pieceworkers, independent
  contractors, sales objectives, target customers, sales tools, sales
  support)
- Distribution
  (direct to public, wholesale, retail, multiple outlets)
- Pricing
  (costing, markups, margins, break-even)
- Promotion
  (media advertising, promotions, publicity — appropriate to reach
  target market)
- Guarantees
  (product guarantees, service warranties)
- Tracking methods
  (method for confirming who your customers are and how they heard
  about you)

Sales Forecast

- Assumptions
  (One never has all the necessary information, so state all the
  assumptions made in developing the forecast.)
- Monthly forecast for coming year
  (sales volume in units and dollars)
- Annual forecast for following two to four years
  (sales volume in dollars)

Note: The sales forecast is the starting point for your project income
statement and cash flow forecast in Part II.

Production Plan (Manufacturing)

- Brief description of production process
  (Don't be too technical.)
- Physical plant requirements
  (building, utility requirements, expansion capability, layout)

- Machinery and equipment
  (new or used, lease or purchase, capacity)
- Raw materials
  (readily available, quality, sources)
- Inventory requirements
  (seasonal levels, turnover rates, methods of control)
- Suppliers
  (volume discounts, multiple sources)
- Personnel required
  (full-time, part-time, skill level, availability, training required)
- Cost of facilities, equipment, and materials
  (estimates and quotations)
- Capital estimates
  (one-time startup or expansion capital required)

Production Plan (Retail or Service)
- Purchasing plans
  (volume discounts, multiple sources, quality, price)
- Inventory system
  (seasonal variation, turnover rates, method of control)
- Space requirements
  (floor and office space, improvement required, expansion capability)
- Staff and equipment required
  (personnel by skill level, fixtures, office equipment)

Corporate Structure
- Legal form
  (proprietorship, partnership, corporation)
- Share distribution
  (list of principal shareholders)
- List of contracts and agreements in force
  (management contract, shareholder or partnership agreement,
  franchisor service agreement, service contract)
- Directors and officers
  (names and addresses and role in company)
- Background of key management personnel
  (brief résumés of active owners and key employees)
- Contract professionals/consultants
  (possible outside assistance in specialized or deficient areas)
- Duties and responsibilities of key personnel
  (brief job descriptions — who is responsible for what)

Risk Assessment
- Competitors' reaction
  (Will competitors try to squeeze you out?)

- "What if" list for critical external factors
  (anticipated effects of strikes, recession, new technology, weather, new competition, supplier problems, shifts in consumer demand)
- "What if" list for critical internal factors
  (effects if sales off by 30%, sales double, key manager quits, workers quit)
- Dealing with risks
  (contingency plans to handle the most significant risks)

Action Plan

- Steps to accomplish this year's goals
  (flow chart by month or by quarter of specific action to be taken and by whom) (Also refer to Checklist 1.)
- Checkpoints for measuring results
  (identify significant dates, sales levels, production levels as decision points.)

PART II: FINANCIAL PLAN

Financial Statements

- Previous years' balance sheets and income statements
  (include past two to three years if applicable.)

Financial Forecasts

- Opening balance sheet
  (for a new business only)
- Projected income statements
  (detailed operating forecast for next year of operation and less detailed forecast for following two years) (Use sales forecast as starting point.)
- Cash flow forecast
  (budget of cash inflow and outflow on a monthly basis for next year of operation) (See Sample 5.)

Financing and Capitalization

- Term loan applied for
  (amount, terms, when required)
- Purpose of term loan
  (Attach detailed description of assets to be financed with cost quotations.)
- Owners' equity
  (your level of commitment to the financing aspect)
- Summary of term loan requirements
  (for a particular project or for business as a whole)

Program		Example Financing	
Leasehold improvements	$ 20,000		
Equipment and machinery	60,000	Term loan from bank	$ 40,000
Vehicles	30,000	Owners' initial investment	
Non-recurring startup expenses	10,000	to fund the company	50,000
		New investor*	30,000
	$120,000		$120,000

*If the purpose of the Business Plan is to attract a new investor, further details would be given here concerning share participation, role in company, etc.

Operating Loan
- Line of credit applied for
  (new or increase, security offered)
- Maximum operating cash requirement
  (amount, timing) (Refer to cash flow forecast.)

Present Financing (if Applicable)
- Term loans outstanding
  (balance owing, repayment terms, purpose, security held)
- Current operating line of credit
  (amount, security held)

References
- Name of present lending institution
  (branch, type of accounts)
- Lawyer's name
  (include address and phone number.)
- Accountant's name
  (include address and phone number.)

Appendix
The following documents *may* be requested by your banker or potential investor:
- Personal net worth statement
  (include personal property values, investments, cash, bank loans, charge accounts, mortgages, and other liabilities. This will substantiate the value of your personal guarantee if required for security.)
- Letters of intent
  (potential orders, customer commitments, letters of support)
- List of inventory
  (type, age, value)
- List of leasehold improvements
  (description, when made)

- List of fixed assets
  (description, age, serial numbers)
- Price lists
  (to support cost estimates)
- Description of insurance coverage
  (insurance policies, amount of coverage)
- Accounts receivable summary
  (include aging schedule.)
- Accounts payable summary
  (include schedule of payments.)
- Copies of legal agreements
  (contracts, lease, franchise agreement, mortgage, debenture)
- Appraisals
  (property, equipment)
- Financial statements for associated companies
  (where appropriate)

FINALLY...

Preparing a business plan will generate a lot of thought and a lot of paper! Keep in mind, however, that the final document is a summary of your planning process. You can always refer to your working papers later on to substantiate a particular point.

Have your key employees and two or three impartial outsiders review the finished plan in detail. There may be something you have overlooked or underemphasized. Also, a critical review will be good preparation for your presentation to potential investors and lenders.

APPROACHING LENDERS

When approaching any financial institution, you are effectively selling the merits of your business proposal. As in all sales, consider the needs of the other party:

- Ability to serve the debt with sufficient surplus to cover contingencies
  (carry interest charges, eventually repay in full) (Cash flow forecast and projected income statement will show this.)
- Track record/integrity
  (personal credit history, management ability as demonstrated in your business plan, company results)
- Your level of commitment
  (your equity in the business or cash investment in the particular asset being purchased)

- Secondary source of repayment
  (includes security in the event of default and other sources of income) (Discuss this subject with your lawyer before submitting your proposal.)
- Lead time
  (Lender needs a reasonable time to assess your proposal — also, the loan may have to be referred to another level within the financial institution.)
- Don't overdo it
  (Be sensible with the amount of documentation you provide initially — for example, the Introductory Page, Summary, and Financial Plan sections alone provide a good basic loan submission if the amount requested is small.)

ATTRACTING INVESTORS

Start first by approaching people you know (i.e., friends; bank, credit union, or trust company manager; lawyer; accountant; doctor). They, in turn, may know of possible investors. If your business concept exhibits high growth potential, a second alternative is to approach a venture capital company. Either way, take a moment to consider the investor's needs, which may differ from a lender's needs:

- Your level of commitment
  (To be sure that you are sharing the risk.)
- Share participation
  (Investors may demand more equity than you are willing to give.)
- Rate of return
  (Investors are willing to take a high risk, but they also expect a high rate of return — e.g., to double their money in two to three years.)
- Involvement in key decisions
  (Possibly as a director or even an officer of the company.)
- Regular financial reporting
  (Investors usually want to see tight financial controls in place and prompt financial reporting.)

SAMPLE 3
(See Chapter 2)

Personal Cost-of-Living Budget

A. Income (average monthly income, actual or estimated)

Salary, bonuses, commissions, dividends $_____

Interest income $_____

Other: _____ $_____

Total Monthly Income $_____

B. Expenses (Average Monthly, Actual or Estimated)

1. Regular Monthly Payments

Rent or mortgage payments $_____

Automobile loan $_____

Personal loan $_____

Credit card payments $_____

Insurance premiums (medical, life,
  house, auto) $_____

Investment plan deductions (RRSP, etc.) $_____

Other: _____ $_____

Total Regular Monthly Payments $_____

2. Household Operating Expenses

Telephone $_____

Heat, gas, and electricity $_____

Water and garbage $_____

Repairs and maintenance $_____

Other: _____ $_____

Total Household Operating Expenses $_____

3. Personal Expenses

Clothing, cleaning, laundry $_____

Food (at home, away from home) $_____

Medical/dental $_____

Day care $_____

Education $_____

Gifts, donations, and dues $_____

Recreation and travel $_____

Newspapers, magazines, books $_____

Automobile maintenance, gas, and parking $_____

Spending money, allowances $_____

Other: _____ $_____

Total Personal Expenses $_____

4. Tax Expenses

Federal and provincial income taxes $ _____

Home property taxes $ _____

Other: _____ $ _____

Total Tax Expenses $ _____

TOTAL MONTHLY EXPENSES $ _____

TOTAL MONTHLY DISPOSABLE INCOME
    AVAILABLE $ _____

(Subtract total monthly expenses from
    total monthly income.)

SAMPLE 4
(See Chapter 2)

Projected Financial Needs for First Three Months

This worksheet will help you to estimate the amount of money you will
need for the first three months of business operation. *Note*: This
worksheet relates to your business expenses only. You will have to also
calculate your personal cost of living expenses on a separate sheet
provided (Sample 3), making certain not to duplicate income or expense
items.

Cash Available

Owner's cash on hand $ _____

Loan from relative or friend   _____

Other: _____   _____

Total Cash on Hand $ _____

Startup Costs

Repairs, renovations, and decorating $ _____

Equipment (including installation costs)   _____

Furniture   _____

Insurance (homeowners' rider, personal
    and product liability)   _____

Inventory   _____

Product materials and office supplies   _____

Advertising and promotion (Yellow Pages,
    business cards, stationery, flyers,
    newspaper ads, etc.)   _____

Other: _____   _____

Total Startup Costs $ _____

Operating Costs

Wages of owner $3 \times$ $ _____ = $ _____

Utilities $3 \times$ $ _____ =   _____

Supplies and inventory 3 × $\underline{\hspace{2cm}}$ = $\underline{\hspace{2cm}}$
Advertising 3 × $\underline{\hspace{2cm}}$ = $\underline{\hspace{2cm}}$
Auto and travel 3 × $\underline{\hspace{2cm}}$ = $\underline{\hspace{2cm}}$
Contingency 3 × $\underline{\hspace{2cm}}$ = $\underline{\hspace{2cm}}$

Total Operating Costs $\underline{\hspace{3cm}}$

Total Startup and Three-Month Operating Costs $\underline{\hspace{2cm}}$

TOTAL MONEY NEEDED FOR FIRST THREE MONTHS OF BUSINESS $\underline{\hspace{3cm}}$

SAMPLE 5
(See Chapter 2)

Cash Flow Worksheet

Month Of:

Cash Receipts (Cash In)	Planned	Actual	Planned	Actual	Planned	Actual
1. Cash sales						
2. Collection from accounts receivable (credit sales payments)						
3. Term loan proceeds						
4. Sale of fixed assets						
5. Other cash received						
6. **Total Cash In**						

Cash Disbursements (Cash Out)

	Planned	Actual	Planned	Actual	Planned	Actual
7. Rent (for premises, equipment etc.)						
8. Management salaries						
9. Other salaries and wages						
10. Legal and accounting fees						

11. Utilities (heat, light, and water) _____ _____ _____ _____ _____ _____

12. Telephone _____ _____ _____ _____ _____ _____

13. Repairs and maintenance _____ _____ _____ _____ _____ _____

14. Licences and municipal taxes _____ _____ _____ _____ _____ _____

15. Insurance _____ _____ _____ _____ _____ _____

16. Other operating expenses _____ _____ _____ _____ _____ _____

17. Payments on purchase of fixed assets _____ _____ _____ _____ _____ _____

18. Interest paid on loans (short-term loans, lines of credit, overdrafts) _____ _____ _____ _____ _____ _____

19. Payments on mortgages/term loans _____ _____ _____ _____ _____ _____

20. Income tax payments _____ _____ _____ _____ _____ _____

21. Cash dividends paid _____ _____ _____ _____ _____ _____

22. Payments on accounts payable/ inventories _____ _____ _____ _____ _____ _____

23. Other cash expenses _____ _____ _____ _____ _____ _____

24. **Total Cash Out** _____ _____ _____ _____ _____ _____

Reconciliation of Cash Flow

25. Opening cash balance _____ _____ _____ _____ _____ _____

26. Add: Cash In (line 6) _____ _____ _____ _____ _____ _____

27. Deduct: Cash Out (line 24) _____ _____ _____ _____ _____ _____

28. Surplus or (deficit) _____ _____ _____ _____ _____ _____

29. Closing cash balance _____ _____ _____ _____ _____ _____

Projected Cash Sales and Accounts Receivable

Month

Projected sales

Cash sales (line 1)

Collection of previous
month's sales

Collection of sales from two
months previous

Collection of sales from
more than two months
previous

Collection from accounts
receivable (line 2)

Projected Accounts Payable

Month

Planned purchases

Payments on current
month's purchases

Payments on purchases
from two months
previous

Payments on purchases
from more than two
months previous

Payments on accounts
payable (line 22)

EXPLANATIONS

Lines 1, 2, and 22 of the cash flow have been completed by the exercises on page 289 (Projected Cash Sales and Accounts Receivable plus Projected Accounts Payable) and their total should now be inserted on the worksheet.

Line 3   **Loans** If you take possession of borrowed money during the month, list this cash receipt.

Line 4   **Sale of fixed assets** If you sell a fixed asset such as a piece of office furniture or a vehicle, list the cash income in the monthly column when payment is received.

Line 5   **Other cash** List all other cash income such as interest, rent, shareholders' loans, etc.

Line 6   Total of lines 1-5.

Lines 7-16   **Operating expenses** Enter the amount of cheques that you write for your monthly expenses. This is actual cash outlay for the month; for example, if you write a cheque in January for the full year's insurance, the amount of the cheque would be put in the January column and nothing would be entered for the rest of the year.

     Other operating expenses The expense items listed in the format may not be applicable to your business. The headings should be changed so that they are applicable to your situation.

Line 17   **Payments on purchase of a fixed asset** If money is spent for the purchase of fixed assets such as a vehicle or a filing cabinet, list the amount for the month when the cheque is written.

Line 18   **Interest paid on loans** This is the interest paid monthly on short-term loans such as bank overdrafts or lines of credit. Since you are in the process of working out the amount of money you will need to borrow, this interest figure may be very difficult to estimate. Consequently, you may decide to leave the line blank for now. If it is likely to be a small amount, you may decide to omit it altogether.

Line 19   **Payments on mortgage/loans** Indicate the monthly payment for the principal and interest on long-term loans. For example, if you borrow $20,000 to purchase a half-ton truck and monthly payments are $550 with the first payment due in March, then $550 will be entered in line 19 for each month beginning in March.

Lines 20-21   **Income tax payments and cash dividends paid** The amounts you expect to pay, if any.

Line 23	**Other cash expenses** The expense items listed in the format may not be applicable to your business. The headings should be changed so that they are appropriate for your situation.
Line 24	**Total cash out** Total all possible cash payments for the month.
Line 25	**Opening cash balance** The amount of money you started out the month with.
Line 28	**Surplus or deficit for the month — cash in minus cash out** If line 28 is a deficit, the operating bank loan should be increased to cover the deficit. Sometimes a bank will require a minimum balance to remain in the account at all times. If line 28 is a surplus, excess funds should be applied on the operating loan.
Line 29	**Closing cash balance** The amount of money you started out with plus (or minus) the amount of cash surplus at month's end. The closing cash balance becomes next month's opening cash balance.

SAMPLE 6
(See Chapter 8)

Media Release

Contact: Joan Brown   FOR IMMEDIATE RELEASE
Smith & Company   May 1, 19___
100 Main Street
Anytown, Any Province X0X 1X0

Consultant Gives Tips on Avoiding House-Buying Pitfalls

TORONTO — David Smith, a property inspection consultant with Smith & Company, will be conducting a seminar on the pitfalls of buying an older home, and how to avoid them. The seminar is being given for the first time through Metro College.

"Many people don't realize the risk of buying an older home until it is too late," says Smith. "By then, the expense of repair or renovation could increase the original investment in the house beyond the owner's budget. The best way of preventing future headaches is to know what to look for in the pre-purchase stage so that you can negotiate realistically and budget accordingly."

The seminar topics include: what to look for in inspecting a home, how to negotiate with the vendor, how to select and negotiate with a contractor, local bylaw regulations, what renovations will provide the best return on your investment, government financial assistance for renovations, and how to avoid construction problems.

During the seminar, students will also have the opportunity to discuss their specific needs, concerns, and experiences relating to house inspection, repair, and renovations.

The one-day seminar will be held on Saturday, June 1, 19___, at Metro College. Cost is $55. Further information and a brochure can be obtained by contacting the Metro College non-credit division at 333-3333.

– 30 –

SAMPLE 7
(See Chapter 9)

Time Log

To accomplish today: Date _____

1. _____

2. _____

3. _____

4. _____

5. _____

Time	Activity	Total minutes	Priority level H/M/L	Comments
a.m.				
p.m.				

Priority Level

High ____hr ____min (____%)   Medium ____hr ____min (____%)

Low ____hr ____min (____%)

_____

SAMPLE 8
(See Chapter 9)

Weekly Time-Use Analysis

A. Planning and Priorities

**Rate on a Scale of 1 to 5
(One Point for Each Day)**

1. Did I plan my day ("to do" lists)?   _____
2. Did I set priorities?   _____
3. Did I stick with them?   _____
4. High priorities:
   - Number achieved   _____
   - Number — some progress   _____
   - Number — no action   _____
5. Overall success score on priority setting   _____
6. Problems encountered _____
   _____
7. Possible solutions _____
   _____

	When?	What Did I Do?
8. Most productive time	_____	_____
9. Discretionary time	_____	_____
10. Did I set a quiet hour?	_____	_____

B. Time Management
1. Delegation:
   - (a) What did I delegate?
   - (b) How effective?
   - (c) What else could I delegate?
2. Paperwork:
   - (a) Handled papers once: How effective?
   - (b) Tidy, clear desk: How effective?
   - (c) How much paper shuffling?
   - (d) Ways to improve
3. Meetings:
   - (a) Effectiveness of meetings I ran
   - (b) Effectiveness of someone else's meetings
   - (c) Problems
   - (d) Solutions

C. Time Wasters
1. Interruptions:
   - (a) Who? What purpose? How long?
   - (b) Ways to cut down or eliminate
2. Procrastination:
   - (a) What? Why?
   - (b) Possible solutions
3. Other time wasters:
   - (a) What? Who? How much?
   - (b) Causes
   - (c) Solutions

N.B.: You may choose to highlight your "solutions" and build them into your plan for next week.

SAMPLE 9
(See Chapter 12)

Evaluating Business Ideas

Needs:
- Financial: (e.g., $1,500 to $2,000 per month)
- Lifestyle: (e.g., evenings and Sundays free)
- Personal: (e.g., creativity, enjoyment, people contact)
- Business: (e.g., challenge)

Business Idea ___ : _____

Criteria	Details (Use additional paper as necessary)	Pro	Con	Neutral
1. Do you have the appropriate background experience/training?	_____		_____	
2. Will additional training be required, and for what length of time?	_____		_____	
3. Can business be operated on a part-time basis?	_____		_____	
4. Approx. amount of startup capital required	_____		_____	
5. Approx. amount of overhead expenses	_____		_____	
6. Approx. length of startup time before revenue is generated	_____		_____	
7. Anticipated revenue for:				
• First 3 months	_____		_____	
• First year	_____		_____	
• Second year	_____		_____	
8. What amount of space is required?	_____		_____	
9. Will you need to hire staff?	_____		_____	
10. Amount of personal interaction with:				
• Suppliers	_____		_____	
• Customers	_____		_____	
• Staff	_____		_____	
11. Degree of support/ assistance required from spouse:				
• Financial	_____		_____	
• Emotional	_____		_____	
• Physical	_____		_____	
12. Degree of personal needs met	_____		_____	
13. Degree of business needs met	_____		_____	

APPENDIXES

APPENDIX A
Sources of Further Information

Introduction

The cliché that "Knowledge is Power" is a fundamental truism in business. Thorough knowledge will greatly assist you in reaching your goals. It will show you are resourceful, enhance the quality of your decision-making, increase your confidence and decrease your stress. Knowledge is a function of research and utilization of available resources. There are many sources and resources to assist your learning curve. The following is a summary of key contact sources to facilitate your search.

Many of the following federal and provincial government departments and agencies have local or regional offices. Check the Blue Pages of your telephone directory. In many cases the government offices have toll-free phone numbers, or they will accept collect calls or phone you back at their expense. This is helpful to keep in mind if you are making general or specific enquiries, or want information sent to you and no local office exists.

The telephone numbers given here relating to government departments change from time to time. If this happens, the correct number can be obtained from directory assistance, or you could call the Federal Business Development Bank (FBDB) toll-free number to obtain information, contact addresses, and phone numbers relating to federal, provincial, and municipal programs that assist small business. You can also phone Reference Canada toll-free to obtain current information on federal government programs, services, and contact addresses and phone numbers. The number is listed in the Blue Pages of your directory under "Government of Canada."

A. FEDERAL GOVERNMENT

Foreign Affairs and International Trade Canada

Info Export Division
125 Sussex Drive
Ottawa, Ontario K1A 0G2
(613) 993-6435
Toll-free: 1-800-267-8376

An excellent and comprehensive information source of all federal government programs, services, assistance, and financial support for the novice or experienced exporter. Also contact for information relating to imports.

Federal Business Development Bank (FBDB)

800 Victoria Square
Tour de la Bourse, C.P. 335
Montréal, Québec H4Z 1L4
(514) 283-5904
Toll-free: 1-800-361-2126

A federal Crown corporation. For information on small business management seminars, clinic, CASE counselling, financing, financial matchmaking, do-it-yourself kits, publications, and government programs (federal, provincial, and municipal).

Industry Canada

235 Queen Street
Ottawa, Ontario K1A 0H5
(613) 995-8900

For information on incorporation, trademarks, trade names, copyright, patent, industrial design, bankruptcy, consumer protection legislation, and federal government assistance and incentive programs for small business, counselling on how to apply for those programs, and publications and directories. Offices in major cities throughout Canada.

Statistics Canada

Customer Enquiries
Tunney's Pasture
Ottawa, Ontario K1A 0T6
(613) 951-8116

For information and statistics on geographic, demographic, and other population characteristics for small business planning and decision-making. Publications and computer data access are available. Offices in major cities throughout Canada.

Public Works and Government Services Canada

Communications Services
45 Sacre-Coeur Boulevard
Hull, Québec K1A 0S7
(613) 997-6363

Toll-free: 1-800-361-4637

For information on how to sell products or services to federal government and Crown corporations, statistical information, and publications. Offices in major cities throughout Canada.

B. PROVINCIAL GOVERNMENTS

For information on provincial small business financial assistance and
match-making programs, free counselling, seminars, publications,
small business reference material, selling goods or services to provincial governments, and management assistance programs.

British Columbia

Ministry of Tourism, Small Business and Culture
760 Pacific Boulevard South
Vancouver, B.C. V6B 5E7
Toll-free: 1-800-972-2255

Alberta

Department of Economic Development and Trade
Sterling Place
#9940 - 106 Street
6th Floor
Edmonton, Alberta T5K 2P6
Toll-free: 1-800-272-9675

Saskatchewan

Department of Economic Development and Tourism
1919 Saskatchewan Drive
Regina, Saskatchewan S4P 3V7
(306) 787-2207

Manitoba

Department of Industry, Trade and Tourism
155 Carlton Street
6th Floor
Winnipeg, Manitoba R3C 3H8
(204) 945-7738
Toll-free: 1-800-282-8069

Ontario

Ministry of Industry, Trade and Technology
Small Business Advice and Counsel
Hearst Block
900 Bay Street
7th Floor
Toronto, Ontario M7A 2E1
(416) 965-5494
Toll-free: 1-800-387-6142

Quebec

Ministére de l'industrie et du commerce
930, chemin Ste-Foy
5e étage
Québec, Québec G1S 2L4
(418) 643-5070

Communication — Québec
Bureau régional du Québec
870 rue Charest est
Québec, Québec G1K 8S5
Long distance: (418)-643-1344
Zenith for toll-free number

New Brunswick

Department of Commerce and Technology
Centennial Building
King Street
Suite 517
P.O. Box 6000
Fredericton, N.B. E3B 5H1
(506) 453-3608

Prince Edward Island

Department of Industry
Small Business Division
Shaw Building
Rochford Street
Charlottetown, P.E.I. C1A 7N8
(902) 368-4219

Nova Scotia

Department of Small Business Development
1690 Hollis Street
Suite 700
Halifax, N.S. B3J 3J9
(902) 424-6660

Newfoundland

Department of Development
Confederation Building
West Block
4th Floor
P.O. Box 8700
St. John's, Newfoundland A1B 4J6
(709) 576-5680

Northwest Territories

Ministry of Economic Development and Tourism
P.O. Box 1320
Yellowknife, N.W.T. X1A 2L9
(403) 920-3349

Yukon Territory

Department of Economic Development
Mines and Small Business
Box 2703
Whitehorse, Yukon Y1A 2C6
(403) 667-5466

C. SMALL BUSINESS EDUCATION INSTITUTE

This organization provides research, consulting and education programs on a national basis, on all aspects of small and home business development. This includes business startup, expansion, diversification, purchase, sale, management, franchising and financing. It also offers extensive consulting services across the country. Contact:

Canadian Enterprise Institute Inc.
#300 - 3665 Kingsway
Vancouver, B.C.
V5R 5W2

APPENDIX B
Recommended Reading

Note: Asterisk denotes Canadian content.

BOOKS

Business Opportunities

Chapman, A. C. *Small Business Opportunities*. Englewood Cliffs, NJ: Prentice Hall, 1984.

Davidson, Peter. *Earn Money at Home*. New York: McGraw-Hill, 1981.

Feinman, Jeffrey. *100 Surefire Businesses You Can Start with Little or No Investment*. New York: Jove Publications, 1976.

Hausman, Carl and the Philip Lief Group. *Moonlighting: 148 Great Ways to Make Money on the Side*. New York: Avon Books, 1989.

Hoelscher, Russ von. *Making Money for Yourself*. San Diego, CA: Profit Ideas, 1987.

Holtz, Herman R. *Profit from Your Money-Making Ideas*. New York: Amacom, 1982.

Kahm, H. S. *50 Big Money Businesses You Can Start and Run with $250-$5,000*. New York: Doubleday, 1985.

Kahn, Sharon and the Philip Lief Group. *101 Best Businesses to Start*. New York: Doubleday, 1988.

Levinson, Jay Conrad. *555 Ways to Earn Extra Money*. New York: Holt, Rinehart & Winston, 1982.

Revel, Chase. *184 Businesses Anyone Can Start*. New York: Bantam Books, 1987.

_____. *168 More Businesses Anyone Can Start*. New York: Bantam Books, 1984.

Stockwell, John and Herbert Holtje. *100 Ways to Make Money in Your Spare Time, Starting with Less Than $100*. West Nyack, NY: Parker Publishing Co., 1972.

Entrepreneur Profiles

Bailey, Geoffrey. *Maverick: Succeeding as a Freelance Entrepreneur*. Toronto: Watts, 1982.

Barnes, Kenneth and Everett Banning. *Money Makers: The Secrets of Canada's Most Successful Entrepreneurs*. Toronto: General Publishing, 1985.*

Carter, John Mack and Joan Feeny. *Starting at the Top: America's New Achievers*. New York: William Morrow & Company, 1985.

Cohen, Albert D. *The Entrepreneurs: The Story of Gendis Inc.* Toronto: McClelland and Stewart, 1985.*

Cooke, Ronald J. *Money-Making Ideas for Retirees.* Toronto: Stoddart, 1983.*

Fiffer, Steve. *So You've Got a Great Idea?* Reading, MA: Addison-Wesley, 1986.

Fraser, Matthew. *Quebec Inc.: French Canadian Entrepreneurs and the New Business Elite.* Toronto: Key Porter Books, 1987.*

Fucini, Joseph J. and Suzy Fucini. *Entrepreneurs: The Men and Women behind Famous Brand Names and How They Made It.* Boston: G. K. Hall & Co., 1985.

Gould, Allan. *The New Entrepreneurs: 80 Canadian Success Stories.* Toronto: Seal Books, 1986.*

Grescoe, Paul, and David Cruise. *The Money Rustlers: Self-Made Millionaires of the New West.* New York: Viking, 1985.*

Henderson, Carter. *Winners: The Successful Strategies Entrepreneurs Use to Build New Businesses.* New York: Holt, Rinehart & Winston, 1985.

Litton, Monica. *Women Mean Business.* Toronto: Key Porter Books, 1987.

Robinson, Jeffrey. *The Risk-Takers: Portraits of Money, Ego and Power.* London: George Allen and Unwin, 1985.

Shook, Robert L. *Why Didn't I Think of That!* New York: New American Library, 1982.

_____. *The Entrepreneurs.* New York: Barnes & Noble Books, 1980.

Silver, A. David. *Entrepreneurial Megabucks: The 100 Greatest Entrepreneurs of the Last Twenty-Five Years.* New York: John Wiley & Sons, 1985.

Witt, Scott. *How Self-Made Millionaires Build Their Fortunes.* New York: Parker Publishing, 1979.

Home-Based Business

Aliaga, Barbara. *Start and Run a Profitable Home Typing Business.* Vancouver: International Self-Counsel Press, 1984.

Atkinson, William. *Working at Home: Is It for You?* Homewood, IL: Dow Jones-Irwin, 1985.

Behr, Marion and Wendy Lazar. *Women Working Home.* New Jersey: WWH Press, 1983.

Blanchard, Marjorie P. *Cater from Your Kitchen.* New York: Bobbs-Merrill, 1981.

Bohigian, Valerie. *Real Money from Home: How to Start, Manage and Profit from a Home-Based Service Business.* New York: New American Library, 1985.

_____. *How to Make Your Home-Based Business Grow*. New York: New American Library, 1984.

Brabec, Barbara. *Creative Cash: Making Money with Your Crafts, Needlework, Designs and Know-how*. Huntington Beach, CA: Aames-Allen Publishing, 1986.

_____. *Homemade Money*. Whitehall, VA: Betterway Publishers, 1989.

_____. *Help for Your Growing Homebased Business*. Naperville, IL: Barbara Brabec Productions, 1987.

Casewit, Curtis M. *Freelance Writing: Advice from the Pros*. New York: Collier Books, 1985.

Contrucci, Peg. *The Home Office*. Englewood Cliffs, NJ: Prentice Hall, 1985.

Drouillard, Anne and William F. Keefe. *How to Earn $25,000 a Year or More Typing at Home*. New York: Frederick Fell, 1973.

Edwards, Paul and Sarah Edwards. *Working from Home*. Los Angeles: Jeremy P. Tarcher Inc., 1985.

Faux, Marian. *Successful Freelancing*. New York: St. Martin's Press, 1982.

Frohbieter-Mueller, Jo. *Stay Home and Mind Your Own Business*. White Hall, VA: Betterway Publications, 1987.

Goodrich, Donna. *How to Set Up and Run a Successful Typing Business*. New York: John Wiley & Sons, 1983.

Gray, Douglas A. *Start and Run a Profitable Consulting Business*. Vancouver: International Self-Counsel Press, 1985.

Hicks, Tyler G. *How to Start Your Own Business on a Shoestring*. Rocklin, CA: Prima Publishing, 1987.

Hoelscher, Russ von. *Stay Home and Make Money*. San Diego, CA: Profit Ideas, 1984.

Hynes, William G. *Start and Run a Profitable Craft Business*. Vancouver: International Self-Counsel Press, 1986.

Johnson, Joanna. *Working at Home for Profit*. Oxford: Basil Blackwell, 1980.

Kishel, Gregory F. and Patricia Gunter Kishel. *Dollars on Your Doorstep*. New York: John Wiley & Sons, 1984.

McConnel, Patricia. *The Woman's Work-at-Home Handbook: Income and Independence with a Computer*. New York: Bantam Books, 1986.

Masser, Barry. *Thirty-Six Thousand Dollars a Year in Your Own Home Merchandising Business*. Englewood Cliffs, NJ: Prentice Hall, 1982.

Rees, Clair. *Profitable Part-Time Full-Time Freelancing*. Cincinatti: Writer's Digest Books, 1980.

Scott, Robert. *How to Set Up and Operate Your Office at Home*. New York: Charles Scribner's Sons, 1985.

Seldon, Ina Lee. Going *into Business for Yourself: New Beginnings after 50*. Glenview, IL: Scott, Foresman & Co., 1989.

Shebar, Sharon S. and Judith Schoder. *How to Make Money at Home*. New York: Simon & Schuster, 1982.

Silliphant, Leigh. *Making $70,000 a Year as a Self- Employed Manufacturer's Representative*. Berkeley, CA: Ten Speed Press, 1988.

Smith Kern, Coralee and Tammara Hoffman Wolfgram. *Planning Your Own Home Business*. Chicago: National Textbook Company, 1986.

Witt, Scott. *How to Make Big Money at Home in Your Spare Time*. New York: Parker Publishing, 1979.

Self-Evaluation and Development

Albert, Kenneth J. *How to Pick the Right Small Business Opportunity*. New York: McGraw-Hill, 1980.

Beard, Mama and Michael J. McGahey. *Alternative Careers for Teachers*. New York: Arco Publishing, 1985.

Bolles, Richard N. *The Three Boxes of Life and How to Get Out of Them*. Berkeley, CA: Ten Speed Press, 1983.

_____. *The 1989 What Color is Your Parachute? A Practical Manual for Job-Hunters and Career Changers*. Berkeley, CA: Ten Speed Press, 1988.

Carnegie, Dale. *How to Win Friends and Influence People*. New York: Pocket Books, 1940.

Crystal, John C., and Richard N. Bolles. *Where Do I Go from Here with My Life?* Berkeley, CA: Ten Speed Press, 1981

Flexman, Nancy A. and Thomas J. Scanlon. *Running Your Own Business: How to Evaluate and Develop Your Entrepreneurial Skills*. Allen, TX: Argus Communications, 1982.

Garfield, Charles A. *Peak Performance: Mental Training Techniques of the World's Greatest Athletes*. New York: Warner Books, 1984.

Gray, Douglas A. *Have You Got What It Takes? The Entrepreneur's Complete Self-Assessment Guide*. 2nd edition. Vancouver: International Self-Counsel Press, 1993.

Hill, Napoleon, and E. Harold Keown. *Succeed and Grow Rich through Persuasion*. New York: Fawcett Publications, 1970.

Kotter, J., V. Faux, and C. McArthur. *Self-Assessment and Career Development*. Englewood Cliffs, NJ: Prentice Hall, 1978.

Mancuso, Joseph. *Have You Got What It Takes? How to Tell If You Should Start Your Own Business*. Englewood Cliffs, NJ: Prentice Hall, 1982.

Schwartz, Lester, and Irv Brechner. *Career Tracks*. New York: Ballantine Books, 1985.

Sher, Barbara, and Annie Gottlieb. *Wishcraft: How to Get What You Really Want*. New York: Ballantine Books, 1979.

Silver, A. David. *The Entrepreneurial Life*. New York: John Wiley & Sons, 1986.

Timmons, J., L. Smollen, and A. Dingee. *New Venture Creation: A Guide to Small Business Development*. New York: Richard D. Irwin, 1977.

Waitley, Denis. *Seeds of Greatness: The Ten Best-Kept Secrets of Total Success*. New York: Simon & Schuster, 1983.

General Business Subjects

Aschner, Katherine. *Managing Your Office Records and Files*. Vancouver: International Self-Counsel Press, 1984.

Beach, Wayne and Lyle R. Hepburn. *Are You Paying Too Much Tax?* Toronto: McGraw-Hill Ryerson, 1992.*

Blake, Gary and Robert W. Bly. *How to Promote Your Own Business*. New York: NAL Penguin, 1983.

Bliss, Edwin C. *Doing It Now*. New York: Charles Scribner's Sons, 1983.

_____. *Getting Things Done*. New York: Charles Scribner's Sons, 1976.

Bromwich, Geoffrey. *Insuring Business Risks in Canada*. Vancouver: International Self-Counsel Press, 1976.*

Christian, Tim and James C. Robb. *Employee-Employer Rights: A Guide for the Alberta Work Force*. Vancouver: International Self-Counsel Press, 1984.*

Coltman, Michael M. *Financial Control for the Small Business*. Vancouver: International Self-Counsel Press, 1982

_____. *Franchising in Canada*. Vancouver: International Self-Counsel Press, 1983.*

Cornish, Clive. *Basic Accounting for the Small Business*. Vancouver: International Self-Counsel Press, 1989.

Dawson, Roger. *You Can Get Anything You Want*. New York: Simon & Schuster, 1986.

Dean, Sandra. *Advertising for the Small Business*. Vancouver: International Self-Counsel Press, 1980.

Dorsey, James E. *Employee-Employer Rights: A Guide for the British Columbia Work Force*. Vancouver: International Self-Counsel Press, 1984.*

Fisher, S. Brian. *The Canadian Personal Tax Planning Guide*. Toronto: Richard de Boo Publishers, 1993.*

Gray, Douglas and Donald G. Cyr. *Marketing Your Product: A Planning Guide for Small Business*. 2nd edition. Vancouver: International Self-Counsel Press, 1994.*

_____. *Start and Run a Profitable Consulting Business*. 3rd edition. Vancouver: International Self-Counsel Press, 1993.*

_____. and Diana L. Gray. *The Complete Canadian Small Business Guide*. 2nd edition. Toronto: McGraw-Hill Ryerson, 1994.*

_____. and Brian Nattrass, *Raising Money: The Canadian Guide to Successful Business Financing*. Toronto: McGraw-Hill Ryerson, 1993.

Grenby, Mike. *Mike Grenby's Tax Tips*. Vancouver: International Self-Counsel Press, 1989.

Grensing, Lin. *A Small Business Guide to Employee Selection*. Vancouver: International Self-Counsel Press, 1986.*

Holtz, Herman. *Great Promo Pieces*. New York: John Wiley & Sons, 1988.

_____. *The Secrets of Practical Marketing for Small Business*. Englewood Cliffs, NJ: Prentice Hall, 1982.

Husch, Tony and Linda. *That's a Great Idea: The New Product Handbook*. Berkeley, CA: Ten Speed Press, 1987.

Jacks, Evelyn. *Jacks on Tax*. Toronto: McGraw-Hill Ryerson, 1994.*

Joffe, Gerado. *How You Can Make at Least $1 Million in the Mail Order Business*. Vancouver: International Self-Counsel Press, 1980.

Johnston, Karen, and Jean Withers. *Selling Strategies for Service Businesses*. Vancouver: International Self-Counsel Press, 1988.

Karrass, Gary. *Negotiate to Close*. New York: Simon & Schuster, 1985.

Levinson, Jay Conrad. *Guerilla Marketing Attack*. Boston: Houghton Mifflin Company, 1989.

Paulsen, Timothy R. *Collection Techniques for the Small Business*. Vancouver: International Self-Counsel Press, 1983.

Richardson, Lois A. *Working Couples*. Vancouver: International Self-Counsel Press, 1983.

Rovet, Ernest. *Employee-Employer Rights: A Guide for the Ontario Work Force*. Vancouver: International Self-Counsel Press, 1985.*

Simon, Julian L. *How to Start and Operate a Mail Order Business*. New York: McGraw-Hill, 1981.

Vipperman, Carol, and Barbara Mueller. *Solutions to Sales Problems: A Guide for Professional Saleswomen*. Englewood Cliffs, NJ: Prentice Hall, 1983.

Wallace Elizabeth. *The Book for Women Who Invent or Want To*. Waterloo, Ont.: The Women Inventors Project, 1987.

Winston, Stephanie. *Getting Organized*. New York: Norton, 1978.

Withers, Jean, and Carol Vipperman. *Marketing Your Service: A Planning Guide for Small Business*. Vancouver: International Self-Counsel Press, 1987.

MAGAZINES

Magazines are an important means of keeping current on trends, ideas, opportunities, and legislation. There are many excellent magazines available at the public library and local newsstands tailored to meet the needs of small- and medium-sized businesses. There are national, provincial, and local business publications in Canada that might interest you. In addition, there are many U.S. publications which provide fresh ideas, trends, and perspectives that can stimulate your imagination. Your subscription costs are tax-deductible as a business expense. A partial listing of suggested national publications follows:

Profit Home Business
C.B. Media
56 The Esplanade
Toronto, Ontario
M5E 1A7

Profit
C.B. Media
56 The Esplanade
Toronto, Ontario
M5E 1A7

Home Office Computing
411 Lafayette Street
New York, N.Y.
10003

Opportunities Canada
2550 Golden Ridge Road, Unit 42
Mississauga, Ontario
L4X 2S3

Entrepreneur
2392 Morse Avenue
Irvine, California
92714

Small Business Opportunities
1115 Broadway
New York, N.Y.
10010

Success
342 Madison Avenue
New York, N.Y.
10173

Income Opportunities
380 Lexington Avenue
New York, N.Y.
10017

Venture
521 Fifth Avenue
New York, N.Y.
10175

Inc.
38 Commercial Wharf
Boston, MA
02110

ABOUT THE AUTHORS

Douglas Gray, LL.B., is Canada's authority on small business law and entrepreneurial development. He has given seminars for more than 250,000 people nationally and internationally and is frequently interviewed by the media throughout North America as an expert on entrepreneurship. He has founded 12 successful businesses, of which 7 have been home-based. Mr. Gray is a consultant specializing in small business entrepreneur stimulation and retention, and community economic development. He is also a recently retired lawyer and author of 12 bestselling books, including *The Complete Canadian Small Business Guide* (with Diana Gray), *Raising Money* (with Brian Nattrass), and *The Complete Canadian Franchise Guide* (with Norm Friend). Refer to the preliminary pages of the book for a list of the books written, and the last page for ordering information. In addition, he writes numerous articles on small business for various publications, including the *Globe and Mail* and *Maclean's*. He has a regular column in *Profit Home Business* and *Opportunities Canada* magazines, and writes a nationally syndicated weekly finance business newspaper column.

Mr. Gray is the founder and president of the Canadian Enterprise Institute Inc.

Diana Gray has founded several successful businesses, as well as acted as owner/manager of them. In addition, she is a business centre consultant. Her various companies provide centralized business services, catering to the specialized needs of small as well as home-based business owners. She has employed up to nine full-time staff. She is experienced in understanding and dealing with problems associated with business startup, growth and expansion.

Mrs. Gray has written many small business-related articles and training manuals, and has co-authored the bestselling book (with Douglas A. Gray), *The Complete Canadian Small Business Guide*, published by McGraw-Hill Ryerson.

She is the Past-Chairperson of the Association of Women Business Owners — an organization committed to encouraging and fostering women entrepreneurs — and has given seminars and presentations to potential and existing women entrepreneurs. In addition, she has participated on various provincial and federal committees which have made recommendations on ways of stimulating and fostering women entrepreneurship.

Douglas and Diana Gray live in Vancouver, British Columbia.

Reader Input and Educational Services/Products

If you have thoughts or suggestions that you believe would be helpful for future editions of this book, are interested in having a seminar or presentation given to your group or association, or would like further information on consulting services or educational material available, please write to the Institute. Refer to the last page of this book for book ordering information.

Canadian Enterprise Institute Inc.
#300 - 3665 Kingsway
Vancouver, BC
V5R 5W2

Ordering Information for Other Bestselling Books by Douglas and/or Diana Gray

Home Inc.: The Canadian Home-Based Business Guide (2nd edition)
(with Diana Gray)
ISBN 0-07-551558-X

The Complete Canadian Small Business Guide (2nd edition)
(with Diana Gray)
ISBN 0-07-551661-6

The Complete Canadian Franchise Guide
(with Norm Friend)
ISBN 0-07-551797-3

Raising Money: The Canadian Guide to Successful Business Financing
(with Brian Nattrass)
ISBN 007-551-490-2

Risk-Free Retirement: The Complete Canadian Planning Guide
(with Tom Delaney, Graham Cunningham, Les Solomon and Dr.
Des Dwyer)
ISBN 0-07-551274-2

Making Money in Real Estate: The Canadian Residential Investment Guide
ISBN 0-07-549596-1

Home Buying Made Easy: The Canadian Guide to Purchasing a Newly-Built or Pre-Owned Home
ISBN 0-07-551560-1

Mortgages Made Easy: The Canadian Guide to Home Financing
ISBN 0-07-551344-7

Condo Buying Made Easy: The Canadian Guide to Buying Apartment or Townhouse Condominiums, Co-ops or Timeshares (2nd edition)
ISBN 0-07-551791-4

Mortgage Payment Tables Made Easy: The Canadian Guide to Calculating Mortgage or Loan Interest
ISBN 0-07-551722-1

Available at your local bookstore or by contacting:
McGraw-Hill Ryerson Limited
Consumer & Professional Books Division
300 Water Street
Whitby, Ontario L1N 9B6
Phone: 1-800-565-5758 / Fax: 1-800-463-5885 (orders only)